MOTIVES, VALUES, AND REALITIES

caste and class. In general, research studies in the behavioral sciences amplified rather than contradicted our theory. Naturally the reading was done over a period of years and the many valuable studies in the behavioral sciences contributed to the results as well as served as checkpoints for the findings.

The third method was observation employing the usual techniques. In addition, we had the opportunity to travel extensively in Asia, Africa, and Europe. Reading about different cultures and values is a vicarious experience. Living with values and customs different from our own gave us the chance to observe them and to develop a new perspective on the values of our own society.

Although a result of research, this book does not have the usual research format. The reader will find no tables, diagrams, vectors, valences, formulae, or statistics because the theory deals with people as individuals. We found no exceptions to the theory presented here; hence there was no need for statistics. We have never believed that a theory that holds for forty-nine or even fifty-nine per cent of the people is of great value to the counselor because he usually finds the exceptions facing him in his counseling room. We also feel that statistics are tools, not ends, and that they often serve to obscure rather than increase understanding. Any researcher in the behavioral—and perhaps many in the physical —sciences eventually reaches that point where human beings cannot be described statistically because "the dignity of man is not susceptible to measurement." [1] *Motives, Values, and Realities* presents the results of research with an emphasis on making those findings meaningful in relation to the individual.

The cases included in the text and the Appendix are illustrative of the protocols used. The book contains only these samples because we hope that each person using it either for his own information or for teaching purposes in classes in "Understanding Individual Behavior," "Theories of Counseling," and

[1] John W. Dodds, "The Humanist Looks at the Doctor," *Medicine and Anthropology*, edited by Iago Galdston (New York: International Universities Press, The New York Academy of Medicine, No. XXI, 1959), p. 38.

PREFACE

Motives, Values, and Realities offers a framework for understanding individual behavior in the light of the behavioral sciences. It focuses on the "normal" individual, the person whom every school counselor meets in his office. Hence the purposes of the book are dual: to supply counselors, teachers, and other educators working with "normal" individuals a basis for understanding them as people; and thus to create a solid groundwork from which effective counseling and guidance-personnel techniques and procedures can logically be derived.

The book is a report of a research study. It contains the comprehensive theory that evolved from the use of several research methods. The first was analysis of counseling protocols and/or descriptive studies of individuals. The group used for this intensive study consisted of over five hundred people of varied socio-economic and intellectual levels and from different geographical locations. Of this group, over 100 were adults; over 350, junior and senior high school students; and over 100, elementary school pupils. The number of interviews with each individual ranged from one to fourteen with five to six interviews the median. The theory derived from the common elements that recurred in protocol after protocol.

The second method was intensive reading of research studies and theories from the behavioral sciences with constant analysis of where these materials might amplify, coincide with, or negate our own developing theory. This analysis had interesting results. We discovered that many psychological theories with different emphases fit within the outline of the theory presented here. Anthropological reports attested to its cross-cultural applicability, and sociological studies illustrated its relevance to problems of

v

Library of Congress Cataloging in Publication Data

Barry, Ruth, 1919-
  Motives, values, and realities.

  Reprint of the 1965 ed. published by Teachers College
Press, Teachers College, Columbia University, New York.
  Includes bibliographical references and index.
  1. Motivation (Psychology) 2. Counseling. I. Wolf,
Beverly, joint author. II. Title.
[BF683.B3 1976]   152.5   76-40268
ISBN 0-8371-9066-5

© 1965, TEACHERS COLLEGE, COLUMBIA UNIVERSITY

Originally published in 1965 by Teachers College Press,
Columbia University, New York

Reprinted with the permission of Teachers College Press,
Columbia University

Reprinted in 1976 by Greenwood Press, Inc.

Library of Congress Catalog Card Number 76-40268

ISBN 0-8371-9066-5

Printed in the United States of America

MOTIVES, VALUES, AND REALITIES

A Framework for Counseling

RUTH BARRY and BEVERLY WOLF

GREENWOOD PRESS, PUBLISHERS
WESTPORT, CONNECTICUT

"Counseling Techniques" will want to add to our illustrations with protocols of his own. Students, especially, can benefit from such analysis of their own materials after finding a method by using ours.

Throughout the book, we have avoided insofar as possible the use of technical psychological jargon. It is a shorthand mode of expression, but it can interfere with the understanding a counselor is trying to develop. Such phrases and words as cognitive dissonance, affect, congruence, and deficiency motive mean little to the counselor, who, struggling to work effectively with individuals, cannot take refuge in jargon. We are attempting to avoid the depersonalizing effects that inhere in jargon.

The process of understanding human behavior is only beginning. Physical as well as behavioral scientists are constantly discovering new knowledge about man. Undoubtedly within the next few years, they will reveal now unknown facts about the relationships of body chemistry and mental illness. We feel that such facts will be indispensable to the counselor but will not directly transform theories of human behavior. What such knowledge can and will do is to supply new medications that enhance, not diminish, the therapeutic function of counselors.

Motives, Values, and Realities is the second in a series of three books. The first, *An Epitaph for Vocational Guidance,* analyzes the current state of guidance practice and highlights areas where change is needed. This second book presents a framework for counseling. The third, *Dynamic Developmental Counseling,* will deal with counseling process and practice as it evolves from theory and as it applies to the day-by-day work of guidance-personnel counselors with their students. The purpose of the three books is to allow today's counselor to analyze his field, to find guidance-personnel theory suitable to his work, and to relate this theory to his practice. The general purpose naturally is to improve the work of the increasing numbers of counselors by helping them better to understand and to counsel their counselees.

Without the research and theorizing of many people in all the behavioral sciences, this book could not exist. Without the challenging questions of our students and colleagues, we probably would not have searched so diligently for answers. We are particularly grateful to those counselors who participated in the study and to all those students who have continued to force us to evolve a theory that we hope will be meaningful to them.

R. B. and B. W.

CONTENTS

1

UNIVERSAL MOTIVATING FORCES

A theory of motivation must lie at the core of any sound approach to personality and counseling. In one sense, each psychoanalytic or psychological approach to personality implies a theory of motivation, whether expressed in terms of psychic energy, drive for power or superiority, mechanistic response to stimulus, or fulfillment of need. Unfortunately, these theories of motivation have not been directly meaningful to the counselor working with the normal individual. Almost all of those presenting a dynamic view derive from and apply to the mentally ill; others, static in nature, deal with laboratory animals. All theories are so ethnocentric that they have no universal applicability. Motivational theorists have seldom, if ever, started with the normal human being and attempted to integrate the findings of the behavioral sciences, thus establishing cross-cultural relationships. Hence the modern counselor working with normal students cannot adapt extant theories in his attempts to understand why his counselees do what they do.

The lack of a universal theory of motivation applicable to normal individuals handicaps the counselor not only in understanding behavior but also in finding a comprehensive, consistent approach to counseling. Without such a theory, counselors must continue to draw upon either the antiquated, static concepts basic to current guidance practice or the limited dynamic constructs underlying therapy for the abnormal personality. Neither really provides an adequate foundation for the counselor working with the normal individual.

Some present-day theorists are beginning to focus on the normal person, but their theories of motivation continue to center

1

around the concept of need. The human being lacks something, feels this lack as tension, and seeks to reduce this tension by meeting the need. Although this concept of motivation serves to explain some of the simple physiological needs, it fails to explain the more complex, interrelated motivations that can be observed in most individuals in many societies. The definition of need as a lack of something has long dissatisfied some psychologists as being too negative, as not providing explanations for many of the positive actions of individuals. As Dorothy Lee suggests, "either needs are not the cause of all behavior, or . . . the list of needs provides an inadequate unit for assessing human behavior." [1]

A. H. Maslow's list of needs and their ordering according to prepotency suffers from precisely the difficulties discussed by Lee. Although his theorizing about needs is gaining wide acceptance, many psychologists and counselors cannot reconcile the idea of lack with Maslow's concept of self-actualization, which is far too positive to permit such a negative base. Essentially Maslow seems to be moving toward a positive interpretation of human motivations, but he has yet to discard the concept of need or to take a broad look at motivation encompassing more than the American scene. [2]

Many authors have discussed motivaton either as need, adjustive response, drive, or under some other rubric. Lists of motivations are becoming as common as lists of instincts used to be before the concept of man's behavior as a product of his instincts fell into disrepute. The authors of most lists fail to recognize that the motives they describe are culturally developed and may well represent only the group supplying them. In a society as large and diverse as the American, no group can be considered truly representative of the whole culture. These lists

[1] Dorothy Lee, *Freedom and Culture* (New York: Prentice-Hall, Spectrum Book, 1959), p. 72.

[2] Abraham H. Maslow, *Motivation and Personality* (New York: Harper, 1954) and *Toward a Psychology of Being* (New York: D. Van Nostrand, Insight Book, 1962).

only highlight the few similarities and blur the important individual differences in motives.[3]

For effective work, counselors need a comprehensive theory of motivation that will help them to explain behavior rather than confuse or negate it. Such a theory must have simplicity, universality, consistency, and applicability. This book presents an approach to motivation that meets these four requirements and provides counselors with a sound foundation for their work and the methods they use in carrying it out. Human beings strive to live, to internalize a culture, to perpetuate internalized learnings, to express themselves within a culture, and to achieve positive experiences. These five kinds of striving incorporate the motivations common to human beings everywhere regardless of geographical location or social group.

TO LIVE

In order to live, human beings strive for the essentials of living and simultaneously struggle to maintain themselves in their particular group situations. In one sense, these strivings coalesce so that it is often difficult, if not impossible, to distinguish where one leaves off and the other begins. Separateness is not a characteristic of any of the motivations under consideration and the discussion of them apart from one another does not mean that they ever exist singly.

The Essentials. For continued existence man has to have food, drink, rest, protection and, in a somewhat different sense, sex. Without these essentials, man as an individual would cease to exist and man as a species would die out. Because of his

[3] As one example, see Jerome Kagan, "The Choice of Models: Conflict and Continuity in Human Behavior," *Behavioral Science and Guidance*, edited by Esther Lloyd-Jones and Esther M. Westervelt (New York: Bureau of Publications, Teachers College, Columbia University, 1963), pp. 63–85. Kagan's lists of motives for the various activities he discusses seem to us strangely limited and expressed in a fashion to indicate that they are mutually exclusive.

physical make-up, man strives for the essentials in response to stimuli provided by his body, but his strivings take many different forms and are directed toward widely varied ends in response to his bodily requirements.

The essentials are the physiological facts of life and are exactly that—essential. In general, the hungry man will seek food, the thirsty man will search for water, and the tired man will sleep. At times and under certain circumstances, other strivings can supersede those for food, water, and protection, but only to the point where either death or the heightened pressure for satisfaction of the bodily requirements intervenes. Gandhi and his fasts provide an example of how an individual can ignore some of the essentials in favor of striving for an ideal. Sleep is perhaps the one exception for exhaustion leads eventually either to sleep or unconsciousness regardless of the will or intention of the individual.

The essentials are the cornerstones upon which men have built their societies and around which they have patterned their cultures. Eating is not a cultural phenomenon, but what one eats, when, with what utensils, where, and in whose company are part of the societal ornamentation of life and differ radically from group to group. Rest and protection are similarly necessary, but the group defines the form they take.

Whether men eat two, three, four, or five times a day is purely a function of the society in which they were brought up. What one eats is largely a matter of societal definition. Americans consume quantities of meat while the orthodox Hindus get their protein from milk, curds, cheese, and nuts. Some Australian aborigines include ants, iguanas, snakes, and certain fungi as staples in their diet—foods repulsive to most Americans. Western society demands variety in food and differences in what is served at the various meals. Man does not need variety in food; he simply needs enough of the basic nutrients to support his body in good health and those can be obtained from a montonous or a varied diet. Food is an essential, but everything else relating to it is cultural embroidery.

Drink is an essential similar to food; everyone has to have a certain amount of fluid intake in order to sustain life, but the kinds of fluid, the amount desired, how taken, and when depend upon a great many variables not the least important of which is the society of the individual. Water is, of course, the commonest way of supplying this essential but every society takes fluids in many forms: coffee, tea, milk, soft drinks, or fruit juices. Alcoholic beverages, which have been in existence since people learned to grow grain, not only supply fluids but also provide needed nutrients.[4]

The essentials of rest and protection go hand in hand. Man has to have a certain amount of sleep in order to carry on his activities and he needs some protection from his environment while he rests. Such protection may simply be a watchman who guards against danger, a fire that keeps wild animals at bay, a crude shelter that wards off snow and rain, or sufficient clothing to protect a person from sharp changes in temperature. The forms of shelter, clothing, and other kinds of protection depend to a considerable extent upon the climate of the individual's environment and the society in which he lives. Houses are adapted to the climate of the area in which they are built and the materials available, but their modifications and elaborations are cultural phenomena. Clothing is generally related to climate, but modified by other societal factors.

Protection, of course, takes many forms. Men strive, for example, to maintain the integrity of their bodies, to preserve themselves against accident and physical damage. Similarly they attempt to protect themselves and their wives and children against the depredations of their fellow men. Even warfare among some groups seems to show strong elements of this motivation toward self-protection and safety and the damage inflicted

[4] Ralph Linton, *The Tree of Culture* (New York: Alfred A. Knopf, 1955), pp. 94–95. Linton claims that beer is an important source of the B vitamins for many peoples of the world. Anyone who has tasted Kaffir beer, the native drink of South Africa, is immediately aware of the yeast content of this glutinous beverage.

on each other by the contending parties is limited by the cultural patterning of war itself.[5]

Probably most important in the strivings for safety and protection is the need of the human infant for care during the years before he is able to care for himself. Among no other mammals is the infant as dependent upon adults for as long a period of time as is the human child. Although this period can be slightly shortened or considerably lengthened by the manner in which the culture defines childhood, nevertheless the human child has to have protection and care for the first three years of his life and probably for considerably longer although the life-and-death nature of this essential decreases as the age increases. This requirement for protection has led to many of the cultural developments in terms of the social group and many of the forms by which the essentials are acquired. The nature of the care provided children differs from culture to culture and group to group,[6] but no society expects children to grow up independent of adult supervision and tending.

Sex is probably another essential although the degree of its necessity to the health and well-being of the individual is still unknown. Certainly for the continuance of the race, sexual relations and procreation are essential. The sexual aspects of life are, however, so circumscribed and regulated by the society in which the individual lives that it is difficult if not impossible to determine what is physiological necessity and what, cultural patterning. Desire and arousal are physiological facts, but for whom, when, where, how often, and how satisfied seem, within limits, to be culturally determined.

Every society has formalized ways in which its members can obtain sexual satisfaction. Usually there is provision for

[5] See, for example, Peter Matthiessen, *Under the Mountain Wall* (New York: Viking Press, 1962), *passim;* Jomo Kenyatta, *Facing Mount Kenya* (New York: Random House, Vintage Books, 1962), pp. 200–205; and Luigi Barzini, *The Italians* (New York: Atheneum, 1964), pp. 91–92.

[6] The many forms adult care of infants and children may take are amply documented in the studies of anthropologists. For a listing of some of these see the Bibliographical Note.

some form of marriage on a more or less permanent basis which furnishes the partners with a somewhat stable sexual relationship. All such statements must be carefully qualified, however, because all societies differ in their patterning of sex behavior and the formal rules and regulations governing its expression vary from group to group.

The motivation impelling human beings to seek sexual outlets has been amply documented by psychiatrists and psychologists of the Freudian school. Their view of sex as the all-important drive of human beings does not seem valid when applied to people in other than Western cultures or even when applied to healthy individuals in American society. Although sex is an important motivation in any culture—and an even more important one in those cultures which try to suppress it—it is neither the single motivation nor has any society patterned its whole culture around sex as a motivating force. By and large, the importance given to sex as a motivation is waning; it will some day take its place as an important motivation among the essentials rather than being regarded as primary.

These five items—food, drink, rest, protection, and sex—constitute the essentials of man's existence. Without them he cannot live and for them he will work, plan, and struggle as long as he is physically able to do so. These are universal motivations, which spur men everywhere to activity and thought. All the essentials are physiological requirements and efforts to provide them are usually responses to bodily stimuli.[7] In American society, these motivations are rarely distinguishable in the actions of individuals. Certainly Americans work to set a good

[7] One question suggests itself: In American society where the automobile and other machines are making physical effort obsolete, is exercise a physiological essential? Physical fitness is needed for good health, but does man need exercise in the same way and for the same reasons he needs food or rest? Does his body signal the need for exercise as it does for food or drink or is physical activity something he needs without receiving stimuli impelling him to seek it? Such questions could only be raised in a highly mechanized, affluent society for in many parts of the world the amount and kind of physical activity is sufficient—or often excessive—in terms of the capabilities of the individuals involved.

table, to have a nice house, and to dress themselves and their children properly, but these motives are a far cry from the direct motivations of hunger or protection. In an affluent society, people are rarely so hungry that food of any kind is the sole good and hunger pangs are not the only reason for eating. In other societies where mere subsistence entails a major daily struggle, man's strivings for the essentials may be more obvious and less adulterated by other motives and learnings, but in Western society the motives arising from the essentials are seldom, if ever, of the simple stimulus-response type.

The Group.   Basic to any discussion of the essentials is the underlying assumption of the existence of a group of human beings. The existence of one human infant presupposes the prior —at least temporary—existence of a group of two adults. Most human groups, however, have been and are larger than the nuclear family of a man, a woman, and their offspring. An extended family or several extended families living in some sort of community seem to compose the group experienced by children in most societies. American society differs from many others in that the basic group is the nuclear family with various relatives peripheral to this fundamental unit.

Some form of group is so necessary in the achievement of the essentials that the group itself might almost be considered an essential except that it has no direct physiological base. Sexual satisfaction virtually requires the existence of a group; securing food and ensuring protection are far easier and more efficient on a group basis. A group of hunters can pursue a large animal with greater chance of success than can an individual; a community is better able to withstand food shortages or extremes of weather when its members pool their resources than is the individual relying only upon himself. A lone adult might be able to sustain life, but he would be far more liable to the many vicissitudes of primitive life than would a group.

Perhaps the most influential factor in man's strivings toward maintenance of a position in a group stems from the long period of dependency undergone by every human infant. For survival an infant has to have at least one adult—usually his mother—who cares for and feeds him. Hence he necessarily establishes with that adult a relationship, which may be warm and friendly, brusque and impersonal, or even inimical. Through this relationship, the infant learns to strive for attention, belongingness, security, love, and/or esteem, first from the person who tends him and later from the other members of the family and community group. The person providing an infant with the essentials also teaches him to seek the security of other people and the feeling that he is one of them and not alone in an unfriendly world.

In almost all societies, a child learns to strive for belongingness and love, but this learning is so closely linked with his strivings for the essentials that it is often difficult if not impossible to separate the two motivations. As the child grows, he continues and elaborates his strivings for group membership and affectional ties and his culture determines the form his strivings take. He may develop intimate family ties that are maintained and strengthened throughout his life or he may learn that intense emotional relationships are to be avoided and that friendly detachment is expected of him.[8] Esteem may take many forms and be accorded for various reasons and kinds of behavior. Whatever the form, however, as children and later as adults, individuals learn to strive to earn and retain the love and esteem of others and their own sense of belonging to some group of human beings.

Some human group may be an essential for the psychological development of an individual in much the same way that food and water are physiological necessities. H. F. Harlow's experiments with monkeys have shown that some social interaction is necessary for them to develop into "normal" monkeys. According to Harlow, monkeys brought up for a year or more in isolation were unable to establish "any kind of effective social relationship"

[8] H. G. Barnett, *Being a Palauan* (New York: Holt, Rinehart and Winston, 1960). Palauan children have a strong emotional tie to their mothers, which is deliberately broken at about age five when abruptly they are expected to take on some independence and emotional detachment.

or to demonstrate "even infantile sexual behavior." [9] Clinicians, doctors, teachers, and others who work with children have long recognized that the child reared in relative isolation suffers some psychological deprivation and fails to develop the skills necessary for his own healthy development and integration into the group. Since children usually live in a group, early experience with and learning from it seem a necessary part of everyone's experience.

The motivation to belong to the group, to earn belongingness and esteem through adequate or successful group membership paves the way for children to learn skills and attitudes. Affection, love, prestige, status, admiration, security, belongingness—whatever the group regards as being of value and providing a sense of oneness with others shapes the directions of the strivings of its members. These strivings, in turn, enable the group to offer learnings and provide experiences that will perpetuate the group and its way of life.

TO INTERNALIZE A CULTURE

Each group has its own way of life. This phrase—"way of life"— includes techniques and skills; relationships and forms of relating; patterns for providing the essentials; methods of communication; explanations of the immediate world and the universe; rules, taboos, and their enforcement; roles and social orderings; myths, legends, and the individual's relation to the supernatural and unknown; appropriate emotional expression; and the practices for coping with day-by-day living. Whatever their way of life,

[9] Harry F. Harlow, "Expert Says Mother May Not Be Best," *Medical World News*, November 9, 1962, p. 62. These experiments raise some interesting questions since the reports imply that the behavior of the isolated monkeys represents "bad adjustment." For monkeys destined to live in isolation, ineffective social abilities and immature sexuality may be "good" if not typical adjustment. Much the same point can be made about the so-called wild child who grows up in isolation or in the company of animals. See L. F. Shaffer and E. J. Shoben, Jr., *The Psychology of Adjustment* (New York: Houghton Mifflin, 1956), p. 402. They conclude that "our distinctive attributes, even our most fundamentally human qualities, are products of our experience with other human beings."

the members of a group view it as right and proper for since birth they have engaged in the process of learning it. The total of these internalized learnings is the culture,[10] for they encompass, shape, limit, and modify all that an individual is and does.

From the moment of birth, a child begins to learn the culture into which he is born. Other group members teach him constantly by a variety of means to become a full-fledged, socialized member of their particular community. The child learns what actions and expressions meet with approval or disapproval, rewards or punishments, smiles or frowns, acceptance or ostracism, praise or ridicule, security or fear, fulfillment or frustration. He observes the people around him and imitates them. He constantly tries to do what they do and these trials result in either success or failure. He practices certain actions until they become habits. He repeats the information, facts, myths, legends, and learnings of the group and knows them so well that what the group deems right and important is right and important to him. The result is a person steeped in his own culture.

A simple example illustrates the nature and depth of internalized learning. In every society, children learn how, when, what, where, and with whom to eat. The learning starts at birth. An infant is either breast- or bottle-fed and learns what kind of activity on his part results in receiving food, when he may expect it, and the closeness of the relationship with the person providing it. When he is older, he internalizes the rituals, values, and skills associated with eating. He learns what foods are good or bad, the amounts and kinds of food he can anticipate having, the times at which he can expect to eat, and the beverages (if any)

[10] Precise definitions of culture have long plagued anthropologists. In this book, we are using a simple but inclusive definition of our own based upon that of Ralph Linton. We have defined culture as the internalized learnings characteristic of a particular society. We are sure that we are saying the same thing that Linton said in defining culture as "an organized group of learned responses characteristic of a particular society" and we are certainly indebted to him. The phrase "internalized learnings," however, seems to us to be broader in connotation and less mechanistic than Linton's phrase "learned responses," which might possibly be misinterpreted. See *The Tree of Culture*, p. 29.

that will accompany his food. Gradually he learns how to approach his food, whether to use his fingers, a single implement, or an assortment of implements; whether to reach into a communal bowl or to concentrate upon a container of his own; whether to hunker, kneel, stand, squat, or sit on a stool, cushion, mat, the floor, or the ground while consuming his meal. He participates in the rituals preceding, accompanying, or ending the meal. He may or may not wash his hands, feet, head, or body, or engage in such elaborate cleansing ceremonies as those of the Yoga. He may learn to invoke the blessings of supernatural powers or to drive away evil spirits by prescribed rites—or may do none of these. He learns what garb to wear for different occasions and what people he may or may not join during a meal. He learns how to show appreciation for his food. Simultaneously he learns the laws governing hospitality, many of which revolve around the serving of food.[11] Whatever he learns, becomes for him right and proper.

Internalized learning involves a strong emotional commitment. A person reacts emotionally when other people do not behave according to his learnings. He feels strong guilt whenever he himself violates his internalizations. An orthodox Hindu eating beef or even with a beef-eater, a Mohammedan or a Jew eating pork, a Catholic eating meat on Friday—all are violating taboos; the seriousness of these offenses depends upon the internalizations of the individual. The non-Hindu, non-Mohammedan, or non-Catholic is unable completely to understand the depth of emotional response evoked by breaking these taboos for he has internalized different learnings. In like manner, a Westerner is nauseated at the idea of drinking cow's urine or eating caterpillars while a Chinese may feel the same way about drinking cow's milk. Burping and belching after a dinner may be the highest expression of appreciation or a cause of intense embarrassment. There are innumerable examples of the emo-

[11] In complex societies, books of etiquette outline the proper, formal laws and chiefs of protocol are employed to see to their observance on state occasions.

tional charge associated with both the observances of and offenses against any individual's internalized learnings concerning food. These reactions range from embarrassment, amusement, anxiety, fear, resentment, disgust, to physical illness, even death.

As the example of eating illustrates, many kinds of learning underlie even an apparently simple act. The child simultaneously assimilates physical skills (postures, gestures, the use of tools), social skills ("politeness," relating with others), emotional skills (attitudes, expressions), mental skills (the "subject-matter" of foods, the social hierarchy, the written or unwritten laws of etiquette and hospitality), and values (the subtleties of right and wrong). Distinctions into various types of skills are more an organizational device than a reality for no convenient demarcation separates the categories. It is impossible to teach a child anything—how to use chopsticks, spell a word, or build a campfire—without also teaching him values, emotional reactions to the task, and attitudes toward himself and others.

The internalized learnings any person acquires include those his society deems important. These learnings range from simple necessary skills to subtle, tenaciously held concepts. How to sit on a chair is an essential learning for the American who will spend much of his life in this act. The school program reflects the skill learnings considered essential for a particular society—driver training is a latter-day curricular addition for an affluent society and relatively less important in an underdeveloped nation. A society based upon the humanist and Judeo-Christian traditions teaches its members so to value human life that they cannot understand peoples to whom the individual is unimportant and life itself has little value. Those groups viewing time as a commodity to be traded in the market place often fail to communicate with people who have learned to contemplate time as nothingness and eternity.

Every society—or each subgroup within complex societies —prescribes proper degrees and kinds of emotional expression and occasions for such expression. In some societies, for example, women learn to view breast-feeding a child as a pleasurable experience; in others, as highly unpleasant.[12] Children learn to express or inhibit partially or fully such emotions as love, affection, hate, anger, fear, grief, pain, happiness, and unhappiness. The Eastern European Jewish man expresses sorrow and joy by weeping and wailing because in the *shtetl* tears are "a part of the vocabulary for expressing grief or joy."[13] Appropriate emotional expression for the *shtetl* would be judged unmanly for a member of American society.

Standards for appropriate emotional expression are neither clear-cut nor consistent in most societies. Differences occur according to sex, place, time, and social class. American women may weep but men may not. Ordinarily men do not kiss and hug each other in public, but World Series winners are expected to exhibit such outbursts of joy and the grieving losers may even weep. Girls may show fear openly and generally learn to be afraid of snakes, rodents, and insects, but boys must not demonstrate fear when faced with similar stimuli. The *sheyneh* Jew in the *shtetl* may argue violently about erudite and impersonal topics and become so angry that "he 'jumps out of his vessels'" but he may not demonstrate the same anger on other occasions for "It is only women and prosteh who 'really quarrel.'"[14] As a result of these inconsistencies and differences, the child has a long period of learning what is and what is not appropriate emotional expression. In a complex society, when a person moves from one social class to another, he must relearn appropriate emotional behavior for his new situation. Such learnings are some of the most difficult for people to internalize because no printed

[12] American women are supposed to view breast-feeding as pleasurable. The women of Tepoztlan and Dobu, however, derive little or no pleasure from breast-feeding. See Oscar Lewis, *Tepoztlan, Village in Mexico* (New York: Holt, Rinehart and Winston, 1960), p. 73 and R. F. Fortune, *Sorcerers of Dobu* (New York: E. P. Dutton, 1963), p. 273.

[13] Mark Zborowski and Elizabeth Herzog, *Life Is With People, The Culture of the Shtetl* (New York: Schocken Books, 1962), p. 303. This study of life in the now nonexistent *shtetl* furnishes many examples of training in emotional expression, far more than many other anthropological works.

[14] *Ibid.*, pp. 148–149.

rules guide emotional behavior. Emotional expression is an integrated part of personality and an individual often does not know why he feels as he does or how to change his expression of those feelings.

Some researchers in various cultures as well as laymen have claimed that particular societies produce characteristic types of people. The stereotypes of the reserved Swede and the excitable Frenchman are examples of this kind of thinking. Certainly different cultures emphasize and favor certain kinds of behavior, but no society produces a prefabricated emotional man. Within every society, there seems to be enough flexibility to allow it to accommodate wide ranges of emotional behavior. Thus among the Arapesh, who strive for control and emotional restraint, the choleric, excitable individual can and does exist.[15] Americans do not admire the fearful timid man and parents attempt to teach their sons courage, but except under extreme circumstances timid men can and do live acceptable lives in the United States. The attempt to characterize individuals in terms of the extremes of emotional behavior favored by their cultures is probably futile and certainly dangerous for it ignores the all-important factors of degree and intensity.

The members of every society attempt to pass on to their children the skills, emotional expressions, and attitudes they consider important and good. The learnings of two children in a single, closely knit society may be similar but they are never identical. The similarities of learnings produce the apparently pervasive trends within a society but should not obscure the individual and his idiosyncratic way of internalizing his culture. Each man, with slightly different internalized learnings, strives for the things most important to him and, within each culture, these strivings may be similar, but more often differ widely particularly in complex societies.

[15] See Margaret Mead, *Sex and Temperament in Three Primitive Societies* (New York: Mentor Books, 1950). Cora DuBois discusses modal personality in her 1960 Introduction to her earlier study, *The People of Alor* (New York: Harper, Torchbooks, 1961), Vol. I, pp. xix–xxvii.

TO PERPETUATE INTERNALIZED LEARNINGS

The third universal motivating force impels man to perpetuate his internalized learnings or his culture. What he judges good, he fights to preserve; what he views as bad, he strives to change or eliminate. Throughout history, men everywhere have struggled to maintain the way of life they have internalized and, proselyting, to change other men's ways of life and beliefs. These attempts to perpetuate one's own learnings create the continuity of culture.

Experts have long deplored the fact that social learnings never keep pace with technological developments. Undoubtedly the nature and depth of internalized learnings create this insoluble dilemma. Man can fairly readily adapt to and adopt new technological developments, especially when their benefits and advantages become apparent, but even so many of these changes are rarely immediate. The horse gave way to the horseless carriage only gradually. In general, however, people adapt far more easily to external change than to those changes that demand new internalizations and undercut "the way things have always been done." Americans, eager for new technological advances, bought television sets, dishwashers, and transistor radios shortly after they appeared on the market. Yet, more than a hundred years after the Emancipation Proclamation, many of these same Americans still hesitate to grant equal rights to Negroes and, a century after Charles Darwin offered his theory of evolution, demand that this counterfundamentalist doctrine not be taught in their schools. Every society offers many illustrations of similar discrepancies in the acceptance of innovations. Change in actions is easy when it does not depend upon corresponding change in internalized learnings, but when new developments hit deeply held beliefs, change is slow indeed, for it involves new internalizations.

There are many examples that demonstrate the power of the motivating force to perpetuate internalized learnings. The battles waged to preserve a culture are legion. Throughout the ages, men have died rather than change their mode of life or go against ways they consider right and good. Their actions cannot be explained by a simple list of economic motivations, although some of these may play a secondary role. Essentially, what people strive to preserve is their way of life in its own peculiar symbolic representation for them.

Often the attempt to preserve a culture entails retreat, one group moving to areas not wanted by the stronger group and there attempting to carry on life as they knew it. The Bushmen of the Kalahari Desert present a continuing example of retreat and the development of special adaptations in order to maintain their culture.[16] The American, of course, need not look beyond the borders of his own country for illustrations. The colonies of Amish in Iowa and Hutterites in Montana demonstrate the point well. Currently, rather than accede to the demands of the state concerning their schools, the Amish are contemplating a move to Canada where they hope their culture can be preserved intact.

Anthropologists have speculated about the depth of the power of the culture upon an individual. There is some evidence that a person to whom identity with a particular group represents the highest good cannot live apart from that group. Bushmen, for example, incarcerated in prisons or separated from their tribe often become ill and die from no apparent physical cause. Dorothy Lee points out that "Recruiting for plantation labor was prohibited in Tikopia when repeated experience showed that almost all the men died when away from home." [17] Evidence seems to indicate that when the state of being a Bushman or a Tikopian becomes an internalized, integral part of existence and represents the highest good, a person may lose even his motivation to live without this essential part of his identity. Much more research is

[16] Although not an anthropologist, Laurens van der Post has studied the Bushmen extensively and his readily available and readable works present an interesting account of these rapidly disappearing people. See *The Lost World of the Kalahari* (New York: William Morrow, 1958) and *The Heart of the Hunter* (New York: William Morrow, 1961). See also Elizabeth Marshall Thomas, *The Harmless People* (New York: Alfred Knopf, 1959) and Jens Bjerre, *Kalahari* (New York: Hill and Wang, 1960).

[17] *Freedom and Culture*, p. 34.

needed before any definite conclusions can be reached and, unfortunately, such evidence continually becomes more difficult to gather because cross-cultural influences are constantly increasing and simple societies are being forced to adapt or disappear.

As cultures overlap and buffet each other, conflict often results for the individuals involved. American Indians live in two entirely different cultures and the conflicts are not only handicapping but often stalemating for the individual. The evolving nations of Africa present many illustrations of the conflicts that ensue when one tribe merges with another to form a nation, particularly when the cultures of the separate tribes are distinctly different.[18] Modern India is continually torn by conflicts among its many cultural groups. Less dramatic but equally poignant conflicts occur everyday between individuals of different backgrounds in complex societies. The member of one group finds himself suddenly having to understand and accept the values of another and the result is more often than not failure in communication, heated argument, even physical violence, for internalized learnings are strong motivations.

Psychological discussions of motivating forces do not ordinarily acknowledge internalized learnings as motivations nor do they recognize the strength of the perpetuation of what is as a motivation. Yet the evidence supporting such an hypothesis is undeniable. Many phenomena can be explained only by the strong motivation present everywhere in all people to preserve the culture as each has known and become saturated in it. New internalizations can occur but vestiges of the old remain. Herskovits claims that even for Africans who have spent much time abroad "their early cultural conditioning" was a major force and "assured the retention of various deep-seated African patterns of behavior and thought, despite the most intensive exposure to other ways." [19]

What is needed is a thorough investigation of the motivating

[18] Melville J. Herskovits, *The Human Factor in Changing Africa* (New York: Alfred A. Knopf, 1962) is a penetrating study of continuity and change in culture. See also Kenyatta, *Facing Mount Kenya.*

[19] *Op. cit.,* p. 453.

trend to perpetuate the culture. When elderly people urge a "return" to the simple life or to "hard" education or to strict moral standards, they are endeavoring to preserve the way of life and behavior they knew or feel they knew. Psychologists have tended to dismiss this reluctance to accept change as purely negativistic and peculiar to old age. Unfortunately, this categorization has obscured the importance of the motivation to preserve one's culture and buried it in lists of behavior mechanisms.

It is hard to explain the ignoring of the major motivation to preserve one's culture when everyone readily acknowledges the importance of "vested interests." People recognize this tendency of others to protect their vested interests but usually limit interpretations of this trend to the economic sphere. A person fighting to preserve his vested interests, however, battles for far more than his livelihood. He fights for his way of thinking and doing not only because he may suffer material loss but also because he believes in the goodness and rightness of his approaches and ways of doing. He often insulates himself against change. The longer he has held a point of view, the more difficulty he experiences in changing it if he has thoroughly internalized it. The attempt to protect one's vested interests is simply one aspect of the tendency to perpetuate one's culture.

TO EXPRESS ONESELF WITHIN A CULTURE

The first three universal motivations do not allow for great individuality either among people within a single group or among societies. Everyone struggles to live, to belong, to internalize a culture, and to perpetuate his internalizations, but none of these strivings serves to explain completely the many differences among people of even the most homogeneous group. Certainly no two individuals make identical internalizations about their culture, but their learnings are similar enough to enable them to be recognized as members of the same group. If men did not struggle toward ends other than those summarized under the first three motives, they would probably show relatively little variation and their societies would not change, progress, or regress. Similarities in internalizations provide for continuity in cultures and for continuation of what has been done; but they cannot explain differences among individuals and changes in cultures.

The first three motives considered as a unit have a further limitation through implying that an individual is entirely the prisoner and product of his culture—and, of course, to some extent he is, but not entirely. If an individual strove only to secure the essentials, to be a member of his social group, to learn his culture, and to preserve it, he would not be an individual, merely an automaton-like creature who performs his social tasks much as do bees or ants. Hence the first three motives are not sufficient to explain man's individuality, his strivings for change, and his ability to oppose some of the traditional patterns of his culture.

When adults teach youngsters the ways of their culture, each child learns something slightly different. Even the learning of physical skills or factual knowledge gives evidence of this idiosyncrasy. Children in American schools spend at least six years learning penmanship. During and after this instruction and the coercion it entails, variations creep into students' handwriting to such an extent that the rigid instruction seems futile. Teachers also try to produce identical internalizations in spelling, but their failures are only too evident. Whatever the reasons for his difference, the student is expressing it through his failure to internalize completely one or another of the learnings his society deems important.

Constantly people learn far more than subject matter, information, and facts. Jules Henry[20] stresses what he calls the "inordinate capacity of a human being to learn more than one thing at a time" and illustrates his point by the American classroom. Here children learn, for example, to regard neatness as the highest good, to compete, to be afraid of certain situations, to cooperate, to keep their ideas to themselves, or to strive for success while dreaming of failure—and some, of course, learn none of these,

[20] Jules Henry, "American Schoolrooms: Learning the Nightmare," *Columbia University Forum,* 6:25, 27, Spring 1963.

but myriad others. In many businesses and professions, adults acquire similar internalizations. The composite nature of all learning tends, however, to be lost in a stress on subject matter, data, pedagogy, or the methods and mores of a particular industry or institution. Unfortunately, parents, educators, and employers as well as others cling to the myth that what they intend to teach is internalized and is all they actually do teach.

Whatever one learns, he uses in his actions, verbalizations, thinking, and feeling. His peculiar internalizations are what he expresses and contribute to his individuality. Each person seeks to express his learnings. The child dashes home from school to share some of his new learnings with his parents or friends; the Bushmen dance and sing the story of the last hunt for eland; the adult American tells his business friends the tale of his latest coup; the researcher writes up his findings. Expression can take any of many forms and all people everywhere share their internalizations and, in so doing, reveal their unique selves. This striving for self-expression within a culture constitutes another human motive, one which explains differences among individuals and societies.

Self-expression is necessarily a function of the culture in which the individual lives. Complex societies provide virtually unlimited ways in which an individual may express himself while smaller more homogeneous groups have fewer ways in which the individual can secure some satisfaction of this motive. All societies, however, influence the forms self-expression can take. Einstein, for example, born in Bali might have been an extremely talented *rabab* player or a complete misfit, but he probably would not have been a renowned physicist because Balinese society would not have provided him with the learnings necessary for theorizing in physics. The person who expresses himself through hallucinations is institutionalized in the United States, but may become a religious or medical leader in other social groups.[21] In all social groups, some forms of self-expression are acceptable,

[21] In this connection, see Ruth Benedict, "Anthropology and the Abnormal," *The Journal of General Psychology*, 10:59–79, 1934.

even honored; others are tolerated; still others are intolerable and involve the individual in conflict with his society. Culture influences self-expression through the learnings and opportunities it provides the individual and through its acceptance or rejection of his expression, but its influence is by no means exclusive.

The capacities of the individual also shape his self-expression for they help to determine his internalizations. Genetic inheritance plays an important role in the learnings of an individual and in the directions his expression may take. Sex, metabolic balance, energy level, physique, appearance, and intelligence-creativity are only a few of the factors filling this role. Some of these exert no influence in and of themselves, but are significant because of the way in which the society treats the individual having them. In groups where boys are educated and girls are not, sex obviously affects the forms self-expression takes. The individual whose appearance differs markedly from that of other members of his group may find himself on the fringe and so have to seek his forms of expression in solitary ways perhaps atypical of his culture. Many genetic factors influence the growth and development of the individual in this manner and affect not only the strivings of the individual for self-expression, but also his other strivings.

Perhaps most important for an understanding of the individual's striving to express himself is his endowment of a capacity for intelligence-creativity. Any mention of this capacity immediately raises the spectres of I. Q. scores, measurement devices, and all the paraphernalia associated with it in American society. Most current definitions of intelligence and creativity were designed to permit their measurement and so are as much artifacts of American culture as pots or baskets or beadwork are of a primitive society.[22] Because of this quantifying orientation, these defini-

[22] I. A. Taylor, for example, states that intelligence tests in the United States demonstrate "how fast relatively unimportant problems can be solved without making errors. In another culture, intelligence might be measured more in terms of how adequately important problems can be solved, making all the errors necessary and without regard for time." "The Nature of the Creative Process," *Creativity* (New York: Hastings House, 1959), p. 54.

tions do not permit their application cross-culturally and frequently obscure some aspects of these capacities even from people accustomed to measurement and its shortcomings. For this discussion, intelligence can be most usefully understood as the capacity to internalize a culture and creativity as the capacity to utilize those internalizations in more or less significant ways. Under these definitions, the individual who learns the ways of his people is giving evidence of intelligence and the idiosyncratic nature of those learnings and their expression show his creativity. Undoubtedly the two capacities are so closely related that separation is virtually impossible.[23]

[23] These definitions represent our attempt to give counselors a concept of intelligence-creativity directly related to cultural factors and concepts of human growth and development. Internalization undergirds what psychologists have long called the socialization process and makes understandable the successes and failures of youngsters trying to learn to think, feel, and behave the way society expects. Current definitions and tests of intelligence are too numerically oriented to allow counselors to consider students in other than linear terms. If counselors can view each individual as having a unique capacity that enables him to internalize some aspects of his culture, then perhaps they can view his achievements of whatever nature as accomplishments for him and expressions of his self.

Creativity has become an extremely muddy concept in the past few years. As Guilford remarks, " 'Creativity,' like 'love,' is a many-splendored thing. Small wonder that few have ventured to define it." (J. P. Guilford, "Potentiality for Creativity and Its Measurement," *Proceedings of the 1962 Invitational Conference on Testing Problems,* Princeton, Educational Testing Service, 1963, p. 31.) By and large, Americans have tended to define creativity in terms of the product resulting from the creative process or in terms of the significance of the contribution to the culture. Such a definition is post facto and useless when counselors try to discern creative potential (whatever that phrase means) in school children. Today the results of some tests seem to indicate that the intelligent, as measured by intelligence tests, are not creative and vice versa. Such a conclusion is patently ridiculous and should lead to a reexamination of the basic concepts and the measurement instruments. Intelligence tests are related to certain skills deemed important in American society, but creativity must be related to other facets of intelligence besides word comprehension, arithmetical ability, and reading skill. We, the authors, believe that intelligence and creativity go hand in hand, but that creativity is not solely a product of intellectual functioning. To a considerable extent, creativity seems to depend on the personality and motivation of the individual as well as his experience and learning in his social milieu. This orientation allows a humane approach to creativity and

Intelligence-creativity affects profoundly the self-expression of individuals in a variety of ways. The internalizations of people depend to a great extent on their capacity to learn their cultures. Individuals of average intelligence seem likely to show more similarities in their learnings than do those of above or below average capacity. Thus the internalizations of very high-ability or of very low-ability persons are apt to be more unusual, bizarre, and singular than those of the average. Everyone internalizes his culture, but the degree of intelligence exercises considerable influence on the nature of those learnings.

Intelligence-creativity also affects the uses the individual makes of his internalizations—and it is here that creativity in modern terms is most evident. The highly intelligent-creative individual tends to develop new ideas, ways of doing, and perspectives. An invention, a novel, a new theory, or an imaginative swindle are all examples of the forms this use of internalizations may take and all are expressions of the self of the individual. Individuals with great capacities are strongly motivated to use them and are capable of ignoring to some extent other motives and the pressures of society in order to achieve self-expression. Great intelligence-creativity seems to heighten and intensify the strivings of individuals for self-expression and serves to explain why some people will go to any lengths to pursue an idea or create a new entity.[24]

Societies tend to remember and applaud or deplore the self-expressions of their highly creative members. They also tend to overlook the evidence of intelligence-creativity in the self-expressions of those members whose capacity is not so great. Expression of it need not entail a significant contribution to society, but may simply take the form of living a "good life" in a familiar milieu

---

permits counselors to view some of the behavior and accomplishments even of the mentally retarded as "creative" in relation to their capacities. If parents, teachers, and counselors could accept and encourage rather than stifle the creativity of all students, they might find that "creative potential" exists in everyone.

[24] Cf. E. Paul Torrance, *Guiding Creative Talent* (Englewood Cliffs, N.J.: Prentice-Hall, 1962), p. 120 and *passim*.

and this in itself can be creative. All too often the intelligence-creativity involved in human relationships and everyday living is ignored in favor of that which leads to the discovery of penicillin or atomic fission. Perhaps most individuals never feel the intensity involved in the strivings for self-expression of the gifted, but they nevertheless strive for expression of their own uniqueness.

Individuals with a small capacity for intelligence-creativity also have a strong motive for self-expression. The internalizations of these individuals are often unusual, even erroneous, but they struggle to make them and their use of these learnings can be creative although society usually does not regard them as significant. Lessened capacity seems to direct the strivings for self-expression along lines suited to it. The mentally slow tend to limit their attempts toward self-expression to simple, obvious endeavors that go unrecognized. Even the less able, however, internalize, utilize their internalizations creatively, and make some contribution to their society even though the limited nature of their capacity may obscure the significance of their self-expressions.

Self-expression can take many forms that may or may not be acceptable to society. The man who murders his mother-in-law or devises a new confidence racket or defies the sanctions of the gods is expressing himself in ways most societies cannot tolerate whereas the man who invents a new vaccine, develops a mathematical theory, or draws a different design on his canoe paddle may be expressing himself in ways his society welcomes— but not always. Not all forms of self-expression are immediately acceptable. The Moslem or Hindu woman who scorns *purdah* and becomes active in politics or social reform often meets disapproval and ostracism. Darwinian theory after one hundred years of controversy is no longer a source of intense conflict although today it is not acceptable to everyone. Smallpox vaccination is still opposed by some groups. Innovations and ideas considered good by a society and fitting its existing patterns find readier acceptance than do those requiring a major readjustment. These conditions, however, are no guarantee of the acceptability of a contribution.

Self-expression finds varied outlets. It can be an idea, a theory, or a process. It can be a tangible work of art, product, or invention, which is functional or aesthetic or both. Sometimes self-expression is sought through a way of life, service to others, or simply being a Trobriander or a Tikopian. Too often there is a tendency to view as self-expression only those activities and products involved in artistic creation. Perhaps the emotional concomitants of such activity are apparent and thus make the involvement of self easily recognizable. The emotional factors are as important in the discovery of a drug or the invention of a machine as they are in the interpretation of a sonata or the painting of a picture.

Men can, of course, express themselves in ways running counter to the accepted mores of society. The criminal, delinquent, anarchist, atheist, traitor—all are expressing themselves in ways more or less intolerable to American society. The atheist is probably the most acceptable of these, but even he will meet some societal disapproval. Even the mentally ill find self-expression in bizarre behavior and fantasy, much of which is highly creative in nature. All societies attempt to direct the self-expressions of their members into socially desirable channels, but none is completely successful.

Like everything else, self-expression is relative to the individual. It is never the same for two people even though similarities may exist because of the opportunities their society offers. All areas of an individual's life are stamped with his uniqueness, which often tends to go unrecognized as societies become increasingly complex and technologically centered.

Man directs his strivings not toward the rewards—nor even away from the punishments—his society offers as much as toward the expression of his uniqueness. Only a consideration of self-expression as a fundamental motive can really explain the phenomenon as it exists in all cultures and continues to exist despite the forces acting to curb it. It is more than a culturally induced or culturally fostered happening; it is an intrinsic fact of life, a basic motivation.

TO ACHIEVE POSITIVE EXPERIENCES

Sensitive observers of "less civilized" groups of people have often noted but little analyzed a quality not easily observed in the Western world or perhaps stultified by the effects of the civilizing process. Eleanor Dark claims

> that we, nine-tenths of whose "progress" has been a mere elaboration and improvement of the technique, as opposed to the art, of living, might have learned much from a people [the Australian aborigines] who, whatever they may have lacked in technique, had developed that art to a very high degree. "Life, liberty, and the pursuit of happiness"—to us a wistful phrase, describing a far-away goal—sums up what was, to them, a taken-for-granted condition of their existence.[25]

Barbara Ward in a recent article discusses life, liberty, and happiness as she sees these qualities in the societies of emerging and about-to-emerge countries. She suggests that civilization "for all its progress, does not yet know how to add to health and long life and knowledge and material plenty the crowning gift of joy." [26] Anthropologists fortunate enough to revisit after a period of time groups they have studied have noted the positive constructive nature of some of the changes that have taken place as a result of time and cultural contacts.[27] In his discussion of the search for

[25] *The Timeless Land* (New York: Macmillan, 1941), pp. viii–ix.

[26] "We May Be Rich But They Are Happy," *The New York Times Magazine*, May 5, 1963, p. 121. The subtitle of the article is equally suggestive, "Western technology is transforming the prescientific communities of Asia and Africa. The question is: will they lose the secret of self-fulfillment in the process?"

[27] See Robert Redfield and Alfonso Villa Rojas, *Chan Kom, A Maya Village* (Chicago: University Press, Phoenix Books, 1962) and Robert Redfield, *A Village That Chose Progress, Chan Kom Revisited* (Chicago: University Press, Phoenix Books, 1962); Margaret Mead, *Growing Up in New Guinea* in *From the South Seas* (New York: W. W. Norton, 1939) and *New Lives for Old* (New York: Mentor Books, 1961).

values in the emerging countries of Africa, Herskovits implies the existence of this same constructive trend despite the expectation of probable negativeness.[28] Hence a novelist, an economist, and several anthropologists see in the human being and some of the societies he has created and elaborated something that points to the existence of strong strivings toward the art of living and the pursuit of happiness.

Until recently, psychologists have discussed only cursorily the relationship between the individual and happiness. They have usually stated goals in therapy as helping the person to achieve better adjustment, improved interpersonal relationships, or better personality integration. Although these changes might contribute to a happier individual, the phraseology has seldom included this idea; the approach has largely been that of improving something bad rather than enhancing something potentially good. Perhaps this limited view stems from the tendency of early theorists to stress one source of motivation to the exclusion of others. Freud, for example, overemphasized sex as a motivating force; Adler saw in inferiority feelings and the search for power the primary source of motivation; Jung with his concept of primal libido presumably linked motivation to undifferentiated psychic energy. These early theorists, however, were handicapped by working exclusively with neurotic and psychotic individuals.

Following the trend already started by Sullivan, Horney, and Fromm, Carl Rogers in his first book gave some general consideration to the satisfactions and the positive decisions of his counselees.[29] Elaborating his view but still theorizing within the framework of the needs concept, he states that "the organism has one basic tendency and striving—to actualize, maintain, and enhance the experiencing organism." [30] Rogers claims that this need includes all others—and possibly it does if one accepts the needs concept of motivation. Rogers' approach has the further disad-

[28] *The Human Factor in Changing Africa,* Chapter 14.

[29] Carl R. Rogers, *Counseling and Psychotherapy* (New York: Houghton Mifflin, 1942), pp. 174–238.

[30] Carl R. Rogers, *Client-Centered Therapy* (New York: Houghton Mifflin, 1951), p. 487.

vantage of mixing those motivations having a definite, distinguishable physical stimulus at their base and those deriving from the culture and experience of the individual. Nevertheless, Rogers' discussion of the positive trend of the organism points the way toward a less negative concept of human motivation.

Maslow has also based his theory of motivation on the concept of needs, but he has made more explicit than Rogers the positive trend of human beings, calling it the need for self-actualization. Maslow describes it as "man's desire for self-fulfillment, . . . the tendency for him to become actualized in what he is potentially." [31] In his later book, he considers motivation under the two headings—Deficiency and Growth Motivations—and seems to be moving away from the stereotyped concept of needs, although it still underlies his theorizing. He continues to consider needs as forming a hierarchy of prepotency and to view the healthy person as having sufficient gratification of his deficiency needs and, therefore, being motivated chiefly by trends toward self-actualization. Here again the objection is to his reliance on the concept of needs and his demarcation between the two types of needs as well as to the static and unrealistic concept of an hierarchy of prepotency of needs.[32]

Maslow has nevertheless performed an important service by emphasizing the constructive aspects of personality and the trend of the individual toward self-actualization. Such a postulation is

[31] *Motivation and Personality*, pp. 91–92; see also Chapters 12 and 13.

[32] A. H. Maslow, *Toward a Psychology of Being*, pp. 19–41, 177–200. One difficulty has always muddied theories of motivation—especially when the counselor tries to apply them to his work with individuals. The early theorists were physicians and psychology arose out of a medical base, which it has never shed. Concepts of homeostasis and equilibrium are physiological in origin and application, but they have colored and influenced psychological theories of motivation. Physiologically, the body may seek homeostasis and equilibrium; indirectly, bodily malfunctions may affect behavior. Psychologically, however, man strives for more than mere balance or maintenance of the status quo. The effects of an inoperative gland may signal the need for medical attention, but these effects in and of themselves are not motives in the way that the universal motivating forces outlined in this chapter are. The subtle influence of medical concepts has often served to channel psychology.

essential when psychologists try to explain the behavior not only of the mentally well but also of the mentally ill striving for improvement. While the idea is not new with Maslow,[33] he is the first to amass the evidence and present it forcefully and cogently.

Hence psychologists, scholars in other behavioral sciences, and laymen are all seeking some way of describing and expressing the positive aspects of men's life and behavior. Self-actualization, full-functioning, and self-fulfillment seem to be psychological expressions for the pursuit of happiness and the art of living. What everyone seems to be saying is that the individual seeks to achieve some positive, personally satisfying experiences in the course of his lifetime.

Much of what has been written about striving for positive experiences is misleading. Maslow, for example, describes self-actualization as a process and implies that one goes through a series of stages leading to an ultimate state. He indicates that self-actualization requires a person to be whatever he is capable of being. [34] Although self-actualization in Maslow's terms undoubtedly contributes to and enhances a person's enjoyment of positive experiences, the achievement of self-actualization does not seem to be a prerequisite for having them. Anyone and everyone—except perhaps the mentally ill and this may be why they are mentally ill—has some positive, satisfying experiences in his life. Perhaps the self-actualizing undergo these experiences more often and feel them more intensely, but they are not the sole prerogative of a select group.

Almost all people experience transitory moments of complete satisfaction and happiness. No one achieves and lives in a state of blissful euphoria for any prolonged period of time. Pleasurable experiences may last for varying amounts of time, but never indefinitely. A person may be generally happy and contented, but recall certain specific moments when he was con-

[33] See, for example, Erich Fromm, *Man for Himself* (New York: Rinehart, 1947) and Rogers, *Client-Centered Therapy*. Unfortunately, Rogers linked his interpretation of constructive trends so closely to bodily growth trends that his readers tended to overlook this aspect of his theory.

[34] *Motivation and Personality*, pp. 91–92.

sciously aware of an intensity of joy quite unlike the calmer emotions of his day-by-day existence.

Such positive moments may or may not be related to a product. A housewife may feel joy in the production of a delicious meal, but she may also experience happiness in the intimacy of her family group. A gifted artist may find total satisfaction in contemplating his newly completed painting or from working on it and lose interest in it upon completion. A sense of achievement may cause the positive moments of some people, but again not always.

Positive experiences may involve sensual or aesthetic satisfaction. The feeling as the golf club hits the ball with a sharp crack provides one example of positive sensual experience probably not unadulterated by satisfaction in achievement. Sexual intercourse may be a source of sensual pleasure although it is probably mixed with joy in the shared experience and the heightened sense of intimacy with another person. The sight of a picture or the reading of a poem may also inspire aesthetic pleasure in the viewer or reader.

Sometimes for some people complete happiness is directly related to dissatisfaction. The artist who after many attempts and great discouragement achieves the right color or line may experience a rapid transition from dissatisfaction to pure joy. The crippled child attempting to hold a crayon and one day managing not only to grasp but to draw with it may shift from utter disgust at his own ineptitude to sheer delight. Perfection is often associated with pleasurable moments, but it is not a requirement for their occurrence.

Such experiences are shaped by the society in which the individual lives. It defines, although often vaguely and tacitly, those that may be constructive, happy, or satisfying. For the Buddhist, self-fulfillment may come only through his loss of self in the contemplation of his God. The Bushman may find his joy in overeating until his belly is far distended to make up for past times of hunger and to celebrate present abundance. Neither act would be a source of joy for most twentieth-century Americans.

In fact, many Americans seem to be suspicious of joy, happiness, and spontaneity. They ridicule the person who describes a meaningful experience and avoid their own and others' attempts to express great joy or satisfaction. Even young children learn not to exhibit too exuberantly their pleasure in accomplishments or experiences lest they appear too self-centered or competitive. Perhaps little has been written about the positive trends of human beings because of this prohibition and the inhibitions arising from it.[35]

Positive moments are a function of the individual and, even to him, largely unpredictable. No one can be sure what will prove satisfying or productive of happiness for another. The counselor informing a student that he scored at the 98th percentile on a standardized test may be disconcerted when the student does not derive satisfaction from this accomplishment, but rather worries about the "large" number of students who scored higher than he. The nonmusic lover dragged to the opera expecting to loathe it, suddenly finds himself caught up in the beauty of the voices. Happy experiences for each individual will depend on the society in which he lives and what he personally has learned from that society. Because each individual's learnings are different, his satisfactions, joys, pleasures, even self-fulfillment will be evoked by many, varied experiences.

All people have the potential for enjoying positive experiences and feelings. Probably most people with the development of greater spontaneity, receptivity to, and acceptance of, such expe-

[35] This trend is noticeable in the poets whom Americans admire. Whereas Browning, now considered passé, claimed that "God's in his heaven/All's right with the world," T.S. Eliot, the new prophet, predicted that we are going out "not with a bang but a whimper." Today Americans regard tragedy as great drama and relegate comedy to the lightminded and frivolous. When they speak of improving television programs, most suggestions deal with covering news in depth or acquainting people with current problems. Pleasurable programs without an obvious didactic purpose are suspect. Yet even in the face of the annihilation of man as a species, individual men continue to seek for and strive to attain moments of happiness, joy, and satisfaction. The experiences eliciting these feelings may vary, but the striving goes on.

riences could achieve more of them. Their strivings serve to explain many of the constructive actions of individuals and even some of their less socially acceptable behavior. Such a motivation lies behind the efforts of handicapped individuals to learn to live with their disabilities and to achieve positive experiences despite the obstacles they face. For the youngster beset by so many difficulties that he sees no way out, stealing or other aggressive acts may be an unconscious and unrecognized striving for help toward a more satisfying life. It makes understandable the efforts of socially, economically, and culturally deprived youngsters to overcome the prejudices of society. This concept illuminates continual striving against seemingly insurmountable odds and many failures.

The striving for positive experiences is a cross-cultural fact. When Barbara Ward speaks of joy or Eleanor Dark of the art of living or Maslow of self-actualization, they are describing man's motivation to seek positive life experiences. Such experiences include the simple pleasures of the child, the ecstasy of the saint, the frantic productivity of the creative artist, or the quiet intimacy of the family man. Regardless of complexity or simplicity, sophistication or naïveté, or spontaneity or inhibition, these positive experiences are intensely meaningful to individuals and they continue to strive for them.

THE INTERPLAY OF MOTIVES

To live, to internalize a culture, to perpetuate internalized learnings, to express oneself within a culture, and to achieve positive experiences—these are the universal motivating forces. Regardless of time, location, society, and culture, men find themselves impelled by these motives. The outcomes of them may vary widely, but the forces causing men to strive are identical.

The listing of motives as discrete entities should not obscure the essential interplay of them, for none operates alone. All are always active because man lives as a holistic being. The outsider viewing a particular society may not be able readily to see all

the motives in operation, but his inability does not mean they
do not exist. The standards of living, the lore of the tribe, the
forms of self-expression, and the joys that furnish positive experiences for the member of a simple community may puzzle the
American accustomed to his complex modes of living, his extensive symbolism, his masses of recorded learnings, and his formally
organized recreations. In both societies, the interplay of motives
is constant. Only ethnocentrism camouflages their existence.

The basic motivations are always intermingled at any stage
of a person's life. The society in which a person lives may accent
one or another of them and thus create the impression that at
certain ages some of the motivations are superordinate. All
societies, for example, stress childhood as a period of internalizing
the culture: the child must be taught those learnings that will
make him a socialized, constructive member of his group. Its
members determine the extent of this youthful period of intense
learning. The individual learner, however, experiences a constant
interplay of and varying emphases on motives not necessarily
corresponding to the one stressed by his culture as paramount.
Moreover, his basic motivation to internalize is life-long. Similarly most societies tend to regard the perpetuation of the culture
as a striving peculiarly powerful among the elders of the group,
but this motive is strong for all people of whatever age. The
child perpetuates his internalizations with the same tenacity as
the adult. Societal emphases can easily obfuscate the constant
and life-long interplay of motives for each individual.

Just as all five motives operate simultaneously so also there
is no set hierarchy of prepotency among them. The strength of
the various motives depends entirely on the individual at a point
in time. Temporarily one motive may seem to overshadow the
others for a certain individual, as he seeks wholeheartedly to
learn, for example, or express or enjoy himself, but such ordering
is never static. Sometimes circumstance determines the prepotency of motive for an individual as when his striving to live
takes precedence over all others. Hence another basic character-

istic of the five universal motivating forces is that their ordering is different not only for each individual but also for a single individual at various points in time.

Herein lies an important approach to a real theory of individual differences. American society favors ordered lists and the recent popularity of the concept of a hierarchy of motives is probably a cultural phenomenon. There is a security in ordering motives and suggesting that one motive after another can be satisfied in a steady progression toward a blissful state of nirvana or self-actualization. Such superimposed hierarchies, however, negate the idea of man as a dynamic being and interfere with a solid approach to individual differences. Concepts of prepotency actually prevent understanding of the individual.

Understanding human behavior depends on a theory incorporating concepts of change and dynamism. Striving is never a single-line endeavor. The constant interplay among the basic motivations means that men establish consciously or unconsciously their own hierarchies at different times and that satisfaction of any motive is temporary and often incomplete. Striving is always a mixture of motivations and only the individual establishes the changing prepotency among them.

Another important characteristic of the motivations is that they always produce conflict for the individual. Man's struggles to live, learn, perpetuate, express, and enjoy himself more often than not run counter to each other. The most dramatic conflicts are often those between the individual and his culture because all cultures punish the person whose expressions of himself and his uniqueness go too far beyond the accepted norms. In an age of great freedom of expression, Socrates was sentenced to death. Semmelweis was persecuted and hounded merely for suggesting that physicians wash their hands after examining one patient before proceeding to the next. To Americans in the twentieth century, such intolerance of free expression and scientific advance is unthinkable, but the Scopes trial, the censoring of textbooks, and the plight of teachers attempting to instruct about Communism provide examples of expression intolerable to this society. The limits on self-expression vary continually not only among cultures but within them and evolve out of the fabric of each. For the individual himself, the conflict is not simply one between culture and self-expression. His conflicts are unique to him and caused by the interplay of motives. Socrates faced a clear-cut choice between death and self-expression, but most conflicts are not so dramatic. The individual seeking to promulgate a new idea is, as Torrance points out, a minority of one.[36] His conflict probably begins with his own struggles to internalize the ideas of others as taught to him while he finds himself questioning and making different combinations. He may struggle for expression or inhibition. He may even face a choice between his expression and way of life, as did Semmelweis or Socrates.

Less dramatic but equally important internal conflicts occur everyday for all individuals. In any society, for example, the individual must do some kind of work in order to live. Working may not provide positive experiences and may curtail self-expression. The worker may find the internalizations of his associates far different from his own and face constant choices between expressing his point of view and alienating his group, even losing his job. The cardiac patient faces a constant conflict between his desires to live and to perpetuate his previous way of life. All strivings carry the potentiality for conflict.

Each individual embroiders basic conflicts with the subsidiary motives learned in his own society. The workman who stays on a job offering him no positive experiences discusses his conflict in such societal terms as security, the good life, concern for family, comparative salary, prestige, and his own age and training. He views his conflicts in terms dictated by his society. The basic nature of these conflicts, however, remains the same: the inevitable interplay of motives.

The nature of the motivating forces not only explains differences among men but also among their cultures. Because each

[36] Torrance, *Guiding Creative Talent*, p. 104.

man has his own ethnocentric biases, complete understanding of another person or culture is perhaps an impossible goal, but partial understanding is both possible and essential. Clashes between individuals are unavoidable when what one man deems right runs counter to another's definition of the "good" and each fights to preserve his own way of life. Recognition of the universal motivating forces and the differences among men, however, can aid understanding of the subtle points that lie at the base of many controversies both between individuals and societies.

The theory of motivation presented here explains both similarities and differences in human behavior. All men are similar because they share the five basic motivations. Groups of men are similar because each society promotes certain specific learnings. Differences arise from men's selective internalizing and the varying capacities they bring to learning. Moreover, the nature of internalization, the interplay of the basic motives, and the ordering of them is individual. Just as important, the conflicts and prepotency among motives vary for the individual from time to time. Herein lies the key to individual differences and dynamism.

A view of man as constantly in conflict may seem bleak and pessimistic. Yet it furnishes a picture of him as an eternally striving being capable of learning, creating, and enjoying, free within the limits of his culture and experience to make his own choices. Only a view of him as truly dynamic can provide a basis for optimism about man.

Conflicts are disquieting, unsettling, and disrupting both for individuals and groups. But these conflicts serve to keep men striving for improvement, change, preservation, and perfection. Motivation and its inevitable conflict perhaps constitute the greatest human good. The Bushmen of the Kalahari explain it simply, "There is a dream dreaming us."

2

SOURCES OF SUBSIDIARY MOTIVES

Every society embellishes the universal motivating forces with other motives representative of that particular group. The exact nature, content, and form of these culturally derived motives vary from individual to individual within a single group. They differ even more widely from group to group. These singular embellishments of the universal motives often tend to cloak them and to obscure their basic nature.

The motives clustering around the universals either singly or in combination are subsidiary. The universal motives operate anywhere at any time and within any person and do not depend on such extraneous considerations as skin color, social class, religion, occupation, experience, geographical location, and tribe. Subsidiary motives, on the other hand, may be common within a particular culture, are highly personal, and depend on many extraneous factors. Subsidiary does not mean less important to the individual, but rather secondary to the universals. The word carries the connotation here of specialized, particularized to a culture, and not universal.

To the individual, his subsidiary motives may seem all-important. Especially in an affluent society, the essentials of food and shelter are frequently so taken for granted that a person directs his striving toward what he considers the best foods served in a proper fashion and what he judges the right home in a desirable neighborhood. The elaborations he, as a product of his culture, strives for may symbolize to him what he and his society deem worth the effort—prestige, status, the trappings of success. Not all individuals and societies favor the same embellishments. The ones preferred by a particular society, however, are more often than not those of which the individual is most aware and for which he strives.

Obviously each society shapes to a certain extent the subsidiary motives of its members, but each individual determines his own by what he internalizes from his culture, experiences, and learnings. In order to facilitate understanding, a counselor must have some realization of his counselee's subsidiary motives, of the forces that drive him and make him different from any other human being. The counselor, in particular, has to comprehend not only the idiosyncratic interplay of universal motives, but also the varieties of subsidiary motives with which each person embroiders the universals.

The key to understanding any individual's subsidiary motives is a knowledge of the primary sources of these motives. These sources are the same everywhere: the values, ways of thinking, and ways of doing that each person internalizes. The content of these areas varies widely but the same basic sources give rise to subsidiary motives everywhere.

Unfortunately, values, ways of thinking, and ways of doing are often not easily distinguished. They are so much a part of the individual that he cannot readily discern his own internalizations of them. Anthropologists studying other cultures often note the difficulties of subordinating their own values and ways sufficiently enough to understand those of another people. Subgroups within a large, pluralistic nation such as the United States pose similar problems. The difficulty of recognizing commonalities and differences in American values, ways of thinking, and ways of doing does not excuse the counselor from the attempt. Without it, he can never begin to understand his counselees and why they do what they do.

VALUES

In every society, men strive for whatever they judge to be good and right. Thus motives and values are virtually inseparable because what men strive for must be worth the physical and psychological endeavor entailed in the struggle. Value may be attached to the tangibles of food or drink or the intangibles of love or prestige. Value may describe a belief that is especially important to an individual or group or it may simply relate to one facet of the way of life of some particular human being. These values are inextricably linked to motives and provide at least one explanation for the relative strengths and changing patterns of motives.

The concept of value is important for it replaces the needs approach to motivation with a positive explanation of why men do what they do. In the needs theory, good is equated with the elimination of a lack. A man strives for love because he does not have it and needs it. Essentially he is struggling to fill a void. The introduction of the idea of value, however, changes this interpretation of man's struggle for love to a striving for something that he has learned is good or right or has value. This substitution of values for needs supplies a positive rationale for motivation where formerly there was only a negative one.

 Essentially a value is a learned belief so thoroughly internalized that it colors the actions and thoughts of the individual and produces a strong emotional-intellectual response when anything runs counter to it. The person operating on the basis of some particular value feels he must think and behave in a certain way because he has learned that that way is "good" or "right." The individual who goes to church every Sunday is demonstrating a value concerning organized religion and may experience strong feelings of guilt and shame when he misses church without some such personally acceptable excuse as illness. The person who believes that liquor is "bad" may be revolted when forced to be a member of a group of people who are drinking. A value is not a value without the connotations of "good" or "bad" or "right" or "wrong" and without the emotional factors integral to it.

Values are learned. Infants do not come into the world equipped with the knowledge that some behaviors and thoughts are "good" or "right." Adults begin teaching values explicitly the

day a child is born and reinforce learning through a never-ending
system of rewards and punishments. Cleanliness is good, lying is
bad, stealing is bad, fighting is bad, sharing is good, and politeness is good are only a few of the values many adults consciously
and systematically try to instill in young children. As children
grow older, value teaching becomes less absolute and they learn
both from adults and for themselves that cleanliness is good, but
not when carried to an extreme and that fighting is bad except
when done subtly and nonphysically to advance oneself. All
these teachings are intensified by such rewards or punishments
as praise, affection, material gifts, humiliation, rejection, and
scolding. These impress upon children the importance of the
learnings they are expected to make.

In addition to the values they are taught explicitly, children
internalize many others. The boy who has been taught that
swearing is bad may learn a different value while listening to his
father chat with his friends or make household repairs. The
youngster internalizes values about appropriate masculine behavior and language that may or may not coincide with those
adults are consciously trying to teach him. The teacher or counselor who asserts that all students are equal and then favors
bright or light-complexioned ones is teaching a value that his
students recognize and may or may not internalize as their own.
In the teaching of values, actions often speak louder than words
and prove more effective than all the moralistic lectures of
parents, teachers, counselors, and other adults.

The child first learns values from the important adults in
his life, especially his parents. Later, school personnel and his
peers take over some of this teaching function with the peer group
assuming major importance as the youngster moves through
adolescence. Association with people of differing values leads the
youngster to examine his own and modify or reinforce them in
the light of his experiences. The process of value-modification
or value-reinforcement is life-long for the individual as his horizons widen and his experiences increase.

The personal idiosyncratic set of values of each individual

is not wholly dependent upon those of others. Each child makes his own interpretation of the values he sees expressed in the activities and speech of others. Some he may internalize, some he may ignore, and others he may use to modify previous learnings. Thus the boy listening to his father swear may learn certain values, but what he learns will depend upon his understanding of the situation, his perception of his father's behavior, and the meaning to him of what is going on. The teacher who shows bias toward Negro youngsters in the classroom may profoundly affect the value learnings of his Negro students at the same time that his actions may have less effect upon his white students for whom such discrimination has less personal meaning. Such a teacher may also, of course, be teaching his white students a set of values concerning race. Each individual internalizes values as they have meaning for him, as he perceives them, and as he has the capacity to understand them. The result of this internalization is unique to the individual and seldom if ever precisely what adults think they are teaching.

An individual's life would be relatively simple if he had a limited number of mutually exclusive values by which he could order his behavior and thoughts. Unfortunately for his peace of mind, he has many values overlapping and conflicting with one another. A youngster learns that he must always be polite to grown-ups and must never lie. Faced with a situation in which he must lie in order to be polite or be rude in order to be honest, the child finds himself in a value conflict that is essentially unsolvable. Children do, of course, squirm out of such situations by lying, by being rude, or by evasion, but the conflict is there as are others similar to it and more serious. Conflicts are inevitable because sets of values are never logical, consistent, or mutually exclusive.

Further complications arise because everyone has two corresponding sets of values—the ideal and the relaxed. The ideal values are the absolutes, which dictate that one must never steal or cheat or commit adultery. The relaxed values are the relatives, which people express when they steal a little or cheat a little (but not too much of either) or have an occasional extramarital excursion. Children, especially in middle-class homes, are expected to live up to the ideal values at the same time that they see their parents expressing the relaxed set in their actions. Thus the child is expected always to tell the truth while his mother lies to a neighbor in refusing an invitation. Or the youngster is expected to be completely honest in his school work while his father shaves his income tax in a highly questionable way and even brags about his cleverness. People generally judge themselves according to the relaxed set of values and others according to the ideal. Such phrases as "Do as I say, not as I do" or "You should practice what you preach" embody people's recognition of the existence of these two sets of values and the differences in their use.

Values differ in their relative importance to the individual. To some extent, relative importance depends upon the distance of the value from the person. Thus most Americans believe in the Bill of Rights and would resist attempts to alter that list of values. And yet these same Americans will attempt to censor school textbooks or to prevent the teaching of evolution in the high school of their town. Freedom of speech and expression is an accepted value for many people as long as its implementation does not too intimately affect their lives. The present civil rights struggles provide many illustrations of this concept of distance in values. For example, many Americans feel that Negroes should be able to buy houses in all sections of a community until one attempts to do so in their neighborhood. The relative importance of some values depends upon the degree of closeness and the immediate effect their application might have upon the individual believing in them.

Relative importance is also a function of the individual, his life situation, and past experiences at the time his values are examined. Thus the upward-striving man may discard some of the values he learned as a child and modify others simply because other things are now more important to him. The person who considers alcohol reprehensible may gradually begin to drink a little and to serve cocktails in order to win acceptance in a social group to which he aspires or to be like the other people in his business group. The value negating alcohol assumes in time less relative importance than the values relating to success, social acceptance, and identification with an admired group. Values change as the person changes in response to his learnings, his experiences, and his contacts with other people.

Values find one form of expression in the judgments people make about themselves and others. Any statement incorporating the idea that something is good or bad or right or wrong is a value judgment. "Divorce is wrong" or "Hard work is good" are obvious value judgments as are the comments teachers are required to make about the work, behavior, and personal qualifications of their students. Parents make value judgments about their children as do employers about their employees and even friends about each other. Individuals also make such value judgments about themselves as "I'm no good" or "I'm a failure" or "I really am a worthwhile person." As they grow older, people seem to judge themselves in terms of the relaxed values and others in terms of the ideal, but adolescents who have not been tempered by time and experience seem to judge themselves harshly in terms of their ideal values. Since the judgments of oneself and others form an important part of the individual's self-concept, this tendency makes adolescence and early adulthood extremely difficult.

Not all value judgments are as obvious as those previously cited. The counselor who says, "You will lose $50,000 during your lifetime if you quit school now" is implying that $50,000 in possible future earnings makes staying in school worthwhile— and perhaps it does to him, but it may not to the student. The counselor is also implying that school and study can be evaluated in terms of dollars and cents, which may or may not be what he wishes to convey to the student. The counselor who suggests to a student interested in languages that she consider the state university instead of a distant college specializing in languages with which he is unfamiliar and to which she wants to go is subtly making a value judgment. Through questions and comments, he may imply the judgment that the distant college is too expensive, too far, an unwise choice, or even that the student is being ungrateful in not taking advantage of the opportunities open to her in her own state. The parent who tells his youngster that he must have reasons for behaving as he does and insists that he state them implies the judgment that everyone has and knows the reasons for his own behavior. The implications of good and bad are present in all these examples even though the words themselves are not used.

Value judgments can be expressed in ways other than words. The counselor whose attention obviously wanders during an interview is implying that this student is not worth his full consideration. The parent who ignores a child in favor of other pursuits is making much the same judgment. The counselor who evades all the efforts of his counselee to introduce the topics of dating and sex into the content of the interview implies that sex is not a suitable topic for discussion. Regardless of how the counselor or parent intended his behavior to be understood, the implications to the youngster remain and have to be taken into consideration in understanding his reactions.

Value judgments are an inevitable part of living. Opinions, advice, discussion, thinking, and actions are all replete with value judgments. In this connection, it is important to reemphasize the emotional factors involved in values and the emotional reactions that ensue when values are questioned or countered. A value judgment is as much an emotional response as anger or fear, but less easily recognized as such. The counselor who believes firmly that woman's place is in the home is reacting emotionally when he belittles a girl's vocational plans and suggests that marriage will be her career. Value judgments are a part of everyday life but in a counseling situation they must be recognized for what they are and avoided.

Values differ radically from society to society and even among groups and individuals within a single society. Anthropologists claim that individuals brought up in one society can never completely understand the values of another. Americans and Western Europeans share much the same cultural heritage, but even among these peoples differences in and misunderstandings of values are frequent and baffling.[1] Individuals internalize the values of their particular society and these internalizations lead to some of the differences among people from various national or geographical groups. The general values of a society are those to which the majority of the members at least pay lip service and which they will defend in times of crisis.

For Americans, the values associated with democracy are the first of many possible general values. Freedom and equality together with responsible citizenship are values about which most Americans would agree, although many do not give evidence of this agreement in their actions. The Constitution guarantees to everyone the right to express his own individuality as long as he does so with respect for the rights of other citizens. That Americans are tending less and less to respect the right of the individual is evident in the writings of some authors and in the growing concern with conformity and stifling of talent.[2]

Americans also share some general values stemming from the Judeo-Christian tradition. The belief in the worth and dignity of each human being is a direct outgrowth of the Judeo-Christian ethic and is basic to many democratic principles as well as to the religious beliefs of many Americans. The Golden Rule, although not the exclusive property of Christians, represents another value deriving from the American heritage of religious and philosophical thinking. The Ten Commandments embody values to which most Americans subscribe although they not infrequently fail to express them in their actions. Whether implemented or not, however, these values and many others are part of the systems taught to many American children and form part of those subscribed to by a majority of the population.

[1] As illustration, see V. S. Pritchett, "The Americans in My Mind" and William Golding. "Advice to a Nervous Visitor," *Holiday*, July 1963.

[2] See in this connection, David Riesman and others, *The Lonely Crowd* (New Haven: Yale University Press, 1950) and *Individualism Reconsidered* (Glencoe, Ill.: Free Press, 1954). Many other authors touch on these problems.

The United States was founded and settled during the Age of Enlightenment in Europe. Inevitably ideas and values growing out of the thinking of the eighteenth-century philosophers became part of the American heritage expressed, for example, in the Declaration of Independence and the Constitution. None is so pervasive, however, as the idea of progress and perfectibility.[3] Most Americans believe that progress must be constantly forward and upward and that man and society are infinitely perfectible. These values are expressed in such phrases as "Tomorrow will be better" or "Society should not allow such things to happen." On a more personal level, the efforts of adolescents to improve themselves and their behavior attests to their belief in perfectibility and progress.

The Puritan ethic also contributes to the general values of American society. Work is good and man owes it to God to work diligently. His efforts should be crowned with success, usually material, and his friends will recognize that he has thereby found favor in the eyes of God and man. The Puritan ethic incorporates a concept of man as sinful and a view of life as a period of preparation for the after-life. Pleasure either physical or spiritual is bad and *joie de vivre* is alien to the Puritan outlook. Many of the Puritan values have been tempered and softened by the liberalizing influences that come with the passage of time, but traces of them remain. The belief that life is grim, that work is good regardless of whether or not one enjoys it, and that joy is slightly sinful are all examples of the Puritan ethic in modern life.[4]

Values change and even the general values of a society are modified over the years. Since World War I, psychology has supplied new values for American society and modified old ones. The May 17, 1954, United States Supreme Court decision on school desegregation expresses some of these in its discussion of the problem. Psychological values are only too evident in the

[3] Carl L. Becker, *The Heavenly City of the Eighteenth-Century Philosophers* (New Haven: Yale University Press, 1959), pp. 119ff.

[4] For a discussion of the Puritan values as they relate to work, see Ruth Barry and Beverly Wolf, *An Epitaph for Vocational Guidance* (New York: Bureau of Publications, Teachers College, Columbia University, 1962), pp. 169–172.

questions posed by a brilliant teen-ager, "Can I have a normal life if I become a nuclear scientist? Won't people think I'm queer?" Psychological normality, the deleterious effects of an unhappy childhood, the harmful aspects of anxiety and repression, and the acceptability of nervousness as an explanation for almost anything are only a few examples of possible psychological values. These merge with the American belief in perfectibility and strengthen the ideas that the mentally ill can be made well and that mental health is a goal for all. The amount of psychological information (and misinformation) current among teenagers continually surprises counselors and provides teen-agers with some handy rationalizations for their behavior.[5]

These examples of general American values are only a few of the many that might be cited. By and large, general values find their place in the ideal sets of values of most Americans. These tend to be distant from the individual and to have for him minimal relative importance unless and until the expression of them impinges directly on his everyday life. Thus some Americans believe in freedom of speech until they discover that a professor at a university supported by their taxes is teaching about Communism. To some people, general values are all right in theory, but their implementation can lead to consternation and controversy. Needless to say, many Americans implement many general values in their actions and daily lives. Some of these values, however, serve more as ideals than as regulators of individual conduct.[6]

[5] See Richard T. LaPiere, *The Freudian Ethic* (New York: Duell, Sloan & Pearce, 1959). LaPiere sees the Freudian ethic as replacing the Puritan and blames many of the current American problems in ethics and morals on the substitution. From our point of view, his extremist position is not defensible. Psychological values, however, seem to have provided the individual with a convenient and welcome way of divorcing himself from complete responsibility for his actions. Psychology provides explanations, but some Americans seem to view it as offering excuses.

[6] H. H. Remmers and D. H. Radler, *The American Teenager* (Indianapolis: Bobbs-Merrill, 1957). According to this study, high school students believed in the Bill of Rights when it was identified as such, but not in its specific provisions when they were not related to the title, Bill of Rights.

Every individual has values more personal to him than the general ones characterizing much of his society. He learns these early from parents and other adults and modifies or replaces them as his experiences broaden. Naturally such values are not his exclusive property for many others in his community, state, or nation share them. Thus the American value lauding bigness as a measure of importance and goodness finds expression both generally and personally. The student who feels he lacks scope in the rural or small-town environment and the youngster who states, "I know I'm a hick" demonstrate their admiration for bigness. Many Americans share this value but it can be more personally meaningful and of greater relative importance to some individuals.

Social class influences personal value systems. During the past thirty years, sociologists have delineated the social classes in American society and demonstrated interesting differences in values among members of the various classes. In their attempts to order and organize disparate materials, some sociologists have defined value orientations characterizing each class and labeled the group in terms of its orientation. In so doing, they have often lost the details of individual values and the vast differences among members of the same class.[7] While social class is a convenient peg on which to hang a discussion of some common American values, these are neither the peculiar prerogative of all members of one class nor are they defined in the same way by all persons of whatever class or even of the same class. Thus a lower-class person may value, strive for, and achieve some measure of grace-

[7] In this connection, see Joseph A. Kahl, *The American Class Structure* (New York: Holt, Rinehart, and Winston, 1961), pp. 184–220. Kahl defines five social classes characterized respectively by value orientations toward graceful living, career, respectability, getting by, and apathy. While such characterizations may be useful to the sociologist, they destroy for the counselor trying to understand his students the many specific values entering into these orientations and the tremendous differences among the values of individuals of the same or differing classes. Far more helpful to the counselor are the various studies of particular communities such as those of Warner, Havighurst, Hollingshead, Seeley, Drake, and Frazier. For complete references, see the Bibliographical Note.

ful living as he defines graceful living—and his definition will not
be the sociologist's. Apathy may characterize the value orientation of some lower-class individuals, but it certainly does not
apply to the behavior of many lower-class students. The dangers
of oversimplification, overcategorization, and overgeneralization
mean a loss of the individual in a discussion of typical class values.

Despite the dangers, studies of class have isolated many
American values. These studies have singled out such middle-
class values as cleanliness, privacy, competition, cooperation, the
worth of education, success, modesty, and planning ahead.[8]
Many middle-class youngsters also learn the value of being the
best or the first and doing better than their parents. Long-range
planning and the postponement of rewards are significant values.
The middle-class youngster is expected, therefore, to work diligently through four years of high school for the reward of college
admission and then to start the process again for the college
degree.

Lower-class values differ markedly from those of the middle
group. Many lower-class people regulate their lives according to
a *carpe diem* philosophy—take what you can get now because you
may not get it later. This approach negates many such middle-
class values as long-range planning, postponed rewards, and the
worth of education. Many lower-class children cannot comprehend the attempts of school personnel to engage them in plans
for the future. Similarly the value lauding education and the
importance of graduating at least from high school are concepts
foreign to many of these students for they seldom learn such
values from their parents or other significant adults.

Kahl characterizes the value orientation of the lower class
under the heading Apathy, but he might better have used Apathy-
Violence. While lower-class members are often apathetic about
their chances for getting better jobs, having better lives, or even
striving for these "ideals," they also react violently to their life

---

[8] Our list does not include thrift because the advent of installment
buying has lessened the strength of thrift as a value for many people—
except possibly the managers of savings banks.

situations. Unlike the middle class, the lower expects its males to be able to fight physically for their rights, their "honor," and their women. The taboo against physical violence is a strong middle-class value that is in direct contrast with lower-class acceptance of fighting and brawling as a way of life.[9]

Values relating to sex also differ by class. Middle-class members value chastity—at least in girls—and faithfulness in marriage and expect marital partners to trust one another and function as a team. Among lower-class members, promiscuity is more common and generally accepted. Serial polygamy without benefit of clergy is frequent and condoned—"it's all right to live with a man"—whereas "hustling" is not.[10] Although middle-class people may frequently fail to express their values about sex in their actions, sexual relationships are stabler, more lasting, and less productive of violence than among members of the lowest class. Needless to say, many lower-class people honor their marriage vows, do not indulge in sexual promiscuity, and struggle desperately to protect their children despite adverse environmental factors.

Privacy, respect for property, and concern about the reputation of the family are other middle-class values that do not find expression in the lives of many lower-class members.[11] Lower-

[9] For an excellent description of violence in marriage, see St. Clair Drake and Horace R. Cayton, Black Metropolis (New York: Harper Torchbooks, 1961), Vol. II, pp. 564–588. The fact that this study deals with the Negro lower class is of no significance to the point we are making. Lower-class whites follow much the same pattern of violence in family relations. Many research studies as well as almost any newspaper contain descriptions of the "friendly family spat" that ends with the arrival of the police and the ambulance. The violence prevalent in marriage is also expressed in many other relationships.

[10] Ibid., p. 595.

[11] Here we should note that W. Lloyd Warner has defined six classes in American society. The two lowest, Upper-Lower and Lower-Lower, differ in values despite similarities in socioeconomic status. Our purpose here is to provide a short summary of contrasting values without going too deeply into the niceties of minute distinctions in class. Actually the exact social class of a youngster is irrelevant to the counselor. What is important is that the youngster may have values differing markedly from those of the counselor. A consideration of class in relation to values should contribute to the coun-

class children almost never have their own rooms, wear hand-me-down clothes, have few personal belongings, and frequently come from families whose major concern is subsistence, not reputation. These children may first encounter these middle-class values when they enter school and meet condemnation for not knowing them. Lower-class children, of course, do not learn as do many middle-class ones that family disturbances that can be hidden from the neighbors are less reprehensible than those that become public knowledge.[12]

A child is not the prisoner of his class and given ability, opportunity, education, and luck can move upward in the social hierarchy. When he does, many of his values change to keep pace with his changing status. Frequently he adopts what he sees as the values of his new class with the fervor of the convert and applies these newly acquired values far more stringently than does one who has been long established in his position in the hierarchy. Educational work is one way by which Americans can change their social status. In the schools, therefore, the lower-class youngster frequently encounters a teacher or counselor whose interpretation and application of middle-class values is highly rigid.[13] Perhaps some of the repeated failures of guidance and school counseling with drop-outs, juvenile delinquents, and motivational problems stem from this source.

Upper-class values center around the maintenance and

selor's understanding, not his ability to classify. See W. Lloyd Warner and others, *Yankee City* (New Haven: Yale University Press, 1961), pp. 35–87; *Social Class in America* (New York: Harper Torchbooks, 1960); and *Democracy in Jonesville* (New York: Harper, 1949).

[12] For a humane and understanding description of slum life, see Allison Davis, "The Motivation of the Underprivileged Worker," *Industry and Society*, edited by William F. Whyte (New York: McGraw-Hill, 1946).

[13] See Natalie Rogoff, *Recent Trends in Occupational Mobility* (Glencoe, Ill.: Free Press, 1953). Rogoff makes the point that the hardest barrier to cross is that separating blue-collar from white-collar work. The schools have long provided one avenue for this movement. For the point about teachers and their values, see David Riesman, "Teachers Amid Changing Expectations," *Harvard Education Review*, 24:106–117, Spring 1954, and Arthur T. Jersild, *When Teachers Face Themselves* (New York: Bureau of Publications, Teachers College, Columbia University, 1955).

preservation of an aristocratic way of life. Values including a sort of *noblesse oblige* toward the less fortunate and the whole community characterize many members of the upper class. The good name of the family is important, but reputation as well as position is the result of birth rather than of the strivings of the individual. In many ways, upper-class members are free of the fears and aspirations of individuals in the middle class and of the economic pressures of lower-class people. They are, however, under great pressure to maintain their position and to enhance their family reputations. The importance of leisure and the wise, often benevolent, use of it are also important values for many upper-class individuals and find expression in their service-oriented endeavors. Not all members of the upper class internalize all these values and some individuals fail notably to express them in action. Some give the impression that money, position, and influence will make any kind of behavior acceptable to the community at large. Currently there is considerable overlap in values among members of the upper class and some middle-class individuals on the way up.

Sociological descriptions do not always coincide with the perceptions of people living in a particular community. A town or small city may have no citizens who are technically of the upper-upper class, but may have several families who are regarded as "upper crust" by their fellow townsmen. Children as young as seven and probably younger can usually give some description of the class hierarchy of their community if allowed to do so in their own way. Informal class groupings expressed by children and adults may include "the nice people," "the not-nice people," "the people who live the way we do," "the people who are no better than we are," "the people who live on the wrong side of the tracks," and "the no-counts." These perceptions of class structure are matters of direct concern to the counselor if he is to work constructively with students from that community. Depending on their place in the social hierarchy of any town, children learn early what to expect from adults. The fourth-grade pupil who, seeing a counselor for the first time, greets him, "You don't want to talk to me. I'm a rat from the Flats" has already learned how members of his community view people who live where he does.

Social class colors but does not entirely determine some of the other values a child may learn. During their school careers, for example, many children learn to value popularity. They want to be liked and in this desire they are not too different from American adults who are perennially surprised to find that foreign aid has not bought them the affection and gratitude of the peoples aided. For the high school student, however, the situation is close and poignant. To be "in" with the group, to have dates with the popular boys or girls, to be included in the important parties or clubs, to be a successful athlete—all are important aspects of the value emphasizing popularity. The unpopular youngster usually values and strives for popularity in some manner peculiar to himself.

Competition is another value children encounter in school if they have not already done so in the home or elsewhere. Getting ahead, doing better than one's classmates, being first (or sometimes last if first is impossible) are all manifestations of the value on competition. For some children, competition makes school a nightmare experience in which they learn, according to Henry, that "To be successful in our culture one must learn to dream of failure." [14] Competition is a nightmare not only to those who lose out in the process, but also to those who manage to get ahead or be first. For these children, successful competition in school may mean loss of popularity and added pressure. In American society, the value lauding competition leads both children and adults into many anomalous situations and conflicts.

Americans drill in not only competition but also cooperation. The juxtaposition of these two leads to confusion and turmoil.

[14] Jules Henry, "American Schoolrooms: Learning the Nightmare," *Columbia University Forum*, 6:27, Spring 1963. Henry makes the interesting point that in a society where competition is pivotal, "people cannot be taught to love one another," but they can learn to hate despite the culturally induced failure to recognize that children do hate. See also, Jules Henry, *Culture Against Man* (New York: Random House, 1963).

A student or adult should get ahead but he should also be a good member of the team, a good organization man. The student must strive to do well in school, but he must also learn to subordinate his own desires and individuality to those of others. The statement that "John is intellectually advanced, but socially retarded" often cloaks the teacher's judgment that John can work well by himself, but finds groups intolerable. John has learned to compete but not to cooperate. Chances are that John will learn to cooperate sooner or later because he will have to do so —the cultural forces operating upon him will be too strong to resist. Then he will walk the tightrope between competing enough and cooperating enough to meet the demands of his particular life situation. American society is not gentle to those who do not walk the tightrope judiciously.

Closely allied with the values on competition and cooperation are those on conformity and independence. Many children learn that they should be like other children. "Why can't you behave in Sunday school as well as your brother does?" or "Why do you always ask questions that are not part of the lesson?" are two examples of how parents and teachers press the child to conform in certain situations. Conformity can even take on the aura of thought control when children are limited to learning only what is in the textbook or forced to make educational or vocational choices at the same time and in the same way. And yet these same children are taught to seek independence, to think for themselves, and when necessary to "stand up and be counted." Americans value independence in thought and action so long as that independence does not impinge too directly upon their lives; then they do an about-face and value conformity. When to conform and when to exert one's independence are problems for every child and adult who has learned to value both.

It is, of course, impossible to detail all the many values an individual may hold. Anything in life is a source of values and may help to determine a value orientation. Some people believe that good women do not use cosmetics or that godly people must not use ornamentation on their clothes while others are sure that improvement of appearance is a duty to God and man. Others believe deeply in such intangibles as tolerance and freedom for all and yet cannot practice them in terms of their own children. Still others value the idea that for every question there is a single right answer to such an extent that the idea that the really important questions have no answers can completely upset their lives. Values are omnipresent and influence everything the individual does.

Pluralism of values is a characteristic of American society. This country was settled by people from all different societies and cultures. They brought with them widely divergent beliefs and commitments and mixed their values with those of their fellow Americans. Hence there is a tremendous reservoir of differing values from which one individual learns only a small sample. In the course of time, certain of these values came to be fairly generally shared and some to be codified in such national documents as the Constitution and the Bill of Rights. Despite the leavening processes of time, however, the individual can still learn some of a tremendously large number of values and those he does learn help to make him the unique individual he is and always will be.

Currently some theorists are discussing "valuelessness" [15] as a means of describing those young people who do not know what they want to do, where they are heading, or what purpose their lives should have. And yet the mere fact that students are worried about these areas is an expression of the values that they should know what they want to do or where they are heading and that their lives should have definite purpose. Even the aberrant in American society has values. The juvenile delinquent shares the values of his gang. The mentally ill values his retreat from the world of reality above the pains of everyday life. Everyone values something because he cannot avoid it.

Valuelessness is impossible and there is no such thing as a valueless person or a valueless classroom or a valueless society. The word valuelessness serves simply to describe a value judg-

[15] For example, Abraham Maslow in a talk as part of the panel discussion on "Socio-Cultural Factors and Counseling" at the Convention of the American Personnel and Guidance Association, April 9, 1963.

ment about values themselves. When one individual describes another as valueless, he generally means that the other does not subscribe to the same values as he and that he cannot understand or accept values differing from his own. The person called "valueless" usually does not accept and express in his actions some of the values currently most important to many Americans. Thus the college student who cannot see the value of college work and wants to withdraw is failing to serve the American value that a college education is good. The school in which no prayers are said and no hymns sung is not *ipso facto* valueless. Every teacher in that school expresses values through his presentation of subject matter and his expectations and treatment of his students. The students recognize and internalize these values even more thoroughly than a moral lecture.

Values are a pervasive influence on the actions, thoughts, and emotions of every individual throughout his life. He acts in certain ways at certain times because he has internalized certain values. He strives for some things because for him they have value and are worth the effort. Values are not, however, the only source of subsidiary motives. Arising as they do from the universal motivating forces, subsidiary motives also have a base in the ways of thinking and the ways of doing of a particular society.

WAYS OF THINKING

The second source of subsidiary motives is the ways of thinking of a people. These ways are so deeply internalized and often so subtle that the individual is not usually aware of them. They are to him the natural ways in which everyone should and does approach a problem, a situation, and his life. Being so engrained and so much a part of the person, he regards them as the only and the right way.

Rationalism. Basic to American thinking is rationalism. Every person of whatever age in American society faces everyday such admonitions as "Think it through," "Be reasonable," or "Use your head" and such questions as "Why did you do that?" or "Why don't you think before you act?" The premise and the implications are clear: man is a rational being and he should behave like one. Presumably he should think through his actions, behave reasonably, know why he is doing what he is doing, and be able to justify his actions. More often than not, the ultimate in apology for some "irrational" act will be a chagrined, "I'm sorry. I just didn't think."

Rationalism pervades all of American life. The young child soon learns to seek reasons and to ask why. Formal education is largely a process not only of teaching skills but also of teaching youngsters to think, to approach subject matter and life logically. The small boy giving vent to his emotions is often enjoined to "act like a man" or at least to be "a big boy"—both catch-phrases for being rational. The pressure to be rational starts early and continues. Even the defeated football coach must give reasons for his loss and Monday morning quarterbacks replay the game "logically."

The depth and extent of rationalism can be seen in the many interesting minor and major splits that Americans make between the rational and the emotional man. In social gatherings, for example, individuals who behave in a highly emotional fashion cause embarrassment because presumably the "emotional part" of man temporarily dominates his reason. The criminal lawyer unable to defend his client in any other way may make an emotional plea to the jury but such a defense is a last-ditch stand.

The split between the rational and the emotional has hampered psychology for over half a century. Faculty psychology, which gained much popularity in America, was predicated on a distinct dichotomy of reason and emotion and branches of psychology dealing with the normal individual have never shed this orientation. This division impedes popular acceptance of holistic approaches to human personality.

An illustration of the effects of the split may be seen in the kinds of counseling help offered to individuals in the United States. For the mentally troubled, the "irrational," there is therapy; for the mentally healthy, the "rational," there are advice and information. The two kinds of help are obviously based on the idea that the first set of human beings is guided by emotion; the second, by reason. Certainly the popularity of vocational guidance in the schools is not accidental for its message appeals to the rationalistic American view of the human being. Even fifty years of advances in the behavioral sciences disproving the split between reason and emotion cannot shake the support given to such an antiquated view.

Rationalism is so much the cornerstone of American thinking that rationalization is a favored defensive reaction. Adults can readily summon up reasons to justify almost any act from buying a new car to dropping an atomic bomb. Children patterning their behavior after that of adults learn to rationalize early. The dividing line between rationalization and reasoning is shifting and nebulous, but so long as a person can give reasons for his actions and choices, they tend to be acceptable to him and his society. Even in their defenses, Americans try to exemplify the belief that man is and should be a rational being.

Pattern. A second characteristic American way of thinking is pattern. Everything must have order—naturally a reasonable order. Together with rationalism, the child early learns the value of order whether it be in arranging his clothes, his toys, his day, or his lessons. He may dash in to tell his parents of the day's happenings and be urged, "Now start at the beginning," so that the events he describes make sense in their relationship to one another. In school he constantly learns all the methods of ordering subject matter and patterning his approach to it. Themes must have beginnings, middles, and endings. Problems must be worked in numerical order. He finds that he progresses in school from one subject to another, from one grade to the next and that life should have pattern and order.

Linearity is one of the most important patterns. Not only is the straight line the shortest distance between two points but also the *sine qua non* of marching bands, queues, and such national institutions as the Rockettes. Businessmen illustrate profit and loss by lines on charts and graphs, which have immediate meaning in and of themselves in terms of "up's" and "down's." A farmer is judged by the straightness and parallelism of his furrows. Linearity is such a familiar way of thinking that Americans react adversely when they cannot find this expected pattern. They straighten roads, align goods on display shelves, and comment on foreign dance groups that do not perform in straight lines. Students would indeed be puzzled if a teacher failed to deal with a list of kings in chronological order. Linearity in all its ramifications is so much a way of thinking that Americans cannot visualize a culture in which linearity is unimportant, or even nonexistent.

Another pervasive pattern is *cause-and-effect*. The immediate reaction of most Americans to a failure whether in business or daily life is to ferret out the causes, to look for the reasons. Most attempts to understand human behavior are essentially ways of distinguishing causes for it. This cause-and-effect pattern is integral to a society subscribing to rationalism. Everything must have a relationship to everything else and, while many benefits and discoveries have resulted from the establishment of relationships, many strange syllogisms also ensue.

Educational planning illustrates a common cause-and-effect pattern. Youngsters are encouraged to pattern their educational plans so that they can enter college or get a job. One of the questions they learn to ask is, "What good will this course do me?" meaning "What relationship does it bear to what I eventually want to do?" The pattern is so pervasive that an applicant for a job may be asked, "Why did you take four years of Greek?" The answer, "Because I enjoyed it" leaves the questioner a little uneasy because it does not fit the cause-and-effect pattern. Seemingly courses cannot have meaning and purpose in and of themselves and should not be taken for such unrelated, almost frivolous reasons as the love of learning something new and different.

Even more interesting are occupational patterns. A résumé should show the relationships among the jobs held and preferably these relationships should demonstrate a straight line of development. Dorothy Lee illustrates this point well. She discusses Sally, a Vassar graduate, who is now "selling notions in Woolworth's" and has held jobs as an assistant editor, "a nursemaid, a charwoman, a public school teacher." This assortment "is a mere jumble; it makes no sense and has no meaning." If, however, one element is added, that Sally "is gathering material for a book on the working mother,"[16] the relationships are apparent and the occupational cause-and-effect pattern is clear. Willy-nilly Americans look at an employment record from a cause-and-effect point of view. Today researchers are trying to discover the general patterns of occupational development, ignoring the fact that a way of thinking can establish a pattern, which, when viewed as good, tends to perpetuate itself. Hence the cause of a pattern can be the pattern.

Equally significant in modern American thinking is another pattern, *scientific method.* Throughout school, students learn to observe phenomena and to draw conclusions from their observations. They set up and test hypotheses. Even advertisers stress that their products have undergone scientific testing, which has presumably proved their worth. The scientific approach is so pervasive that almost all Americans are impressed, if not convinced, by such statements as "Science teaches" or "Research points out."

As a student progresses in school, scientific method becomes increasingly important. He distinguishes early, for example, between the writing of themes and research papers. Training for advanced degrees emphasizes the exploration of narrowed fields of learning culminating in the writing of a research paper of some sort. This sequence holds whether the student is majoring in physical science, natural science, or one of the humanities. Insofar as he can, however, the student is expected to adapt the "scientific method" to his studies. The adaptation of the scientific

[16] Dorothy Lee, *Freedom and Culture* (New York: Prentice-Hall, Spectrum Book, 1959), p. 118. Lee's discussion of linear patterns is perhaps the best to be found anywhere; see pp. 105–120.

method to all fields of learning has tended to hamper some in the search for research methods particularly suited to them.

The academic disciplines are not alone in feeling the impact of the scientific method. Science is a part of every man's everyday life. Americans believe that statistics are scientific and that numbers are something definite, precise, and scientific. When trying to be scientific, they use numbers like language. Pollsters conduct studies of opinion covering all areas from politics to preferences in television shows, where a rating of 20.9 presumably means more than 19.8. College students speak of their grade averages in numbers; businessmen discuss sales volume in numbers; vocational guidance experts discuss occupations by DOT classification numbers; and counselors and teachers speak of students by grade numbers and intelligence-test scores. The numbers 36–22–36 conjure up an entire figure. The sports page of a newspaper is nothing but a study in numbers—batting and pitching averages, runs batted in, times at bat, games won and lost, games to be played, scores of games, *ad infinitum*. Those people who do not turn to the sports page first often concentrate on another set of numbers, the financial page. Americans can probably quote more numbers which to them have unquestioned meaning than any other people on the face of the earth. A number to them is an inviolate fact, something certain and scientific.[17]

Another common and often troubling pattern is *authoritarianism*. Americans have had consistent difficulties in reconciling the authoritarian pattern with the general value placed on the freedom of the individual. Certainly no pattern is more troubling to relationships between parents and their children, teachers and their students, and employers and their employees than authoritarianism. The extremist fads in child rearing illustrate the dilemma. Discussions and disagreements about discipline and the independence-seeking of adolescents further point up the deep concern relating to authoritarian patterns.

[17] Those Americans who have absolute faith in numbers might be disconcerted to know that they are based on the Peano postulates, a set of assumptions.

In general, Americans tend to view authoritarianism as a bit of a dirty word at the same time that they implement it in their actions. Many Americans become shoppers for advice and just as many Americans become the authoritarian advisers. People call in an expert to solve their problems on the theory that the specialist has all the answers. The person who can show his expertise by analyzing and diagnosing a situation and prescribing a cure is the authority.

Cartoons and skits lampoon the sycophant but serious writers express deep concern about the organization yes-man and the emphasis on conformity they see everywhere. The recent development of group dynamics and human relations as academic fields of study and inquiry acknowledge the prevalence of authoritarianism as an American way of thinking. The small discussion group represents an attempt to break down the old authoritarian conference, but its influence is slight. Many university professors are troubled because graduate students have apparently been trained throughout their school years to accept anything on the printed page as fact and hesitate to express an opinion not backed by an authority. The parent too busy to spend much time with his children turns them over to a succession of "authorities" to teach them values and skills, to help them select colleges and jobs, to discipline them—even to turn them into socialized human beings.

Rationalism and the various patterns are often inseparable. A person arranging the agendum for a meeting will study the topics logically, examine the relationships among them, and arrange them linearly according to some order. More likely than not, he will then number the topics and plan to approach them in a scientific fashion and hope that he can run the meeting well. Fundamental to his thinking is the assumption that the meeting, like all of life, will have a beginning, a middle, and an end. As an Indian scholar commented, "You Westerners always have to have a beginning and an end. You cannot conceive of Oriental philosophy where life has no beginning or ending. We cannot communicate on philosophy and values because we start from different points." Whether it is a meeting or religion, the difference exists. "In the beginning was the word" and in the end, the revelation. Rationalism and pattern form the basis of American and much of Western thinking.

Comparison and Contrast. A third way of thinking is comparison and contrast. American children grow up being compared with each other, with relatives, even with complete strangers. Rare, indeed, is the visitor who can refrain from remarking that the new baby has Uncle John's nose or looks more like father than mother. The comparisons continue throughout a life-time. Students are compared with each other and graded accordingly. Employers continuously compare employees with each other. Comparison influences American thinking so deeply that one cannot imagine a society in which it does not exist.

Comparison by objective means, including numerical classification, is especially popular. In the schools where teachers and administrators are dealing with large numbers of students, standardized tests are in great vogue because they fit so well the comparative way of thinking. Faced with the question, "Why do you give so many tests?" an educator will often answer that they allow him to compare his students with each other and his school with others.[18] Comparison for the sake of comparison can often be a justification in itself.

Comparison is an engrained American way of thinking because it reinforces the value on being first and the accent on competition. Almost all American games and recreations as well as work involve competition and comparison. Many anthropologists have pointed out the difficulties in understanding societies where competition is relatively nonexistent. Polynesian tribes often have exhibitions of boating skill in which there are no winners or losers—simply demonstrations of boating ability. Americans who see five boats skim across the water automatically begin to cheer for one to cross the finish line first. Teachers who have

[18] For a discussion of tests, see Barry and Wolf, *An Epitaph for Vocational Guidance*, pp. 26–56.

tried to instruct Hopi youngsters in some of the common American games find it puzzling that Hopis can play basketball merely for the sport without keeping score. The American golfer has to justify his not scoring a round by calling it practice—and most golfers score practice rounds for there is no other way for them to play. If he is going to play, he must at least compete with himself or par.

Similar to and often a part of comparison is contrast. Americans are less apt to concentrate on subtle differences in points of view than they are to oppose opinions and ideas demonstrating right and wrong by sharp contrast. In the ever-popular Westerns the "good guys" clash with the "bad guys." Detective fiction, an original American art form, contrasts the upholders of the law and the lawbreakers, good and evil. In the tradition of "standing up and being counted," most Americans find that they must take sides; they must be for something or else they are *ergo* against it.

Most Americans feel more comfortable with sharp contrasts between good and evil than with shadings of values. Children are reared with admonitions to be good not bad, the definitions of which are established by the individual parents and their value judgments. Writers have pointed out the "value security" men find in times of war when the enemy is bad and a soldier can without question or reservation hate all men wearing the enemy uniform. Americans tend to like their values stated in blacks and whites, to ignore the shadings of values, and to avoid examining subtle differences.

The emphasis on contrast tends to erase the middles; attention is given to the extremes. Many cities, for example, have built excellent schools for the gifted and for the juvenile delinquents, but have done much less for the "average" student. Parents urge their children to get "A's" and "B's" and forget the "normal curve," which, if it means anything, insures that most students will receive "C's." New housing in large cities usually consists of low-rental and luxury apartments. Contrasting the extremes, the ultimate in comparison, is the common American approach.

Most advice-giving utilizes extremes: "If you don't study

hard, you'll flunk"; "If you drop out of school, you'll be a failure all your life"; "Be a good boy or Santa Claus won't come." The either/or premise is usually an integral part of advice as it is of the interpretation of advice. Recent reports on the dangers of smoking demonstrate well the tendency to interpret in terms of extremes. The common conclusion is that if one smokes, he will get lung cancer or shorten his life. Certainly some people will, but not all. The popular Gesell averages for the growing child demonstrate the same kind of interpretation. A young mother views her child as deficient if he or she does not begin to walk during the "average" period or as advanced if he or she toddles before the designated age. The "average" in itself of course may be relatively meaningless.

A subtle use of advice occurs in suggesting alternative courses of action. Here the adviser points out the possible extremes that occur to him. All advice-giving is predicated on the assumption that for every situation there is a limited number of alternatives all of which the adviser can foresee. Actually almost every situation has a wide-range, perhaps an infinite, number of alternatives, but the American emphasis on contrast overshadows this fact in the giving and interpreting of advice.

Time. A fourth way of thinking is in terms of time. Every society has its own view and uses of time. Thus the Scottish ship captain who wants his cargo unloaded according to schedule has difficulty impressing his concept of time on the Arab stevedore who believes firmly that the ship will be unloaded "when Allah wills." The Scot calls the Arab "lazy" and the Arab views the captain as an "unbeliever," one unaware that a higher power guides the unhurried path of man. Communication breaks down because each has a different concept of time.[19] In like manner, Americans have so completely internalized certain ways of thinking about time that to them there are no other ways.

[19] One of the best discussions of differences in points of view toward time is found in Edward T. Hall, *The Silent Language* (Greenwich, Conn.: Premier Books, 1959).

To Americans time has great economic worth. The process of employment consists of the buying and selling of a person's time. Heated arguments can ensue between employer and employee over the length of time for a coffee-break or arriving a few minutes late to work. Many labor contracts and strikes hinge around working hours, length of work week as well as wages and fringe benefits. Time is a commodity that is constantly figured in terms of dollars and cents.

A charge that can raise guilt feelings in almost any American is that he is wasting time. Since time has material worth, it should not be wasted. Nothing will so irritate an American as having to wait for a tardy friend, a delayed dental appointment, or a behind-schedule train or plane. Adequate reasons for the tardiness may soothe him a little, but the feeling that time is being wasted remains. Even sports events are subject to time-saving measures. Baseball relief pitchers ride to the mound in cars in order to "save time" and fans ridicule delays in games. One serious criticism of an employee or a student is that he wastes time.

The importance of time to most Americans can be seen by the stress placed on it in the education of the young. Parents start early to teach children how to "tell time." A child's ability to grasp the American meaning of time is even cited as an indication of his giftedness. In order to make Sioux Indian children aware of time, their teachers have large clocks prominently displayed and stress punctuality because Sioux concepts of time differ widely from those of the broader American culture. Throughout the early years, parents admonish children for being late and schools have buzzers ringing loudly to signal the beginning and end of class periods. Guidance counselors often devote much energy to teaching students adequate study habits, most of which center around the proper utilization of their time. Life throughout the United States is geared to the clock without which no household is complete. Almost every person wears a watch and every desk has a calendar. The absent-minded professor who loses track of hours and days is a subject of tolerant ridicule.

With a concept of time as a commodity and the wasting of it as a sin, speed and efficiency logically have high value. Anything done speedily is automatically better than something done well but more slowly. Americans have made a science of time-and-motion studies and have experts to improve speed and efficiency in businesses and industries. In almost every field, time is devoted to discussions of how to do things efficiently. The minimal amount of time necessary for an optimum counseling interview is a constant source of debate as if time itself were the supremely important factor. Americans read digests of novels, stories, news items, and technical literature and take courses to increase their reading speed. Advertisers stipulate that their pills work seconds faster than those of their rivals. Students compare the amount of time spent on homework and give the kudos to the one finishing the assignment the fastest. According to general American thinking, speed and efficiency are virtues in themselves.

A not surprising emphasis on youth accompanies this view of time. The individual must make his mark early and earn his success young. With the growth of retirement plans and the firm establishment of age sixty-five (or younger) for retirement, the cult of youth is widespread. Youngsters learn at home and in school that they must formulate their career plans early in order to get started toward success. Paradoxically, people are living longer and more healthily and vigorously than ever before and yet they are constrained to succeed young. The worker past forty often experiences difficulty in changing jobs or vocations despite the fact that he has almost half his life yet to live.

Concepts of time combine with the values on progress and perfectibility to make the American (if he is not an antique addict) consider anything new better than anything old. He produces cars with built-in obsolescence knowing that most buyers will trade them in every year or so. The new appliance is always more desirable than the old. A highly technological society geared to the production of new or improved goods fosters this emphasis.

Surprisingly the high value placed on the new does not

carry over from the technological to the ideological area. Here Americans tend to prefer the traditions of the past and to strive to maintain the *status quo*. Despite the teachings of the modern behavioral sciences, people cling to the idea that "Bad blood breeds bad blood" and that the child whose parents were "no good" will necessarily be "no good." Many educators assume that what a student is today he will be tomorrow, that his current test scores are what his scores will be five years hence, that today's world of work will be his in the future. Perhaps with change the hallmark of technical development, Americans find security in the ideological *status quo*.

All aspects of thinking in terms of time coalesce in the stress on "keeping busy." What keeping busy means differs from individual to individual but usually connotes some form of doing something. Sitting and contemplating the abstract is usually not considered keeping busy. Americans have made a big business out of do-it-yourself and hobbycraft products, which insure that the buyer will keep busy during his "idle" hours. Americans cannot understand the Navajo boy who developed a great interest in painting and had almost finished a canvas when his summer vacation began. His teacher fully expected him to work on it during the summer. He returned to school with the painting untouched and explained, "I didn't have time to work on it." The teacher asked, "What were you doing?" The boy replied, "I was sitting on the fence watching my sheep grow." Hardly the general American approach to keeping busy!

The common American ways of thinking—rationalism, pattern, comparison and contrast, and time—are those internalized by most people. They become so much a part of the person that they are values to him. Rationalism, linearity, order, scientific method, comparison, contrast, authoritarianism, saving time, and keeping busy are good and right. They are, in a sense, American values.

Not every one, of course, internalizes the same ways of thinking and the same attendant values. Some people never learn a linear approach to living. Most Americans have difficulty in dealing with their emotions in a society where the emotional is always supposed to be subservient to the rational. Some Americans never learn the value of time and can never seem to be "on time," to "save time," or to "keep busy." Some people cannot seem to internalize the great American value of getting ahead, of competing, and of comparing themselves with others. For them competition has little value. In a pluralistic society, there are many varieties and combinations of ways of thinking.

In general, however, the person who internalizes the common ways of thinking is most acceptable. Others may be tolerated; still others, ridiculed, scorned, or even ostracized. The disorderly housewife is a subject of gossip for her friends who cannot understand why she does not at least put her house in order for company. The worker who has trouble taking orders from his boss often loses his job. The person unable to live at least in part "rationally" is consigned to a mental institution. Every society establishes its own limits and within these limits it can tolerate greater or lesser deviations from the accepted ways of thinking.

Ways of thinking are a source of subsidiary motives. Not all are motives in and of themselves but all color other motives. The rightness of his way of thinking spurs a person to such action as summoning up reasons to justify a stand, tidying up his desk, running for an appointment, curbing his anger, or toying with an idea until it satisfies him. Often a way of thinking will color other motives as, for example, when reaction to comparison will be a factor in a person's dieting or choice of clothes. Ways of thinking in combination with values form two important sources of subsidiary motives in any society.

WAYS OF DOING

Subsidiary motives have a third major source in ways of doing. Like the other sources, ways of doing are individual and idiosyncratic but patterned generally by the society in which the person lives.

Perhaps fundamental to American society is the concept that doing in and of itself is good. A person should not just "keep busy" but "do something" and preferably have "something" to show for his labor. Almost any American would recognize and agree with the expression, "Don't just sit there, *do* something!" Soldiers complain bitterly not about the action in war, but about having to wait for it. Perhaps in a nation of doers the reassurance of the final line makes one Milton sonnet his most frequently memorized piece of writing: "They also serve who only stand and wait."

Doing affects all American life. A person joins clubs and organizations in order to have something to do and is usually happiest in the group that supplies it. Some of the popularity of the committee approach lies in the fact that it offers more people something to do. Americans seem to enjoy speeches if they are allowed to participate in some fashion whether by questioning, stamping, parading, or singing. A "good" teacher involves all her students in the class activities. Schools support clubs to foster a wide range of interests and the "well-rounded" student exemplifies "doing" in many areas. Active kibitzing takes place not only around the card table but also on any project or effort. If the American cannot be an active participant, he can at least do something by offering his advice and suggestions.

Doing is best if and when it produces a product. The employee has a satisfied feeling when he sees the finished work literally pile up. Every committee must produce a report as evidence of its activities because discussion for the sake of discussion is not doing. The product is the tangible evidence of having done something and without it doing has little tangible purpose—even so, doing of any kind surpasses total inactivity.

The emphasis on doing naturally results in a suspicion of thinking as a worthwhile endeavor. The Puritan preached that the "Devil finds work for idle hands" and frontier sagas laud the man of action. The "egghead" even today presents a public image alien to American taste—he is not a doer. Somehow reading is not doing and the college professor feels a little guilty when caught with his feet on his desk reading a book for he is not engaged in doing. Anti-intellectualism and all it implies are a part of the American scene and find a strong stimulus for continuation in the primary emphasis on doing, not thinking.

In a pluralistic culture, there are naturally many individual ways of doing. Each person as he grows up internalizes ways that he learns so well he is often not aware of them. These ways of doing are his own habit patterns. If he has always eaten dinner at noon, he wants his big meal at noon. If he relaxes by smoking a cigarette, he will especially want a cigarette in moments of relaxation. If he puts on his clothes in a certain order or sits in a chair in a certain way or drives his car with certain set movements, any interruption of his habitual patterns causes a minor or major upset for him.

Habit as a subsidiary motive can be most easily demonstrated by the action it gives rise to when the usual habit pattern is interrupted. The person accustomed to washing his face or bathing when he first arises in the morning will spring into action if he turns the faucet and no water comes out. He may turn the tap several times, try another one, kick the plumbing, or, if he lives in an apartment building, call the manager or custodian to find out what is wrong with his water supply. Actually he is reacting to an interruption in his habitual way of approaching the day. Similarly if a person is accustomed to having a napkin on his lap before he eats, he will summon a waiter and obtain a napkin even though his food may be growing cold.[20] Habitual ways of doing can and do serve as self-perpetuators and, therefore, as subsidiary motives for the individual.

Regardless of what the habit is, the person possessing it tends to perpetuate it, often unknowingly. Because a habit or its disruption leads to an overt or covert action, it serves as a

[20] The dividing line between habit and compulsion is shady. One blends into the other and certainly compulsion is self-perpetuating and a strong subsidiary motive. The housewife who cannot let dirty dishes stand in the sink but must wash them before she leaves home is a borderline example in which perhaps only the reasons for breaking the pattern might be the distinguishing point between habit and compulsion.

subsidiary motive for the individual. There are, however, varying degrees of motivation involved and differences in the kind of action caused by habit patterns. The child learns how to hold a knife and fork and will continue to handle it in the internalized fashion unless and until later learning introduces a different pattern. O S S agents engaged in intensive training to use a knife and fork in the European, not the American, way. One level of habit is the automatic way of doing.

Another illustration of level of habit is for some people the eating of fish on Friday. The person may have learned from childhood that he cannot eat meat on Friday but this habitual way of doing is conscious. It is geared to his value system and dependent on his knowing which day is Friday. Not eating meat at certain times may be a life-long and deeply held conviction that seems almost automatic but it is a different level of habit. It is at the same time a strong subsidiary motive for the person. Change in the pattern, however, depends on relearning values and beliefs, not just retraining.

The line between levels of habit is rarely clear-cut for habit more often than not entails a concept of being "the right way." Any simple task done in a group immediately elicits comments from viewers about the right way to do it: "Here, let me show you how I do it"; "It's a lot easier this way"; "You're going at it backward." The ways of doing are similar to the values and ways of thinking of a person. They carry with them an emotional commitment and are for him right and good.

Groups as well as individuals have established ways of doing. A frequent comment in any business is "We do things the X way" or "That is not the X way of doing it." The secretary changing jobs has to learn the new office patterns and routines. Her secretarial skills are the same, but she must learn how her employer wants his letters typed, his reports filed, and all the other minor methods that make up the ways of doing of his office. Clubs, associations, and informal groups of all kinds establish their own patterns and the members soon learn whether to sing songs at a meeting, wear insignia, expect entertainment, or salute their officers. Ways of doing are often the distinguishing marks of various clubs.

In a broader sense, many ways of doing depend on group affiliation. Often being a member of a national or religious group may determine them. The vestiges of other cultures brought by immigrants to the United States are passed on to their children. Especially in large cities, the clustering of such groups produces, nationally, a Chinatown or a Germantown or an Italiantown or, religiously, a Jewishtown or a Lutherantown. Cultural vestiges often influence such ways of doing as working hours, kind and size of business, and approaches to food and cooking. Another influential group "affiliation," although informal and often unrecognized, is social class for it may shape not only values but also ways of doing.

The section of the United States a person lives in influences his ways of doing as does living in an urban or rural environment. Meals furnish a simple example of differences. The person from the Midwest is likely to eat a heavy meal at noon and another at six o'clock. The Easterner tends to eat a light lunch at a later hour and a large dinner also at a later hour. The farmer, regardless of his location, tends to eat more frequently and in greater quantities than the city dweller. Whatever the way of doing, interruption of it causes an emotional reaction of varying intensity for the person involved.

Certain ways of doing are common throughout the nation with only slight variations. Cleanliness and a high level of sanitation are in most parts of the United States the expected way of doing. State and federal laws enforce compulsory sanitation in food processing and service and water supplies. Although working hours may not be identical, they tend to be similar for similar occupations. Many ways of doing that seem right and natural to most Americans seem so because they are Americans.

Values, ways of thinking, and ways of doing are so interwoven that they never exist alone. The ways of thinking or doing that a person internalizes are to him good and right. Hence they become values. In like manner, a value determines ways of thinking and doing. A change in one usually entails changes in the others. To the individual his values are often synonymous with his ways and in combine give rise to his subsidiary motives.

THE DYNAMIC TRIUMVIRATE

There is nothing static about the triumvirate of values, ways of thinking, and ways of doing either for the individual or for his society. Especially in a pluralistic nation, one individual finds his values and ways continually subject to assault as he views and tries to understand and work with those of others. The process of internalization, modification, and amplification is life-long.

Changes in values and ways are never easy or instantaneous. Reinternalization demands new emotional commitments and at least the partial shedding of old. No person is probably aware of the full range of his values and ways or of those of others. His own are to him right and good and he judges others according to them. Similarly he is often not aware of the subtle changes taking place within his own system for such change is steady and insidious.

Societal values and ways also change. Some of these changes can be seen most vividly in nations other than one's own. Margaret Mead visited the Admiralty Islands in 1928 and found a Stone Age people. She revisited these islands in 1953 and observed vast differences entailing fundamental changes in values and ways of thinking and doing. Here a people with little realization of the patterns and rationalism of the Western world, with "no alphabet, no knowledge of history or geography, no political organization" adaptable to a large group were grasping the principles of electronic devices and their own political-economic relationship to the rest of the world. Given the "cultural equipment" extending into all facets of life, change came about amazingly rapidly for many of these people.[21]

Within the United States, similar though perhaps not such

[21] Margaret Mead, "A Look at Human Capacities," *The Lamp*, 45:16–17, Summer 1963. See also *New Lives for Old*.

obvious changes are also taking place. Change, however, is not easily distinguished by the person living in the midst of it. Oftentimes its recognition appears in the puzzled statement, "I just can't understand this younger generation. They don't believe in the things we believed in. They don't do things the way we did." And they don't. Each new adolescent society in the rapidly changing United States is almost a distinct subculture with values and ways different from those of the previous generation just as the culture of that generation differed from that of its predecessors.

The person growing up in a dynamic society faces many problems and conflicts in understanding and communication. The youngster engaged in the process of internalizing values and ways sees many inconsistencies, which he cannot understand and reconcile, for values and value systems are never consistent. He must learn to live with the inconsistencies and differences at the same time that he tries continually to shape a system of his own. This task is perhaps the most difficult any person faces, regardless of age. It is the task that causes more problems in mental health than any other for it entails learning to live with the sources of motivational conflict.

The counselor unaware of and unequipped to deal with the infinite array of difficulties arising from values, ways of thinking, and ways of doing cannot help a youngster with his fundamental developmental problems. Neither can he understand a student's motivations. For the student, the externals of subject matter, vocational information, and study skills are always the superficial aspects of his deeper concern with a way of life. Only the student himself, given suitable help, can examine his own values and gain the understandings which will lead to resolution of the questions, "Who am I?" "What kind of a life do I want to live?" These are rooted in the sources of subsidiary motives.

3

SUBSIDIARY MOTIVES AND THEIR DIRECTIONS

Values and ways of thinking and doing as they cluster around the universal motivating forces shape the individual's subsidiary motives. Every society has its unique values and ways just as each individual has his unique internalizations of them. Hence subsidiary motives may appear to be pervasive throughout a society, but can be understood only as they relate to the individual. Understanding any person's subsidiary motives means recognizing the values and ways of his particular society and what that individual personally believes to be right and good.

How values and ways give rise to subsidiary motives is the starting point for a knowledge of how each individual acquires the motives important to him. This process constitutes the derivation of subsidiary motives. Since these motives are often abstractions they can have myriad meanings, and terminology tangles often obscure their differences. Subsidiary motives not only impel the person to action but also forge the directions in which he will strive. In a sense, a statement of motives is a statement of personal goals and aims. Lastly, man continues struggling in order to achieve some positive experiences such as satisfaction, which, therefore, is integral to a theory of motivation. These concepts—the derivation of subsidiary motives, the myriad meanings, personal aims, and satisfaction—are essential to understanding why a person does what he does.

THE DERIVATION OF SUBSIDIARY MOTIVES

Values, ways of thinking, and ways of doing are the sources of any individual's subsidiary motives. These three sources become motives both directly and indirectly. Rarely, if ever, do they act

alone because the individual has internalized and uses them as
interacting entities. The simple transformation of some values
and ways into subsidiary motives, however, serves to illustrate
the process as does the complex intermingling of the two to shape
other subsidiary motives.

Values in and of themselves can function as subsidiary
motives. If, for example, a person holds the value that the body
should not be violated by the introduction into it of another
person's blood, his emotional commitment to this value will impel
him to reject blood transfusions. Occasionally a person will
refuse to permit the blood transfusions that will allegedly prolong
or save his life. Here a value acts directly as a subsidiary
motive.

Many values function as subsidiary motives and the forms
they take and their importance to the person determine what he
does. Many Americans abhor war, but will fight to defend their
country. Some Americans hold the belief that taking of a life
under any circumstances is bad and, therefore, become conscientious objectors. Many Americans view drinking liquor as good;
many, as bad. Some will tolerate others' drinking; some will fight
to prevent the sale of liquor within their community; some will
battle to prevent the sale of liquor on Sundays; and some, like
Carry Nation, will declare war on all saloons. The nature of
the value held, the depth of the emotional commitment to it,
and the importance of it to the individual will determine the
subsidiary motives arising from it.

As they shape subsidiary motives, values are not logical or
realistic. Many children, for example, are taught that they should
always love their brothers and sisters and that hate is bad. Yet
the existence of sibling rivalry is unquestioned. This contra-
diction leaves the child with conflicts about his feelings, which
are usually a shifting mixture of both love and hate. The child
is motivated to try not to hate and may even feel bad or abnormal
because he finds himself occasionally hating his sister. He
struggles to suppress or repress his feelings of hate and to feel
only those sentiments his values tell him are appropriate.

Children are practically never successful in these attempts to feel the emotions they think are right, but their struggles are pathetically apparent. Guilt associated with his feelings of hate may further motivate the child to develop ways of dealing with it that may or may not be psychologically healthy or socially acceptable.

Ways of doing also give rise directly to subsidiary motives. A person strives to keep busy and not to waste time because keeping busy is good and wasting time is bad. The retired person often seeks a time-consuming hobby because he cannot suddenly be idle after a life-time of internalizing and acting upon some of the basic values of his society. Some ways of doing become subsidiary motives as directly as do values.

Ways of thinking can serve as subsidiary motives in a subtle sense. In a recent publication, for example, Tiedeman and O'Hara claim that "It is possible to choose educational and vocational pursuits on a rational basis," although they also add the rider that "Not everyone does so every time, of course; we note only the potential." [1] The value permeating this statement is clear: rational choice is good. The motivation that results is also simple: the impossible striving to make purely rational decisions. Rationalism has so influenced the development of a subsidiary motive that many Americans are suspicious of emotions and thereby unwittingly deny the holistic nature of man. In a sense, the desire to make man a purely rational being is similar to the attempt to prevent children from hating for both deny the emotions and the important role they inevitably play in constant interaction with the intellect.

Those cited are simply a few of the many possible examples that seem to arise directly out of a single important value or way. Subsidiary motives, however, seldom actually derive from a single value or way. A particular value may at one time or another be extremely influential, but ordinarily the subsidiary

[1] David V. Tiedeman and Robert P. O'Hara, *Career Development: Choice and Adjustment* (New York: College Entrance Examination Board, 1963), p. 34.

motives of an individual are shaped from the complex composite of their sources as they relate to the universals. In this as in every other way, the normal individual acts in a holistic fashion. An intermingling of values and ways produces even the superficially simple subsidiary motives. Suppose an individual seems to strive constantly to be a winner. Many values and ways varying from person to person may enter into this motive. American society is highly competitive and the kudos, trophies, and rewards go to the person who is first whether it be in an athletic contest, a scholarship ranking, a club election, or a parlor game. The value placed on being first enters all such striving as, indeed, does rationalism when the winners analyze their victories and the losers explain away their failures.

Along with competition, comparison and contrast influence the striving to be a winner. The individual brought up in a society where comparison is continual learns to evaluate himself as he competes with others. The results of the evaluation and their importance to the individual often intensify his striving. Linearity and order naturally enter this striving. Being first is better than being second; second is better than third and so on down the line. Interestingly, if being first seems impossible for an individual, the achievement of last place in an orderly sequence can often take on some of the aura and distinction of being first. Regardless of rank, however, some position in an orderly linear sequence is an object of striving and "firstness" is the ultimate objective.[2]

Still other values and ways help to shape the striving to be a winner. Perfectionism often plays a part. Puritan values dictate that one should do any task as well as he can do it and doing it perfectly is best. Scientific method aids in differentiating among winners and losers. It permits scorers to distinguish tenths of

    [2] In this connection it is interesting to recall that most of the astro-
nauts, in describing their reasons for joining the first group, cited their
desires to be the first to do something important. Similarly it is no accident
that George Washington is described as the first President and as "first in
peace, first in war, and first in the hearts of his countrymen." History in
the United States is often taught as a catalogue of "firsts."

seconds in races and tenths of points in grade averages when judging the fastest human or the valedictorian. In turn, the athlete and scholar strive for that minuscule difference between winning and losing. Often, too, the striving to be a winner reflects the values placed on being a leader for leadership carries with it the distinction of authority. These and many other values and ways merge to shape the subsidiary motive to be a winner.

Values and ways of thinking and doing form various combinations that are basic to subsidiary motives. Because only the individual determines the combinations, no one can be sure how they will affect his strivings except as they are shown in his behavior. Although some general strivings can be anticipated on the basis of common American values and ways, these expectations can never be viewed as certainties. Not everyone strives to keep busy, to be rational, or to be first, just as not everyone struggles for prestige or upward social progress. Subsidiary motives arise only out of each individual's personally internalized values and ways. Essentially, subsidiary motives are highly individualized and their meanings to the person and the aims they embody lend real difference and variety to them even though the words used to describe them sometimes tend to give them a spurious appearance of similarity and to obscure their myriad meanings.

THE MYRIAD MEANINGS

Suppose a student says, "I want to be successful." He is talking about his motives, but what does he mean by this statement? What is success to this student? Does he mean he wants material possessions, happiness, recognition, control over others, or all of these and many more? Meaning is one of the most important problems in connection with subsidiary motives. An analysis of strivings for success will illustrate the problem of meaning and the many meanings that a single word can include.

For many Americans, striving for success means striving for money and material possessions. In a materialistic society, success almost inevitably carries monetary connotations, but money is by no means the sole consideration. Some students will claim that they do not want "lots of money," just "enough money to live comfortably." Such statements do not clarify the monetary aspects of strivings for success because they leave the listener with the question, What is enough money? What is living comfortably? Certainly material considerations enter into strivings for success, but the extent and intensity of their influence is virtually impossible to ascertain. Success even in its purely monetary aspects can mean so many things to so many different people that no one can prejudge what it will connote to a particular individual.

Strivings for success frequently incorporate strivings for security. When a person says, "I want to be successful," he may mean that he is seeking to establish security for himself and his family. Strivings for security usually include some financial concerns, but equally, if not more, important are the strivings for what might be called social as opposed to financial security. Being wanted, needed, welcomed, and accepted in the family, social, and work groups are an integral part of these strivings as are those for psychological or personal security. Many people view the "successful" man as having confidence in himself, the ability to be decisive, and the capacity to deal with others with wisdom, patience, and fortitude. These strivings for personal security are often linked to those for success under the assumption that monetary success will automatically lead to personal security or acceptance by a group. Hence for some individuals, success may mean security of many kinds and degrees.

Success can also connote achievement. The student who asserts that he wants to "do something" or "accomplish something worthwhile" may be defining success in terms of accomplishment. But accomplishment may include such diverse endeavors as discovering a new drug, building a bridge, joining the best club, getting one's name in the newspaper no matter how, being promoted, learning a language, putting an upstart in his place, closing a big deal, winning the barroom brawl, giving up smoking, even thinking a new thought. Achievement is defined in individualistic terms closely related to the values of the individual and those of his society. For many Americans, success and achievement are virtually converse propositions in the sense that success implies and can include achievement and that achievement can imply and include success. This relationship, however, does not lessen the problem of meaning—for, unless meaning is particularized to the individual, one risks defining one indefinable in terms of another.

In American society, success frequently means status and prestige. As Mike tells it, "A guy's just got to feel important," [3] and Mike gets his sense of importance from his card-playing abilities and his work in the store. A place in the social hierarchy, a sense that one is good for something, a feeling that one is an important part of the social structure, even perhaps a belief that there are other people who are less important—all enter into the strivings for prestige and status. The American value on competition naturally fosters these strivings as does the national tendency to compare and contrast individuals. The woman who says, "She needn't be so snooty just because her husband is a carpenter and mine is a laborer" has met with frustration of her strivings for status and prestige and is trying to enhance her own view of the social status in which she feels trapped. The examples indicate that prestige and status can have two different, although overlapping, meanings to two different people and these examples could be multiplied indefinitely. Strivings for security are not separate from those for status or for accomplishment, which may well include social advancement, recognition, and importance. Subsidiary motives are never discrete, nonoverlapping, independent of each other, or easily defined.

Strivings for power, control, or mastery may also be factors in strivings for success. To some people, success may mean control over machines or money, mastery of ideas or subject matter, or power over people and their actions. Power may mean control over one's children or over vast industrial or financial enter-

[3] See the case of Mike in the Appendix, line 322.

prises; it may mean mastery of one's body as with the Indian yoga or a kind of personal and emotional discipline. In a society with a heritage of authoritarian patterns and Puritan values, power in some form or another is not an unexpected focus for strivings. Children subjected to considerable controls during their early years often grow up with the expectation that they will exert similar control as adults; from being the mastered, they will become the masters. What power and control mean to them depends on their early learnings and the modifications made in those learnings by their life experiences.

Often strivings for success include strivings to be of service to others. Teen-agers and young adults express these strivings in such a statement as, "I want the world to be a little better for my having lived in it." The deeply religious may describe themselves as "called" to undertake a way of life dedicated to service to others—another way of expressing their values. However these strivings are described, there is no question that some people cannot separate success from service. Success to them means being of help to others, serving others in some capacity, or following the directions they feel are indicated by God. The American background of values insures that many people include service among their subsidiary motives although they may not exhibit the zeal of the missionary or the ardor of the reformer.

Strivings for success may also incorporate strivings to be a successful human being as opposed to a successful man. The struggle to become a worthwhile person, to find contentment and satisfaction, to establish warm rewarding relationships with others, to explore many facets of experience and knowledge, and to grow in maturity and wisdom seems to be an integral part of the strivings of many people for success. Maslow describes these strivings under the rubric of the "need for self-actualization" and seems to suggest that the struggle terminates in a state of completion.[4] Against the background of the materials in this book,

[4] See Abraham H. Maslow, *Motivation and Personality* (New York: Harper, 1954), pp. 199–234 and *Toward a Psychology of Being* (New York: Van Nostrand, Insight Books, 1962), *passim.*

such a position is untenable. Strivings for self-improvement continue and remain strivings throughout the life of the individual. Teen-agers are especially likely to look ahead to adulthood as a time when they can become the kinds of people they would like to be. All too often, adults listening to high school or college students talk about success interpret their conversations in terms of materialistic rather than personal psychological success.

Sometimes success means independence and individuality and strivings for one are inextricably mixed with those for the other. American society values independence and expects people to express their individuality within reasonable limits—sometimes even within unreasonable limits. But what is independence? What does being an individual mean? Here again the tie-in with success is obvious. To many teen-agers, the successful man, whoever he is, has acquired independence, whatever that is, and is an individual in his own right. Since many teen-agers view independence from parents as the nirvana in which they can for the first time really be themselves and express their own individual uniqueness, they tend to equate success with independence and individuality. These sentiments are, of course, not limited to teen-agers, but may also serve adults both as rationalizations and as foci for their strivings.

Strivings for success may also include strivings for challenge and interest. Particularly for the gifted teen-ager, the desire to be successful often means that he is struggling toward a challenging job or an interesting life. His strivings may be directed toward utilizing his abilities in activities that require him to do so. Whether these activities are scholarly, administrative, or technical seems to be of relatively little importance provided they offer the individual the opportunities to extend himself. Strivings for challenge and interest are not, however, limited to the gifted although they may be more easily understood in connection with them. All people apparently strive to introduce into their lives something novel, something different, something that will perk up their interest or challenge them to think, feel, and do in unaccustomed ways. These strivings are sometimes difficult to recognize in people of low scholastic ability because they direct their strivings toward thoughts and activities others tend to view as too mundane to be challenging or interesting to anyone. Against the background of a theory that postulates strivings toward internalization of the culture and self-expression and in a society that values challenge, interest and creativity, strivings in these directions are inevitable for many people.

What then does success mean for the student who says, "I want to be successful"? The truthful answer is that no one but the student knows and perhaps not even he could completely define or describe what he means. People are never completely aware of their value systems or their motivations. Meanings are, therefore, highly idiosyncratic to the individual. There are probably as many meanings of success as there are people in the United States.

Any or all of the topics discussed as possible meanings for success can in and of themselves serve as subsidiary motives. A school child can strive to master subject matter and his efforts can be interpreted as strivings for power or for prestige or for interest and challenge or for pleasing an adult or even as strivings for success always depending on the point of view of the interpreter, not that of the individual involved. Perhaps all of these enter into the child's struggle to learn; perhaps some; perhaps none; perhaps others not mentioned. Meaning in connection with subsidiary motives is personal, not general, and does not lend itself to categorization except possibly in terms of the most commonly held societal values and ways of thinking and doing.

Lists of subsidiary or culturally derived motives are by and large misleading because of the problem of meaning. A listing represents a tremendous loss in personal meanings. It also gives the false impression that the motives included are discrete and independent, which they are not. One purpose of the discussion of strivings for success is to show how an individual may operate from a basis of many intermingled motives not necessarily harmonious and rarely consistent among themselves. No normal person has singular, unadulterated motivation.

Subsidiary motives then are complex, interwoven, and not easily recognized for what they are—a mélange of many motives of varying strengths and importance to the individual. Meanings are idiosyncratic and such subsidiary motives as success, prestige, power, service, and challenge can have as many meanings as there are individuals striving for them because meaning depends upon values and ways. As these change, so meanings can and do change and the dynamic nature of human beings is constantly reinforced.

THE PERSONAL AIMS

A discussion of meanings is virtually a discussion of aims. What motives mean to the individual determines the aims embodied in them. A man strives for the intangibles that have value to him and these are his aims. How he describes his aims constitutes their meanings.

Like motives and values, aims are never singular. An individual may strive toward such varied aims as happiness, knowledge, fame, excellence, popularity, or any of the other aims inherent in subsidiary motives. Or he may strive for none of these, but many others. Whatever shape strivings take, they have many meanings and incorporate many aims.

Aims are usually intangibles and never completely attainable. Happiness, success, service, knowledge, acceptance, and challenge provide a few examples of the intangible nature of aims. Happiness, for example, is not a concrete, finite thing that can be measured, doled out, and turned off or on at will. Nor can one determine whether or not he or anyone else has "enough" happiness. Aims are generally vague, ill-defined, large, untidy concepts that do not lend themselves to precise definition. Often the individual is only semi-aware of his aims and finds great difficulty in discussing them. Sometimes he resorts to the platitudes and clichés of his culture, which inadequately describe what he really means.

Aims are rarely, if ever, entirely consistent. A man may

strive for security for his family and himself and for close-knit family relationships and discover that his job consumes most of his time and energy. Or he may seek excellence and popularity and find that the first prevents his making any progress toward the second. Conflicting aims are common and lie at the base of many of the difficulties in which people find themselves embroiled. Sometimes the life situation of an individual can temporarily introduce some consistency into his aims, but aims change as do values, motives, and meanings and such apparent consistency is probably not permanent.

Aims incorporate tangible goals as part of the encompassing motive. Goals are finite, relatively concrete, and, as the word itself implies, terminal or possible to attain. The man striving for success may attain the goal of full union membership, the teen-ager seeking maturity may finally get the car he has been working for, and the housewife may be able to hire the baby-sitter who will free her to seek outside activities. Goals are possible to attain for some people at certain times in their lives and under certain circumstances. Not everyone attains his goals and probably no one ever attains all his goals. Goals are, however, more attainable than aims and lend an aura of concreteness to the concept of aims.

Goals may serve as symbols of progress toward the attainment of aims. The woman seeking social status and prestige may view the acquisition of a new house in a desirable neighborhood as a concrete symbol of progress toward the intangibles she is striving for. A man may regard his promotion as a definite indication of his power and control within a business organization. A high school student may consider his admission to membership in an illicit fraternity as a symbol of his progress toward real popularity. For many people the attainment of tangible goals symbolizes progress toward intangible aims. The failure to attain at least some of his goals means to the individual that he has failed not only in terms of goals but also of his far-reaching aims.

Aims and goals are frequently confused because for some individuals the immediate goal can take on an importance and a symbolism out of proportion to its role in the life of the individual. The teen-age boy who views the ownership of a car as the only important thing in his life is an example of the confusion between aims and goals. For him, having a car symbolizes a solution of all his problems, his immediate maturity, the improvement of his relationships with his parents and peers, and his importance as a human being. Car ownership guarantees none of these things, but the teen-ager sees only the symbol. He fails to understand that he is really striving toward such aims as independence, maturity, and achievement. Adults, too, can center their strivings on symbolic goals. The new house, the promotion, membership in *the* club, a leadership position in a fraternal group, or an intellectual discovery can take on a symbolic value similar to that of the car for the teen-ager. The attainment of the symbolic goal often leaves the individual with a flat empty feeling and a sense of not knowing where to go next that are far different from the satisfactions he expected to result from his strivings. Failure to attain a significant symbolic goal can assume monumental proportions.

Some goals are superimposed upon the individual. The parents who insist that their child must go to college, the wife who nags her husband to earn more and more money, or the employer who expects his employees to dedicate all their activities to promoting his business are attempting to superimpose their goals on other people. The youngster who claims he wants to be a doctor may really be striving toward this goal or he may be verbalizing a goal that his parents have convinced him is his. Superimposed goals complicate the life of an individual because he cannot readily distinguish them from his own. The result is often frustration of his own personal goals and aims.

In the foregoing discussion of aims and goals, the emphasis has been upon those that are socially acceptable. Aims need not, however, be good or societally approved. The man whose aim is revenge for real or imagined wrongs, the woman who seeks adulation and applause at the expense of everyone else, the person who strives ruthlessly for money and power, the teen-ager who seeks belongingness in a gang through antisocial actions—all are examples of people whose aims and goals are warped according to the values of American society. Either or both aims and goals can be at variance with those commonly regarded as good or acceptable.

Goals and aims can and do change. Because of their relatively tangible quality, specific goals can shift fairly readily as the individual develops new symbols and attaches importance to different representations of his aims. A person can also experience a change in aims but such a change entails fundamental alterations in his values, ways of thinking and doing, and his derivative subsidiary motives. An alteration of aims does not appear overnight but rather usually results from a prolonged period of personal turmoil and reinternalization. A man striving for success and defining it as money and prestige may have many tangible goals along the route, all of them fairly consistent within his basic framework of aims. When, however, his aims alter and he no longer strives for success as he previously defined it, this change is far-reaching. The definition of success as money and prestige may become one of service and self-expression. The violinist may become a medical missionary or the haberdasher, a politician. Such changes in aims result from and demand alterations far more extensive than those entailed in changing goals and involve motives and their sources.

Aims and goals are seldom singular. Most people seem to strive toward many aims simultaneously and have many goals that signal their progress toward these various aims. Occasionally a particular individual will apparently strive for only one aim, usually related to his own personal enhancement, but this tendency seems to be exceptional and may characterize the aberrant personality in American society. Normal people have a variety of aims, some of which may be more important than others at a particular point in time. This multiplicity of aims and goals provides the individual with a variety of sources of possible satisfaction as he attains some goals and fails to attain others. This repertoire of aims and goals allows the individual to be flexible and adaptable in his progress toward at least some of his aims. Since he can probably attain only some of his goals and make partial progress toward only some of his aims, these qualities seem to be requisites of the healthy person.

THE SEARCH FOR SATISFACTION

Obviously man struggles for various goals and aims in a search for satisfaction. A universal motive impels him to seek such positive experiences. Theoretically, satisfaction should be a simple concept capable of definition in terms of the goals reached, but unfortunately simplicity is alien to that complex concept.

Satisfaction is one of the vaguest concepts in psychology. The word implies a state of being, of having arrived, of being finished that is antithetical to the sensation itself. Difficulties are compounded by the differences between physiological and psychological satisfactions. Scratching a bite that itches or soothing thirst with a cooling drink are usually physically satisfying; in being so, either can supply a psychological sense of well-being. Gaining pleasure from a fine painting or from listening to a well-played concerto can supply a somewhat similar feeling of pleasure and well-being undoubtedly more psychological than physiological. At times, the two can be practically inseparable as in the combinations deriving from sexual intercourse. Not every person, however, gains satisfactions in the same way to the same degree from the same experiences, objects, or acts. Hence satisfaction has tended to elude specific definition in terms of a complete theory of motivation.

Satisfaction seems at best to lend itself only to broad definition. In the framework of the theory of motivation presented here, satisfaction is the positive feelings that come to an individual at various points in his strivings. With this definition as a starting point, the characteristics of satisfaction become the significant aspects of that concept.

In view of the definition, the first characteristic may seem tautological, but its essential core is only too frequently ignored. Satisfaction is an emotion. It is not adjustment or adaptation; it is not reason. It is a feeling and, as such, individually derived. Satisfaction comes from the individual's universal and subsidiary strivings and arises from his emotional commitments to his particular values and ways.

As an emotion, satisfaction does not lend itself to quantification or measurement, but only to individual analysis by the person experiencing it. Just because the amounts of food and water necessary for life can be measured, there is a tendency to apply the same quantitative approach to satisfaction. When a parent asks, How much love does a child need? How much attention should I give him? What will produce a happy child? —his questions are quantitative. In essence he is asking, What things in what quantities create an emotion? When a researcher seeks to find and analyze the components of job satisfaction[5] or to designate the salary levels, working conditions, and fringe benefits that produce satisfied employees, he, like the parent, is trying to measure an emotion quantitatively. Both examples assume a state of completion and ignore the dynamic aspects of society and the individual's motivations. Emotions are individual subjective feelings—not objective quantities, and satisfaction is an emotion.

The second characteristic of satisfaction is that it is unpredictable. Not even the individual himself can accurately predict when or how he will secure his moments of satisfaction—except, of course, for the physical satisfactions like scratching or eating and sometimes even these activities do not lead to the anticipated pleasurable feelings. Mike,[6] for example, expected to find satisfaction in beating the athletes in a card game, but his prediction was wrong for their playing did not challenge his ability and he

[5] Most vocational researchers skirt a definition or discussion of satisfaction. Donald Super, for example, does not attempt to explain the concept, but refers the reader instead to such categories as "job adjustment," "vocational adjustment," and "needs." (*The Psychology of Careers.* New York: Harper, 1957, p. 360.) This reference is typical of the work and thinking in this area. Obviously the basic theories used do not permit the researchers to deal with satisfaction—or perhaps with emotions.

[6] See the case of Mike in the Appendix. One might also cite the teen-ager who, on emerging from the local cinema, exclaimed, "That was a wonderful movie! I cried all the way through it."

hated "playing a guy for a sucker." Satisfaction may come with
the attainment of a concrete goal or it may not. It may result
from socially acceptable behavior or from extreme antisocial actions. It may even result from no apparent action on the part of
the individual. The important point is that no one, except occasionally the individual, can predict what will produce satisfaction
for him.

Oddly enough, dissatisfaction seems easier to predict than
satisfaction. American Negroes, economically depressed for over
one hundred years, are currently expressing their dissatisfaction
with their condition. It was predictable that this dissatisfaction
would manifest itself. It is not predictable that economic better-
ment will automatically produce economically satisfied Negroes.
Many of the job-satisfaction studies of the past few years can be
interpreted in this same way for the assumption behind them is
that satisfaction will result from the elimination of sources of
dissatisfaction.[7] Satisfaction is more than the absence of dissatisfaction and as such cannot be predicted.

A third characteristic of satisfaction is that it is seldom, if
ever, terminal or complete. Satisfaction as a word seems to imply
a completed state, something finished or accomplished, but this
implication is never true even of the physiological motives, which
recur constantly. The man who seeks prestige may achieve some
and he may derive some satisfaction from it, but he continues to
struggle for more. The goals from which he expects to get satisfactions may change, but he seldom reaches a state of having
enough prestige or enough power or enough affection. He may
secure enough for the moment, but satisfaction is transitory and
he will resume his strivings almost as soon as he experiences some
modicum of the sensation.

Satisfaction is never complete in another sense: it is never
pure. Some dissatisfaction seems always to adulterate the feelings of satisfaction. The artist who finishes a painting may be

[7] For a convenient summary of some of the job-satisfaction studies,
see Robert Hoppock's annual surveys in *The Personnel and Guidance
Journal*.

relatively satisfied with it, but he can also see flaws in it. The man who gets a salary increase may be proud and pleased, but he would have liked a larger one. The high school student who makes the first team will be dissatisfied until he stars in a game. Dissatisfaction colors many of the pleasurable moments of satisfaction and insures that individuals will continue their efforts toward their aims.

Dissatisfaction is, of course, closely related to changing goals. Once a goal has been attained, a new one appears and dissatisfaction with the one just reached begins to rise. If the over-all aim of the individual is success, then the many goals related to this aim illustrate the possibility of several of them taking the place of a goal that has been reached. The attainment of one out of a number of goals may also introduce dissatisfaction with the failure to attain the others and intensify the strivings for them. Ever-changing goals necessitate a concept of satisfaction as dynamic and transitory.

Some authors have related satisfaction to satiation in the sense that an individual can acquire too much of something for which he is striving. This seems at best a psychologically dubious interpretation of what is essentially a doubtful physiological concept. A man may overeat, but satiation does not mean he will not seek food again; he may secure sexual satiation, but he is not thereafter celibate. Actually satiation seems to be linked to changing aims in much the same manner as satisfaction is related to changing goals. Aims change slowly as a result of experience and learning, often without the individual being aware of the changes taking place. Satisfaction with the attainment of goals related to the old aims decreases and dissatisfaction increases, until the individual "has had it." Satiation may occur in the interim before new or modified aims supersede the old. This process of changing aims is the outcome of the dynamic qualities of human beings and reemphasizes the nature of values, ways of thinking and doing, subsidiary motives, aims and goals, and satisfactions.

Closely related to the third characteristic of satisfaction is the fourth: satisfaction is rarely linear in nature. Because of the American emphasis on linearity, there is a tendency to regard satisfaction as a feeling that is acquired through a steady, orderly progression toward a single aim. No one says to himself, "I am going to become a powerful man" and then ticks off his satisfactions in such terms as the number of people he can order about, the amounts of money he can control, and the political influence he can exert. Satisfactions come in a helter-skelter fashion in connection with various aims, but in no set, orderly pattern. Thus the individual may find some satisfactions in his job, his family life, his recreations, and his civic and religious activities. Few people find their jobs entirely satisfying; their family life, idyllic; and their recreations and activities providing as much satisfaction as they had expected. Rather, satisfactions come to them in myriad disorganized ways, from many sources, and in connection with various goals and aims.

The fifth characteristic of satisfaction is its close relationship with the last universal motivating force—to achieve positive experiences. Satisfactions seem to provide some of the necessary positive experiences that make the individual's life worth living. Satisfaction in any area of the person's life seems to provide him with a needed and valuable reinforcement of his own feelings of worth and importance in his particular sphere. In this way, satisfaction provides a link between the universal motive and the self-concept and identity of the individual.

The healthy, normal individual seems to be able to acquire some satisfaction of all five universal motives. Such satisfactions are rarely reached simultaneously or continuously. Rather such a person's life offers him the opportunities to live, to internalize and perpetuate his culture, to express himself and his individuality, and to gain positive experiences at varying times and in varying degrees. No universal motive is constantly frustrated.

The happy, creative individual seems able to acquire a variety of subsidiary motives and a wide repertoire of goals and aims and thereby maximizes his own opportunities for satisfactions. Such flexibility seems to be a *sine qua non* for happiness and personal freedom. Perhaps the lack of satisfactions of some of the universal motives and inflexibility of subsidiary motives, goals, and aims can predispose the individual to mental illness. Undoubtedly an affluent, pluralistic society can offer its citizens opportunities to secure many satisfactions so long as the myriad meanings of motives, goals, and aims remain a reality. Certainly what any society must furnish its citizens is the freedom to attain satisfactions. The concentration of any science like psychology should be on the production of a healthy, normal, happy, creative individual. The aim of counseling must be to help the individual not merely to tolerate but to enjoy life.

4

THE INDIVIDUAL AND THE THEORY

A comprehensive theory of motivation and behavior has to have applicability as well as simplicity, universality, and consistency. It has to have meaning when related to the individual and meaning such that the latest findings in the behavioral sciences fit within its scope and amplify it. The theory has to apply to all individuals, preferably without exception. Perhaps only the test of time can determine the existence of exceptions.

The first three chapters have presented the general outline of a theory with some illustrations showing its applicability. This chapter demonstrates how the theory relates to a single individual and the explanations it offers for individual behavior. The starting point for understanding why any individual does what he does rests willy-nilly on a theory of motivation. Hence the starting point here is to allow an individual to talk about himself, his motives, values, ways, feelings, goals, aims, satisfactions, problems, and conflicts—the very things that anyone would discuss if allowed to do so.

What the individual says is the source material for understanding him from his own point of view and frame of reference. What Bob says will show not only the applicability of the theory, but also furnish the basis for working into the theory generalizations about the nature of problems and conflicts, the role of emotions, and the ways out. To a troubled individual and to those who want to help him, these are the immediate and gripping concerns.

BOB

Bob is a high school junior and his concerns are not atypical of those of many able students who usually see school counselors

only for program and college planning and test interpretation.
Bob's teachers and his former "guidance man" have viewed him
as having no problems except a tendency to overwork. Their descriptions of and judgments about him are contained in the words
"talented," "able," "popular," "mature," "responsible," "excellent
student," "intellectual curiosity," "well-rounded," "gifted," and
"well-adjusted."

As he entered the office, Bob appeared to the counselor to
be a neatly dressed, good-looking, well-built and well-coordinated
youngster, over six feet in height. He tapped his fingers on the
table as the interview started. The counselor did not structure
the interview and the following excerpt starts with the third response Bob made.[1]

> I like to keep in shape. I go out for all the sports and
> when I don't have sports, I usually do a lot of exercises. I enjoy
> basketball a great deal. I got a little unlucky because last year
> in the middle of the season I had to discontinue because of a
> 5   knee injury. Next year I plan to be going strong in sports. It's
> kind of a worry though because now I've not got the best of
> knees. I've always had trouble with one. I could hardly walk
> when I got off the basketball court. When I got home to study,
> it was terribly nerve-wracking. Besides I worry. I worry a great
> 10 deal about studying, too. I'm a perfectionist, I guess you'd
> call it. If I don't get everything right it bothers me, too, I guess,
> and not participating, too. It bothers me. I don't know why this
> is, why I should be so concerned with doing everything and
> doing everything perfect. Like there's band and my school day
> 15 last year was completely filled up which left homework to be
> done at home and everything to be done at home. And I've got
> to get a diploma next year. Even in debate just to show you
> how much of a perfectionist I am—I took debate for the first
> time last year. I had never had an interest in debate until our
> 20 speech teacher said that would be an extra project and to get
> an A in her course, you'd have to take debate. So to get an A,

---

[1] Since the counselor is unimportant for the purposes for which we
are using this interview, we have deleted his remarks in order to focus
attention on Bob. Paragraphs indicate entire statements. The material is
verbatim except where slight alterations have been necessary in order to
prevent identification. The excerpts are from the first two interviews.

I took debate and to the surprise of everyone including myself
I made the team. Our team won everything until the big tourna-
ment and there we missed out by one point. I don't know
25 whether it would be abnormal to really feel hurt about this,
especially for a boy, but it bothered me. It didn't exactly
bother me so much, but I had this complex, I guess you'd call it,
of what the other people would think. And as far as schooling's
concerned, maybe it's too much of what other people think.
30 Take the A honor roll for instance—well, I started out in high
school and I made the A honor roll the first time and the second
and the third and since then I haven't missed—but maybe I
worry about it and worry about missing for the same—well,
other people will know that I miss for the same—well, this last
35 year the studies have been so complicated that only one other
kid has made it even for the same two times. Then out of the
whole school, there's only been six kids who even make it as an
average because of our strict complications we're running into,
the subjects necessary and all. Another thing, I seem to be
40 taking as many subjects as I can and the hardest subjects which
naturally complicates the thing more. I don't know, I seem to
do well in it, but I still seem to have the feeling of an inferiority
complex, it seems. And this bothers me an awful lot. I'm
bothered by being—well, by worrying about people almost. I
45 don't feel average, I guess. I don't know why. I guess part of
it comes from—I could look a little overweight. I don't know.
I am overweight as far as that goes. On the scale I am overweight, but I try to make it muscles not flab. I could still lose—
lose a little. Too much fat around the middle, I guess. And this
50 bothers me tremendously. It bothered me so much that during
eighth grade—I was not so much muscle as fat then—it
bothered me so much that during the summer I virtually starved
myself and lost—ah—thirty pounds, I believe. When I came
back to school, everybody thought I'd been sick and I guess I—
55 then I guess I began to feel a little more—a little more in it
and I started not watching my weight again and I gained some
more. Now I weigh 187, I guess, which is much too much, but
everybody says I don't look like I weigh 187, but I feel so
conspicuous and—and so abnormal—well, not abnormal, but
60 just not average and I *feel* abnormal about it. I don't know. I
just feel a lot of times that I'm just not in with the kids, but to
hear someone else say something, I'd be considered popular,
et cetera. But I don't have that feeling and maybe it's because

I participate in all sports and I'm in everything and because
65   I try to do so good—well, it happens that I do excel. I'm not
trying to brag because I do have an inferiority complex and
things. But I just can't see how I can do so well and still feel
inferior and have an inferiority complex. It—it puzzles me.

I have this feeling of not being in it and I guess—I guess
70   it comes mainly from—well, I like to do everything and I like
to do everything in perfect—I like to do it perfect, just perfect
—and this as you can see creates a problem. When I get going
I have all—everything at one time and I force it—subjects
which are very hard. I don't see how I'm going to do it. And
75   then you get to that point where everyone expects so much
from a person. Next year now they've put on me editor of the
paper. I accepted—I don't really know why. I guess I accepted
just—I don't really know—just—I didn't really accept it because
I wanted it. It's what other people induce me to do. They say
80   I have the ability. They say I can do it better than anyone else.
Maybe I do it to prove to myself that maybe they're right.
That's why I probably take—took it on. The biggest problem
on my mind now is how it will be in college, I guess. Like even
in studying, I know that 95 per cent of the time, I could study a
85   third as much and get, a majority of the time, the same grade, A.
But there's always going to be some time that you have to study
a little more. And I know that I could study even half as much
and get A's but they would not be one hundred per cent. Why
this even gets to be a contest once in a while with some of my
90   teachers. Well, on examinations, my English teacher's put in
two or three questions pointed at me to see how much I studied
and he wasn't able to fool me all year. I haven't missed a question in English. I'm not that smart. I'll admit that. I don't
think I'm very smart, but it's just the principle of working at it.
95   Last year our guidance man called me into his office and said
that I evidently was working too hard. He tried but—I just
learn everything and when I get to college I know there's going
to be so much material I just can't learn everything. But in high
school I've learned everything. I take a sentence from the book
100   and—history, for example—by giving me the topic, I can con-
struct the whole subtopic. Dates included. Everything included. And you can see how much of a nervous strain this
would be. When you're learning all that history and then comes
—well, there's one kid in our class who must have a phenomenal
105   I.Q., way over a hundred. All these examinations that come out

that we've all got to take, he always gets tops. He didn't study
too hard. I got a lot better grades than him 'cause I studied
real hard. Well, I unnecessarily worried about the test and
what probably provoked a lot of my mental anguish was that
110   the test wasn't supposed to be based on the book. But I took
the book and read the whole thing again. Then I went over the
highlights and after that, I went through the tests. I took the
test and I knew everything in it. It was a standardized
eleventh-age test and the teacher said that mine was the highest
115   grade ever got on a test administrated at our high school. But
still, even though I excel at things like this, I still got that—
this worried complex. It's hard. Like even the beginning of
this year, I saw all those hard subjects coming up. I worried
about them. And to make things worse, I went to a party and
120   everybody called me the brain of our class. Well, after I got
home that night, this worried me. It's unexplainable. I know
I'm not a brain and I didn't know whether I could do it—
whether I could continue to get grades like this and—but I did.
I came home with straight A's again. And next year, I don't
125   know if I've improved any, but it'll be just as much of a problem
as before. Just like I said, I'll be editor of the paper. Besides
that, they elected me president of our church society. And they
voted me president of our honor society. Then there'll be more
elections next fall and I don't know whether I'll get any of them
130   or not, but maybe I will and then there'll be that, too. Besides
that, there's all the social functions and then my sports take
about two hours after school. I usually come home about six
o'clock and I start studying and I study awful late. Have to
—have to—to comprehend what I do get because—I study too
135   hard I know that. Schedules don't help. I tried that. Even my
folks don't like it. I have trouble with my eyes, you know. I've
been making them worse. I've had glasses all the time I've been
in high school. They're getting worse from studying too much
and he said that—the eye doctor I went to—he said that I
140   needed at least eight hours of sleep per night. But if you study
till twelve and you get up at six, that's only six hours. At examination time, there's even more. The worst thing is that I know
when examination time comes, I wouldn't have to study even
one bit of the information—I could still get an A. But I have a
145   reputation, I guess you'd call it, and so I go over it all again and
study it and come out with a hundred. Actually when I look
back on it, I didn't have to do it.

Maybe if I didn't excel so much in something—it would bother me naturally, but maybe my biggest concern is what
150 other people expect and think. I don't know what would happen—how much mental strain it would be if I happened to miss the honor roll one time. It—it seems so impossible to make the honor roll with a straight A that actually when you start and get everything right and you don't miss anything and it seems
155 that you should fall into a pattern and expect it yourself as does everyone else. But I—I—I worry and sweat over every test as much as someone who had not opened his book. It's—it's a problem, I think. Sometimes it gets to the point where I do—where I don't enjoy it at all. But everybody expects it. And I
160 don't really know what the problem would be and this college bit, I don't know what that's going to be like. It'll be awfully hard. But as I said, I don't believe I have the mental ability to get straight A's in college as I've got all the time in high school. I'm smart enough to know that there is a great difference.
165 I have the feeling that, if I start to study the way I do in high school, I know I'll just come to a point and go down and get flunking grades almost. If I try to cram in everything, I won't get anything because when I take a book I don't read it, I study it. That presents a great problem. I don't know how
170 much—I don't realize my ability maybe. But the way I study it's a terrible mental strain. It's hard to keep up.

It seems I always studied hard. One year we had a teacher who had a policy of never giving over a B+. That is the only thing that brought my grade average down. And that
175 —that kind of burns in me actually. But no one has ever graduated from our school with an average as high as mine. So you can see how much farther ahead I must be than anyone else but I've still got that worry and if I don't—like the guidance man told me last year, I shouldn't even have to study outside of
180 school because of my ability, but I see no ability and yet I know I must study unnecessarily. But I see no dividing line and this is what I'm worried about in college. Even next year, where's that dividing line? Where is that dividing line where you pick out what is important? I pick out what is important and I learn
185 what is unimp—virtually what is unimportant, I guess. But I don't think you're going to stump me on anything I've had in high school—on any problem I've had or any questions actually. The kids'll ask me questions. They'll just ask me the name of a person who's come up in a story in their literature book only

190   one time. They'll ask me what the name was and I can tell
them and they think it's kind of a game because they really
think it's fun, you know. They'll sit there and try to stump me.
They couldn't do it actually. And I—that's one of the joys I
guess you get from learning it. But maybe it's unnecessary to
195   learn it like that, but I—I learn so much and do so much extra
work, too, alongside that—that I must know a lot, but I don't
feel like I know too much at all. And I don't know how I'm
going to do it next year actually. But it's the same way every
year.

200   I wouldn't take debate next year, but everybody will want
me to because they know that I'll probably go farther than anybody else, but I don't see how I could possibly. But I suppose
I'll take it because everybody will be insisting on it. Like this
year, I didn't want to be in that play at all because I know—it
205   —it'd run for five weeks, the practice sessions from seven until
eleven at night. I didn't want to take it at all and I wasn't
going to try out. Here comes the director and says in a nice
way, "Are you coming tonight for the tryouts?" I says, "No.
My schedule does not permit it." And I believe he was mad,
210   literally mad, and I said, "No. I'm not going to." And he said
that, well, it'd look awful funny to everybody else if I didn't
even come to the tryouts and they gave me a part. They had
already decided the part that I was to have. So I tried out for
the play and I still come out—I studied hard. That was even
215   harder on my eyes because I had to study after I got home after
eleven at night. And get up in the morning at five to study to
keep up. Little sleep and all that studying and I was in the play
and was acclaimed the best one in the play so you can see what
happens. But still—although—all the recognition I get—and
220   another thing, they induced me to write for the paper. I write
up the sports news and I write—just write, you know, for the
paper. And so there's that, too, now. And then there's band
and chorus. It's just tremendous what I've got to do. I don't
see how I do it, but still I've got—everything I do do must be
225   exact and to the best of my ability. And to the best of my
ability I know I can do it in perfection—so there's perfectionism coming up again.

       Last year my—my mother I know was really worried be-
cause she knew I was doing too much and she thought I worried
230   too much. I even went to see the doctor but he just told me to

get more sleep. But I'd sit and study and I'd just perspire. It'd just run off me. And—like taking a test—I go into the test room and I know the materials backward and forward, but I walk into that room like I don't know anything. I sit there waiting
235   for the test and as soon as I get the test I—my hand is just shaking. I see the questions and I could answer them in my sleep. It's supposed to be a hard test. After the test is done, I get a hundred and nobody else gets above eighty or ninety. And all the questions that were so easy, the kids talk about like
240   they were so hard. Now if I was very intelligent to go along with this, which I feel I am not, I would probably have an easier time. But I don't feel I'm any more than average. I—I must be more than average, but I just can't see it. I can't see any more than average in speaking ability, yet I got the speech
245   award. And that's just the way it goes. And I got a journalism letter and a music letter, too. And some people say my writing's clever, but I don't think so. But they decided that I should be editor of the paper and they asked me, "Would you consider"— so naturally I took it, I guess. And each of them, each of the
250   teachers even expect so much more out of me and I'd just like to go to school sometime and just not do anything. But I know how I'd feel like. It's how I'd feel afterward. But I guess it's my nature and it's terribly nerve-wracking.

I get this—this sort of feeling a lot of times. I don't know
255   what it is, what the problem would be. Nerves or mental. But I just get it. When I'm sitting there studying and I look at the day tomorrow and I anticipate a test in every subject—I antici- pate a test every day. That's why I do everything the way I do it. If I stop and think of my work, there's something that
260   rushes through me. I just get—I get just like a hot flash. Just makes you red all over almost. Just rushes through you. And if I sit there and think about it, it just—well, it's just to the point of almost breaking up. But I've just got to put everything out of my mind and do what I've got to do and just take the matter at
265   hand and just work at it like I would naturally. Then set that aside when I do get it done and take the next thing and the next and then the next. That's how I know they say I should work. And it turns out late but I—normally I get it done. And it just gets to be a problem because—last year I had two teachers that
270   became immune because of me to write out answer sheets to the tests. They'd take mine, run through it, and use mine as a key. And so you can see the mental strain. I just have to get

everything right. When the teacher begins to use my paper as a key, it's—it's very bothering I guess you'd say. And it bothers
275 me a lot. And another thing that bothers me. I don't know why. I've probably expressed this to you before. That's just not being in it with the kids. I just feel like I'm not one of them, I guess. I feel—well, I feel more or less abnormal. I don't know why. But it seems like when I go some place, I don't feel like the
280 others want me, you know, to mix. And it's like that even at school. Actually I don't feel like just going up and talking to them. I kind of get to be—even during the noon hours and after school—it bothers me because I just don't—well, I just don't seem like I can mix. And as soon as the bell rings, a lot
285 of times it's just a relief. Just to go sit down and you don't have to try to talk to anybody. But once I get to know someone, I guess it's a lot different and I don't know whether I'm—popularity, that bothers me a lot, too. I try to be popular—very popular. And I don't know if I am. But then again, I must be.
290 And it's difficult.

We have a group in our class—I mean of boys. We have a lot of popular boys, I guess you'd say. These boys would excel our—our girls in our class. And I just don't feel like I'm in it, I guess. But then again, I could be more in it than any-
295 body else, but I don't realize it or something. I just don't feel like I am. I just feel like I'm not with them, I guess. And I feel like they don't ever want to be with me. And that I'm not just as good as anybody else. And I—I think this. This reasoning of mine must come out a lot because my folks tell me,
300 "You're just as good as anyone else. You've just got to think you're just as good as anyone else." But it's—it's there just the same. It doesn't help what people tell me. It's a problem. So I don't know what to think.

I feel that maybe my brother, the one that's in college,
305 maybe he's got something to do with it. Maybe it's—it's that he sets my ideals, maybe subconsciously if not consciously. He's an A student and excelled in athletics. And anything else he was—in my mind, he was just the most popular kid in his class. He always held a class office. He was student council president
310 and president of his class. And he was just real popular, I thought. He was ahead of me in school, but I realized it and I could see it. But it didn't—like it didn't seem to present a problem like grades to him. Twice I think he did miss the A

honor roll, but I don't think he was as conscious of being on the
315 A honor roll. Yet I get the feeling that he must have been a lot
smarter because he didn't seem to study as hard and didn't
worry about it. But I guess maybe that was the ideal that I set
up when I went to high school, him and his record. And now
when he comes home, he says how much he had been reading
320 about me in the paper and how much better I had been doing
than him. And this just kind of grabs me because I don't feel
that I've been as successful as he has. Grade-wise, I know I've
had straight A's and he didn't have straight A's because it
didn't seem to bother him. Still I think he came out with an
325 A average. But there again, he didn't get a hundred every time
and he didn't make the A honor roll every time. He missed it
twice. But it seemed like he was more one of the group. They
considered him as one of the group. Whenever I'm along with
somebody, I just feel like I'm not one of them. Just maybe a
330 shadow or a tag-along. Nobody knows what a mental strain it
gets to be. I'm just the worrying kind, I guess.

Popularity—I guess that's one of the main goals I set up
for myself to have and if I don't seem to be reaching it, then
it's there bothering me. My grades, I reached that. And I
335 accomplish it. But this is a great problem. It's the first time
I've talked about it. I just don't seem to be—I just don't think
the kids are with me. But there isn't any upper classmen that
won't talk to me like last year. And I seem to be with them,
but I've just got that feeling that I'm just not like them. Take
340 our honor society. They voted me president of it and it was
unanimous. But still I got that feeling. And sometimes I wonder. Maybe things that are so little can bother me so much and
then when things get rather big—you can imagine how much
they would bother me. I've always had this—getting on the
345 subject of girls. My freshman year, I never attempted to even
go—I never went with a girl. I never went with a girl in my
sophomore year. I had that feeling that if I asked one, she
would never go with me. Not even a one. And there again I
set my ideals—that girl's got to be pretty nice. She's got to be
350 good looking. She's got to be, you know, real nice, a real nice
girl. And I figured all the girls that I looked at, you know how
it is, I didn't think that they would ever go with me in the
whole world. And there's one especially and she was in my
class. And you know how that goes for a high school boy to
355 date a girl of your own age. It's even harder than just going

with one younger. Well, I don't know what ever got into me. This one kid wanted me to—to ask her. He knew that I liked her. And I knew that she wouldn't go with me naturally. So he wanted me to double date with them. So in a state of not
360 thinking, I guess, I called her up. And she went with me. I've been going with her ever since, but I don't know why she keeps going with me. All evidences are that she likes me, but I just feel that she don't. Now I discover that she has a record of every one of our dates and that we had gone together 43 times
365 and that must be a good indication. I don't know what else it could be. Naturally she has girl friends and her girl friends are friends of mine naturally and they tell me—but I just feel that she wouldn't go with me. That's the only girl I've really ever gone with. And now I'd feel like I'd like to try somebody else,
370 but I don't think anybody else would go with me. I don't like to say that to anybody because that would just be tearing down the girl I'm going with now and she is real nice and everybody thinks she's real nice and considers me lucky. But there I go again. I know any kid would go with her if he could. A lot of
375 kids have gone with her, but no one has since I started going with her. But I just don't feel that she really and truly can like me. I can't see how that would be possible. And then again, she has kind of set me up on a pedestal because she thinks I am so popular and do so well and everything and am so well liked,
380 but I just can't see that either. I guess when I walk around school everyone on the side lines envies me, but I would give a lot to be one of them. But then again, I don't—I suppose I could put myself down there by not studying at all. I imagine my grades would go down. I know they would naturally—by
385 not studying at all. I could drop out of everything. I could stop participating. I could stop being friendly. It seems like I would give anything to do it, but still I want to be up on top. And as it is, I guess I am on top, but it's just so nerve-wracking and just so hard that it seems hardly worth it. And then the reputa-
390 tion I've built up. I can't do any little thing that I don't have to do it to complete perfection because if I don't, it's going to drop my reputation. There's no way to go higher it seems. Grade-wise I couldn't get over an A. But popularity—there I I just don't feel in it at all. That's my big problem, I guess.

395   You just start something and you've got to keep it up to perfection. When I stop to think about it, ten years from now, what difference is it going to make anyway? But now it's real

big. And I guess that's natural, too. But I see no sense in going to school and just being a run-of-the-mill student and not getting
400 good grades and not caring. When you do something, I suppose you should do it up good. I just hope it isn't as bad in college, but I would imagine that it's going to be worse. I don't know what—well, last year I talked to the guidance man once in a while. Just happened to go into his room. He starts talking
405 sometimes. He said that you can never do it up this good in college. You could never learn anything that way in college. He said I shouldn't—I should stop now. Just like I said, he could tell I was studying too much. But I just can't see drawing any line like he said I should do. You can't draw any line
410 if you expect to get one hundred in everything. I know that I'm definitely knocking myself out too much, but it'd be worse to my way of thinking if I didn't knock myself out and went down. So I just keep it up, I guess. It's a strain actually. Naturally it's mental—I know that. I realize that. That guid-
415 ance man told me that. But I can feel it like I said. Like if I'm studying and I'd stop, I'd just get hot flashes all through the body. But I suppose I should see that I don't have to study as much because for a while I studied about half as much. Three times as much worrying but half as much studying and I came
420 out with the same exact grades. But I know from experience that if there's a test, I just cram in every available minute before and most of it with—with worriedness and the longer it gets, the more worried I get. Actually I just hate a lot of times to go to things that should be fun. Like during the night—and enjoy
425 them. They keep telling me to just go and enjoy yourself and forget about the books while you're there and have fun but it —it—it's almost impossible it seems like. I just put in too much time on my books. I must. I don't think other people study that much. Maybe they do. But they don't get the same results
430 on it anyway. Like I see it, I can see I can get the results, I guess, but I just keep doing it. I guess I should consider myself fortunate that I do get those results, but I don't get them as easy as other people draw conclusions to. That's something that bothers me, too. People expect it. They say that you wouldn't
435 even have to read the book. That's the general attitude of a lot of people I know. But it's a long way from the truth. I could probably get the same grade even if I did just read it, but I've got to read it and study it.

Sometimes it's just a misery. Like every night at play
440 practice, I'd drag my books along and try to study between
lines. But what would I get done? Nothing. There I'd have my
books in front of me all the time, try to drill on them, try to get
something done, but I don't get anything done because that's
impossible almost. For a few of these kids maybe it'd be profit-
445 able to bring their books because they just have a couple of
lines, but when you're on the stage all the time except for a
little while, you can't get anything done. Then everybody's
running around and trying to rehearse. I don't get anything
done. I could have just as well left my books at home, but had
450 I left my books home I'd have worried because I had left my
books home. I don't know why but night after night I'd keep
taking them because if I left them home, then if I had a free
minute to sit there, I'd probably worry some more. I can't stand
not to be working. Even to walk slow—if I got something to
455 do, I like to get at it or else I feel—or else it's worse than
doing it.

I think a lot of the things I try to do is—I don't know. I
read a couple of psychology books once and I guess I'm trying
—well, to compensate for all the things that—just to compen-
460 sate for—I don't know—a lot of things I'm inferior at I guess.
But I want to do good. I worry a lot that it's wrong for me to
complain. It's not right at all because basically I realize, I
suppose, that I have nothing to complain about. But still there's
all those things I do complain about and I know I shouldn't com-
465 plain because that's wrong. It's just not—well, Christian, I
guess. I do degrade myself terribly—I know that. But it's just
that—well, I don't want to end up feeling sorry for myself either
or get a lot of complexes or something. I could be in a lot worse
shape than I am, but so why do I have such a complex then?
470 But it seems like whether I do or don't, the feeling is still there
and it doesn't help what people have told me. I try not to let
it bother me what people say, but it's just kind of a stab, I guess.
Kids can be real cruel that way. I imagine I am myself, but just
don't realize it. If you say something to somebody else, they
475 become mad. I try to forget it and I act like it doesn't bother
me at all. But down deep I guess it really does. Then a lot of
things I say, too—you know, once it's said, you can never take
it back and I worry about it. That's another thing. You say
something and you just happen to think about it later and that

480   about drives you batty, too. It's impossible to take something
you say back, but sometimes you end up saying it anyway and
you regret it a lot of times. The kids—maybe lots of people do
that, but they forget about it. I just don't.

Another thing worries me. Like if I act—I don't know—
485   if I act like I'm smarter than everybody else. I mean, it seems
like sometimes when it comes out what other kids say, it seems
like I act that way and I worry about acting conceited. I'm just
about the farthest thing from being conceited that I've ever
known of. Envious would be more the type I would say I am,
490   I guess. But that's wrong, too, again. That bothers me because
I—it's just a whole mess. And then I worry about being envious. I shouldn't be and it's just all complicated. But I just
envy about every—everybody it seems—I just—like some of the
boys in our class—it seems like—I don't know—they're so
495   much better looking, I guess. That bothers me an awful lot.
They just seem to be able to get along and seem to be in with
the group. They've got it—but then I know I shouldn't complain. But more than anything else maybe—I don't know.
Every time I start thinking about one thing it seems like that's
500   predominant over the other, but it's all in a big heap at the top.
All working together. One time that will be real big and then
another time something else. I just try to—try to keep telling
myself that I'm just as good as anybody else, but it don't work.

Sometimes I think I'd feel more comfortable if I just went
505   off by myself, but that's—I tried it. You get such an empty
feeling alone. I just want to be part of them, but I just don't
feel like—I feel like I'm rejected and I don't feel like I'm—I
try to have fun and all that and I'd like to have fun and I'd
like to be part of the group. Oh, everybody's friendly I guess,
510   but—I don't know—I'm just not in it. That's another thing I'm
envious of somebody having a real close friend or something.
But it seems like I never have. I mean they do something and
they call on somebody to go with them or something, but I just
feel like they never call on me or anything like that. I don't
515   know. I'm just defeated before I start I guess. Everybody else,
I suppose, thinks I got it made. But actually I'm more miserable
than anybody. I suppose a lot of people would be surprised if
they ever heard me express any ideas like this.

Like on the basketball team. Out on the court you just
520   get into a mechanical process actually. But I don't feel like any

of the kids—then, too, I think I'd get out there and really try and I couldn't do anything anyway because I'd be thinking about books, too. And I've got bad knees. I think a lot of it's the way my brother played, I guess. I can remember when he
525 was playing. If I could play like him, I'd have it made. I know I could, but I just don't and I don't know why. Maybe I'm just a little reluctant when I get out there. I just know I can't. But I'm even—actually I'm more stout and muscular and taller than he was when he was my age. But I feel like everybody
530 else has got more push and speed than I've got. They push me around and run circles around me. Instead of me pushing them around—anyway I just don't amount to anything, I guess. But I'd really like to get out there and play as good as he did. Boy, he'd get in there and he'd score on anybody. Then he got hurt,
535 but that didn't stop him. He played anyway. Maybe basketball isn't so important after you get out of school, but now I'd really like to go out and do a good job. I know I—I know I can right now. I could score on anybody out there. But when I get out there, it's going to be a different story because then I'm
540 going to feel that incapability again. Oh, I really want to go out there and get on the first team and do a good job but then I don't really want to go out because I know that when I get out there I probably won't do anything anyway, but now I know I have to. I don't know what I'm going to do. I'm not
545 afraid—not exactly. But if I did get hurt, it'd probably be a relief. Maybe I'd have to quit or something.

I'd like to do it like my brother. Basketball mainly and just being in with the kids. It just seemed like he was real popular. One of the—if not the most—one of the best—most pop-
550 ular. I think it's bound to come out at home if you're feeling somewhat like that. If I mention something about him, my mother really feels bad because she keeps telling me I'm just as good as he was and I can do anything just as good as he did. I'm doing a lot of things better and I realize that. If I mention
555 him, she don't like it at all because—well, she just says I can do anything as good as he did. He was no better than I. But once in a while, you know, my mother gets mad at me, I think. Because I mention what he did. He was in everything, everything and anything. We got along real fine, but I guess it's just put
560 up to me—just put up like too much of a goal it seems like. He set too high a goal for me to try to follow. I don't know. Of course, I'm getting better grades. I'd feel terrible if I didn't

get better grades. But it's—it's just—it seems like he was just in it.

Essentially Bob is talking about what is important to him, his problems and conflicts. These are incorporated in a discussion of his feelings about himself and others, his values, ways, motives, goals, and aims, the meanings these have for him, the symbols he establishes, and the satisfactions he derives from his strivings. These elements can be identified and their analysis constitutes an essential preliminary step to understanding the true nature of Bob's problems and conflicts. This identification provides some understanding of the interrelationships and interdependencies of Bob's difficulties, how he feels about them, and how he has tried to cope with them. Such an analysis leads to generalizations about problems and conflicts, emotions, and the ways out that extend the theory of motivation directly to the individual.

THE NATURE OF PROBLEMS AND CONFLICTS

Besides serving as an illustration of the interrelationships among motives, values, ways, aims, goals, and satisfactions, Bob's remarks provide a concrete basis for the consideration of some generalizations about problems and conflicts. People have long recognized that a situation creating problems and conflicts for one individual may be completely untroubling to another. The question, Why? remains. To find the answer, a consideration of the nature of problems and conflicts as it emerges from the background already presented is necessary.

Perhaps the most important fact that appears both from the case and the theory is that *problems and conflicts are always motivational in nature.* The possible conflicts within and among universal motivating forces, subsidiary motives, and their sources have already been noted and their potential for creating difficulties for the individual needs only be reemphasized here. The case of Bob provides an opportunity to see some motivations in operation and to understand how they cause problems for the person.

Bob's striving to do things perfectly is a constant theme. He values perfection and it has become an important aim for him in all areas of his life. At the same time, Bob also values competition; it is a way of thinking that he has internalized particularly as it relates to his brother and the things his brother has done. Through his strivings, Bob has managed to maintain a higher academic record than his brother, but his successes in sports, peer relations, and extracurricular activities have not—at least, to him —measured up to his brother's performance. Hence Bob is a youngster who is constantly striving to achieve a standard of performance that he values and that for him means perfection. As he says, "There's no way to go higher it seems." (392)

Bob's strivings for excellence are complicated by his strivings for popularity. Competition with his brother is influential and so is the meaning popularity has for Bob. There is evidence that Bob is popular in the accepted sense of the word, but from the statements he makes popularity means something more to Bob than winning elections or being included on double dates. Presumably he wants to be perfectly popular, whatever that may mean to him. Excellence and popularity are not always compatible in American society and the attainment of goals related to one may require the individual to make some sacrifices in striving for the other. Problems and conflicts grow out of incompatible motives.

Bob struggles, too, to express many middle-class values in his actions. The healthy body, the "nice" girl friend, the importance of reputation, what other people think, and authority —all represent values Bob tries to implement in his strivings and they inevitably lead to conflicts and problems. Can he really be healthy and normal when he has bad eyes, tricky knees, and "hot flashes"? Why isn't he content with his "nice" girl? Why is reputation so important to him that he will do things he does not want to do in order to maintain it? Why can't he accept and internalize what the authorities (doctor, mother, and "guidance man") tell him? All these questions center around motivations, values, and meanings and make every problem motivational.

Some of Bob's difficulties stem from the motivations growing out of his religious and psychological values. He wants and struggles to be "normal," but he never feels that he is. He is envious of others more popular than he and tries to suppress his envy because it is wrong. He complains about his lot and labels his complaints unchristian. He thinks he must not tear down his girl because that is not right, but he wants to do so. Bob is trying to look at the good side, the bright side of his life for that is what his religious values have taught him to do. And he further tries to pattern himself after the psychological and contemporary stereotypes to which he has been exposed—the average, the normal, the popular, the hero-athlete, the student, the good brother. Here again Bob's problems are motivational and their roots lie in the universal motivating forces and in the sources of subsidiary motives.

Bob's problems are also influenced by the motives and values that other people seek to impose upon him. He should be able to go to parties and forget about his studies while he enjoys himself, but he cannot. He should be able to temper the amount and intensity of his studying, but he cannot. He should be able to feel that he is as good as anyone else, but he cannot. He struggles to implement all these "shoulds" and fails. He has tried schedules, attended parties, and attempted to internalize his mother's advice about his worth and none of them has helped him to change his values or his motives.

Essentially Bob is no different from any other youngster with problems. Any of the cases in the Appendix or any unstructured counseling session with a youngster would illustrate equally well the contention that difficulties stem from conflicts in values, ways of thinking and doing, and motives. Paul wants to do something good, something that would please his mother and tries to do so, but he also wants to fool around with cars because they have meaning and value for him. Laura struggles to conform, to be respectable and her sister's dereliction leaves her frightened and shaken about the worth of the things she has considered important.[2] None of these youngsters can resolve his difficulties by adopting the "shoulds" suggested to him by adults. Rather each has to examine his values and motives and undergo the slow and arduous process of changing or strengthening them for himself.

The case of Bob illustrates a second generalization about problems and conflicts. Like motives, *problems and conflicts cannot be arranged in a set hierarchy.* Throughout the case, Bob tries to assess his problems in terms of their importance to him. His inferiority complex "bothers" him "an awful lot" (42–43); his weight bothers him "tremendously" (50), his "biggest" problem is studying in college (83); his "biggest concern is what other people expect and think" (149–150); popularity is "a great problem" (335). Throughout Bob is trying to arrange his problems in some sort of order according to their importance and poignancy to him. He has learned that something should be most important to him and that other difficulties should fall neatly into place in some kind of tidy sequence, which he should be able to determine. But he cannot.

Actually Bob cannot establish a hierarchy because his problems and conflicts are so interrelated and intermixed that they cannot be separated one from another. Neither can they be judged according to their order of importance or immediacy. Indeed, no real purpose would be served by ordering his problems. Once ordered, the problems and the question of what to do about them still remain. Talking about them helps Bob to clarify his thinking, ventilate his feelings, and reach one insight into the nature of problems. He says, "Every time I start thinking about one thing it seems like that's predominant over the other, but it's all in a big heap at the top. All working together." (499–501) In other words, even he cannot determine which of his problems is most important or most troublesome. Rather he is beginning to understand something of their interrelatedness and interdependence and this understanding may help him to work out his problems and conflicts.

[2] See Appendix.

The expectation that problems and conflicts can be organized in a hierarchy is, of course, totally unrealistic in light of the theory presented here. If universal motives, values and ways, subsidiary motives, and goals and aims cannot be ordered, then the problems and conflicts stemming from them certainly cannot be organized into the neat patterns so dear to scientific classifiers. Here the classifiers are trapped by one of their own ways of thinking—that pattern and order and hierarchy always exist and take forms similar to those of the phyla and genera of Linnaeus. Unlike the physical structure of plants and animals, the behavior and feelings of human beings are changing and dynamic and their problems and conflicts are equally dynamic.

Third, *problems and conflicts are purely individual in nature.* No two people experience the same problem. Bob, for example, is worried about college, but not in the same way as many other teen-agers. He is concerned about the amount of studying he will have to do and whether or not he will be able to learn everything as he always has. Other youngsters might worry about whether or not they will get into college or how they will make friends once they do. These concerns Bob never mentions.

Bob is in competition with his brother and so are many other youngsters his age. But not all high school students who have older brothers compete with them, their records, and their reputations. Some teen-agers feel as strongly as Bob about what they view as their own lack of popularity, but their reactions to these feelings and the reasons for them are far different from Bob's. Problems and conflicts, stemming as they do from motives, are purely personal and peculiar to the individual.

Certainly there is a similarity of problems and conflicts among youngsters growing up in the same or related cultures, but these similarities are more apparent than real. Popularity, dating, inferiority, independence, and human relations are all possible teen-age problems, but how each teen-ager views them is purely an individual function. Some teen-agers may experience difficulties along these lines; some may experience none of these conflicts, but many others. Problems and conflicts are as peculiar to the individual as are his values, ways, and motives; precisely this individuality makes his problems always different even when they are most similar.

A fourth generalization is that *problems and conflicts defy categorization*. Guidance workers often seek to label a student's difficulties with the traditional tags of educational, vocational, social, and personal without giving much thought to whether or not the tags serve a useful or even a justifiable purpose. Bob, for example, is not a student who would usually be viewed as having educational problems. And yet, in a sense, he does because he works too hard, is indiscriminate in what and how he studies, and gets little joy or satisfaction from his work. But does this label adequately describe Bob? From his own point of view, Bob has social problems, which may well intensify his educational struggles. Obviously Bob has personal problems of the sort engendered by perfectionism, extremely high standards, and sibling rivalry to list only the most obvious. On the basis of the material included, Bob has few if any vocational problems, although this apparent absence does not mean that he might not develop some at a future date. But what purpose does this labeling serve?

By tagging Bob's difficulties as if they were jellies and jams, one loses sight of Bob and of the fact that he is a unitary human being who feels all these things at once and experiences them as "just a whole mess." (491) In Bob's case, as in that of any counselee, categorization cloaks the interrelationships of problems and conflicts and obscures the way in which one difficulty can augment and contribute to another. Bob's problems are peculiarly Bob's and labeling them does nothing to advance an understanding of Bob or to help him to work his way through them.

Categorization leads to further difficulties. As Bob tells it, the "guidance man" has told him that he will not be able to study everything in college and that he should not have to do so in high school. It seems likely that Bob has been labeled as too hard-working, possibly even as an overachiever.[3] The "guidance man" expects to settle this problem by offering facile, superficial advice. In so doing, he adds to Bob's problems, gives him something more to worry about, and perhaps even makes him feel guilty about his intensive studying. Other people also reinforce these feelings when they urge him to go to parties and forget his work, but the "guidance man" not only should know better but should make the effort to gain some knowledge (not information) about Bob before he offers his opinions. Categorization of problems and conflicts makes them look too easy, too readily susceptible to the quick, superficial solution that American values teach people to want and expect. Americans are only now beginning to learn, although perhaps not yet to internalize, that human problems have no quick, ready solutions.

Categorization may sometimes have a legitimate research purpose, but research that depends on a distortion of the human personality can hardly be valid. In direct work with people, such labeling can only lead to confusion, misunderstanding, and prejudice on the part of the counselor. If he has labeled a youngster as having a particular kind of problem, he tends to see only that problem and to miss others contributing to or growing out of it. More serious, he tends to see the label, not the person. For the counselor who labels, his counselees become not Joe, Mike, Mary, or Pam, but the study-habits problem, the vocational problem, the culturally deprived problem, or the delinquent problem and the tags lend a spurious similarity to counselees. The problem cannot and should not take precedence over the person.

A fifth generalization about problems and conflicts states that *they do not necessarily occur at specific times in the lives of all individuals.* Bob, for example, as a high school junior might be expected to be concerned about college choice and admissions, but in all the interviews with him he never mentioned college

_____

[3] Overachiever is probably one of the most misleading of labels. If Bob is really working as hard as he thinks he is he may well be an under-achiever rather than an overachiever regardless of his innate capabilities.

except as it related to his intensive studying. Other difficulties were more important to Bob and any attempt to introduce the topic of college would probably have met with little interest and have served to produce further anxiety. For some children, the transition from elementary to junior high school is routine; for others, it is an extremely upsetting and frightening experience. No one, however, can state that all children will have problems and conflicts connected with a change in school level or precisely what form they will take.

Oddly enough, problems and conflicts do not seem to occur at the time of some of the significant crises of living, but rather before and after them. The family in which illness fells one of the parents, carries on despite the difficulties involved. After the crisis is over, motives that were relegated to the background reemerge and difficulties reappear. Jim apparently did as he was told during his father's last illness probably without too much questioning and now is troubled because he was not at home when his father died. Sharp crises seem to leave people with fewer rather than more choices and are perhaps easier to deal with than the less dramatic but persistent kinds of crises related to everyday living.

Certainly some youngsters find some of the designated school crises troubling, but not all. Moreover many youngsters face difficulties and conflicts that are seldom, if ever, mentioned as representing crises in their school careers. No one can assume that, because an individual is at a particular age or a specific point in development, he automatically has or will have a certain problem. Problems and conflicts arise out of the experiences and internalizations of the individual and no one but the individual himself can be sure what will trouble him and when. Of late, too much attention is focused on the problem and not enough on the person and this mistaken focus has led to a loss of perspective on the origins of problems and conflicts and the determining role of the individual in them.

Two other generalizations are so obvious as to require only the briefest mention: *problems and conflicts are inevitable* and *they are never singular.* In the approach to motivation presented here, conflict among the universal motivating forces becomes an unavoidable part of being human and singularity of conflict, an unlikely outcome. The addition of values and ways to the universals and the existence of many subsidiary motives merely emphasize the unavoidable contention that problems and conflicts will exist and will be plural.

One last generalization about the nature of problems and conflicts remains: *problems and even conflicts are not necessarily bad for the individual.* Psychology has amply demonstrated the harmful effects of problems and conflicts on the mental health of the individual but, in so doing, there has been a tendency to underplay the benefits that accrue both to the individual and to society from his attempts to deal with problems and conflicts. The youngster who works his way out of a difficulty or resolves a conflict has learned something about himself, about how to tackle similar difficulties, and about the satisfaction that may result from trying to work things out. Jim, having talked out his feelings and the problems associated with his father's death, has learned to understand himself and his mother a bit better and to develop confidence in his ability to cope with other problems of living. Mike, caught between his impatience with the grocery customers and his fear of losing his job and the sense of well-being it gives him, is making some progress in learning to control his temper.[4] Conflicts and problems create opportunities for learning experiences of a highly personal, individualized kind provided the individual can take advantage of those opportunities.

Even the conflict that is highly productive of guilt can offer the individual an opportunity to learn a valuable lesson that may make significant contributions to his future mental health. The person who knows something about handling guilt, which is as inevitable as are conflicts, has learned an important lesson that will serve him well throughout his life. Counselors and others who work with people in trouble have tended to look on problems and conflicts as difficulties that must be eliminated

[4] See Appendix.

from the life of the individual and this, of course, is impossible for they either recur or new ones develop to take the place of the old. Problems and conflicts offer counselors the challenge to help the person learn ways of dealing with such difficulties that will enable him to meet his present problems and equip him to deal with those to come.

Essentially problems and conflicts seem to provide a certain stimulus to the individual to reexamine his values, think through his motives, assess his goals and aims, and evaluate his satisfactions. They supply an impetus for change and are certainly one factor in the dynamism of the human being. Without them, human beings would be static and progress, however defined, would be nil.

The preceding discussion is not intended to imply that problems and conflicts are good. The deleterious effects of severe and prolonged conflict on human personality are well-documented in the literature and only too evident in the protocols of counselees. Perhaps the best statement about problems and conflicts is that they exist and always will and no one can safely make value judgments about them. Value judgments enter only after the fact as the individual himself assesses how he has solved or resolved the difficulty and what he has learned from the process that may serve him next time.

THE ROLE OF EMOTIONS

For a person like Bob, caught in a tangle of problems and conflicts, understanding his own emotions is one of the most troubling aspects of his difficulties. Emotions play an integral part in any experience, but youngsters are rarely taught to deal with emotions as effectively as they deal with multiplication tables, spelling, or rules of etiquette. Emotions pose different problems that involve an understanding of feelings, a subject rarely discussed in modern America despite its long history of psychological orientation.

Emotions exist. Every "normal" person experiences a broad

panorama of such emotions as joy, pleasure, love, affection, disgust, hate, envy, fear, anxiety, boredom, displeasure, suspicion, guilt, happiness, sorrow, satisfaction, hurt, triumph, like, and dislike. He may even experience most or all of them in a single day without being manic-depressive or abnormal because for the "normal" person, emotions change as situations change.

Often members of American society act as though emotions do not and should not exist. Small children, especially boys, are cautioned not to cry and not to express joy obstreperously. Many youngsters like Bob have learned that complaining is wrong (461–466); that envy, too, is wrong (489–493); that boys should not feel "hurt" (25–26); that feelings of superiority, confidence, conceit (487), and inferiority (*passim*) are all bad, as are fear, trepidation, and anxiety (*passim*). The result for the youngster experiencing these emotions, as all people experience them, is worry and unhappiness. "I'm more miserable than anybody," says Bob (516). But like all people, Bob cloaks his emotions in public because society tends to deny their existence.

Even counselors try to sweep emotions under the rug and hope the bumps will not show.[5] The "guidance man" to whom Bob refers obviously tried to cope with Bob's problems by ignoring the ramifications of emotional entanglements when he told Bob that he was working too hard and apparently suggested new means of studying (95–96, 134–135, 263–267, 403–409). Yet a half century of psychology has taught that the counseling room serves its real purpose as the place in which to express emotions freely and learn how to deal with them.

Perhaps the very phrase "emotional problems" has led to the tacit assumption that all emotions are somehow wrong or bad —at least, that they should not be allowed to show. Accounts and stories of juvenile delinquents, drop-outs, and emotionally disturbed people discuss aggression, hostility, hate, suspicion, fear, anxiety, and guilt as though they should not exist. And yet, all people experience them at one time or another.

The "bad" emotions are even at times admired and con-

[5] See Chapter 3, p. 79.

sidered useful. How can one be the American ideal, the "go-getter," without being aggressive? Suspicion is often a protection and a part of many activities, because few people engage in a "willing suspension of disbelief" all the time. American society would certainly label the completely unsuspicious as immature, naïve, and overcredulous. Similarly, fear is a great protection and it, like anxiety, can heighten one's performance and sharpen one's reflexes. Feelings of guilt serve to prick the conscience and to help man to live by his values. Hate can lead to reforms and changes in the existing pattern of things. Emotions in and of themselves are neither good nor bad. Society and the individual furnish that judgment.

An important societal distinction between the "bad" and the "good" emotions is that a person can express somewhat more openly (provided that expression is not excessive) his feelings of love, affection, and satisfaction than he can his feelings of hate, hostility, and unhappiness. Perhaps in a society where psychologists often speak of a disturbed person's inability to express emotion, to give and take love and affection, there may be a significant relationship between the curbing of exuberant and "bad" emotional expression and the failure to learn "good" emotional expression. The child cannot distinguish societally approved emotional expressions from those frowned on without a long process of learning, which may be neither clear nor consistent. The four-year-old may be comforted when he cries; the eight-year-old scolded for unmanliness. The child may be allowed to have temper tantrums at home, but not in public. The possible illustrations are many. What many a child learns is that emotional expression is dangerous. In learning to curb his expressions of jealousy, frustration, and hate, he may also learn that expressing love, affection, and happiness can be perilous. The result is lack of emotional spontaneity—and perhaps, intellectual, too.[6]

[6] In this connection, the following comment by a nonpsychologist seems relevant. "This kind of 'Anglo-Saxon' emotional control has won battles, crushed mutinies, faced down tyrants, and won through many other storms in history; it is splendid in a storm. The only trouble is that most

Unfortunately, the outcome is usually a Bob, a worried, unhappy boy. Bob has learned to curb and to bottle up his feelings
of anxiety, guilt, and envy, and to behave and express himself
the way he thinks people expect him to behave. The process
leaves him unhappy and unable to experience real feelings of
satisfaction, belongingness, and worth.

All strong emotions trigger physiological reactions. The person who discovers he has eaten some *outré* food may feel nauseated or become ill. The person suddenly plunged into a fear-
inducing situation may shake, tremble, stutter, stammer, and
sweat. The angry person trying to control his anger may clench
his fists and tighten his muscles until he has to hit out to reduce
the tension. The anxious football player or actress may become
actively ill before the performance starts. The worker who dis-
likes his job may develop a variety of hypochondriacal and psy-
chosomatic ailments. The youngster like Bob may find that he
reacts physically to his anxiety. Whatever the emotion, it triggers
and influences physiological reactions that, in turn, often augment the problems already existing.

Emotions are seldom pure. Only rarely in American society
does a person experience an unadulterated feeling of hate or fear
or love. Even the boy who has learned that society rejects him
and fights back with a shield of bravado and hostility does not
feel pure hostility. In a situation such as school where he faces
values far different from his own, he may demonstrate hostility
at the same time that he wants to be a part of this alien society
and envies those who are. He cannot understand its rejection of
him, and he feels himself "a stranger and afraid in a world he
never made." The mask he uses to cover his emotions may be
hostility, but the real emotions underlying it are almost always a
mixture.

As with Bob, ambivalence of emotions is typical of most
_____
of life isn't a storm at all, and this control can make all the rest of life on
the drab side, produce misunderstandings between people, chill humanity
and be a great fertilizer for hypocrites." John Knowles, *Double Vision,
American Thoughts Abroad* (New York: Macmillan, 1964), pp. 162–163.

people because there is no consistency or compatibility among values and motives. Bob both wants to be on top and yearns to be average, not different. He desperately wants to attend and enjoy parties, but finds no satisfaction in them because he worries about his work, not belonging, and popularity. He has the nice girl he thinks he should have, doesn't want to give her up, and simultaneously wishes he dared to search for another and could do so without hurting his present girl and leaving himself dateless. Bob's feelings about himself are equally ambivalent and inseparable from his values and motives. He describes himself as "abnormal," "unlucky," "bothered," "worried," "overweight," not good looking like the other guys, "unpopular," "inferior," and "not very smart." At the same time, he realizes that "I degrade myself terribly" and "it happens that I do excel." These mixed feelings are closely linked to his view of his brother, what he thinks other people expect of him, and the perfectionistic motives that he feels drive him on.

Actually Bob feels ambivalent about almost everything. As he talks, Bob demonstrates this ambivalence by the constant use of the word "but." He wants to do this, *but* . . . ; he wants to feel this way, *but* . . . ; he knows he should feel one way, *but* he feels another. This constant and continual ambivalence intensifies his worries and feelings of abnormality because it persistently raises the unanswerable question for Bob, Why then do I feel this way?

The answer is that most people feel ambivalent about most things, but the reality of ambivalence is too often ignored. Motives and values are made simpler than they are. Few people approach an experience or make plans or live through events with totally pro or con feelings that can be neatly summed up as purely adient or avoidant. They live as total human beings who may attempt to weigh the rationalistic pros and cons but find themselves puzzled by the mixture of emotions with which they actually greet each new experience. These mixtures cannot be weighed in a balance because they are the various degrees of emotional commitment with which each person invests his systems of values and motives and his views of himself, others, and the world.

Bob demonstrates well the person who because of his mixtures of feelings and motives cannot seem to gain much satisfaction from his endeavors. He wins elections, but never the right or important ones and probably not the next one. He makes the A average, but he sees only the danger of failing the next time. He acquires an array of symbols of popularity, but they are never adequate and he feels as though he is "not in it." He receives the best reviews for his acting, but he carries his books to play practice like a barricade against the world. He answers the questions with which the students try to stump him, but says pathetically, "that's one of the joys I guess you get from learning it." (193–194)

What is happening to Bob is a frustration of a universal motive: to achieve positive experiences. Satisfaction as it reflects the universal is for most people fleeting and temporary, but necessary and sometimes there. Bob's feelings of ambivalence are so great and his motives so relatively singular that he finds only very little satisfaction and much anxiety in reaching his goals or trying to fulfill his aims. Without satisfactions, he remains a worried and troubled youngster.

Some feelings of guilt are common among all people in American society. For the disturbed person, they can be traumatic. These feelings of guilt arise when an individual judges consciously or unconsciously that he has thoughts and feelings or has acted in a way that contradicts values he feels he should uphold. Guilt feelings run like a leitmotiv throughout Bob's comments. He feels envious but he knows he should not. He worries about things he has said to others and wishes he could take back. Bob constantly contrasts his values and his performance and finds they do not agree. In a sense, his fear of guilt becomes an additional spur. For many deeply disturbed people, the feelings of guilt may be definite and overwhelming. For the normal individual, guilt is a continual but less handicapping state of being, for

the potential for guilt exists whenever an individual makes resolutions that this time he will live up to his values. He will try,
like Bob, to be good.

As Bob discovers repeatedly, no one can reason away emotions. Bob has tried and failed and continues to try and to fail.
As he talks to the counselor, Bob almost compiles the evidence
that he must often have reviewed for himself and that should
demonstrate to him that he is all the things he wants to be. He
even claims that "everybody else, I suppose, thinks I got it made.
But actually I'm more miserable than anybody." (516–517)
Despite the arrays of proof and what other people say, Bob constantly finds himself caught in feelings that are uninfluenced by
evidence and statements. "I just try to—try to keep telling myself that I'm just as good as anybody else, but it don't work."
(502–503) No matter how hard he tries, Bob is unable to reason
away the feelings that disturb him. He is attempting an impossible task.

Reasoning away feelings is impossible because one cannot
reason away values and motives. Without personally gained
understanding of why one does what he does or believes as
he does, the best that can result is a bewilderment such as
Bob has about the feelings that just seem to remain. The pres-
ence of such "unreasonable feelings" tends to lead an individual
to feel different and somehow abnormal. A cyclic build-up results
in that the more the attempts at "reasoning" fail, the more the
individual misunderstands his own reactions and feels others
misunderstand him. Feelings cannot be eliminated by applying
reason or rationalization to them.

The general tendency is for misunderstood feelings and the
attendant anxiety to heighten and generalize.[7] Bob, like the
others in the Appendix, illustrates this point well. Bob's feelings
of inadequacy have generalized to many areas. Laura's fears and

[7] Although published in 1950, perhaps the best single reference on
anxiety is still Rollo May, *The Meaning of Anxiety* (New York: Ronald
Press, 1950). Certainly his account of the history of meanings of anxiety
in various approaches to personality has not been duplicated or surpassed.
Even though May's definition is limited, his approach is not.

feelings of hurt intrude on many areas of her life. In all cases, feelings of whatever nature generalize just as does the anxiety the person experiences worrying about his problems and feelings.

Psychologically it is an accepted fact that fear and anxiety heighten and generalize the longer they exist. Strangely, the carry-over effects of any strong feelings are rarely mentioned. Yet in everyday life, everyone has experienced this carry-over effect. There are days when everything seems to go well. There are "blue Mondays," just as there are days when one tends to feel kindly toward or suspicious of everything and everyone. There may be "reasons" for these feelings, but the important point is the carry-over they have. The person who has failed often tends to view each new attempt as another potential failure; the person who has just experienced success and satisfaction may approach the next trial optimistically. The person who has received love and affection or rejection from other people will allow these past experiences to color his present and future learnings.

There are ways in which outsiders can heighten the feelings a person already has. Bob illustrates well one of the most effective ways in which such heightening can take place, for he has received advice, words presumably of solace and encouragement and actually of misunderstanding from several significant people. Bob apparently sought a way out of his difficulties through outside devices: the new pair of glasses or the quick medical panacea. He left the doctors' offices with the words of advice, "get more sleep." Bob now worries about not getting sufficient sleep to keep him from ruining his eyes and his health. Although no doubt the doctors' advice was sound, Bob's problems remain and are augmented by that advice.

Even more significant are the words of the "guidance man" from whom Bob sought help with his problems because the guidance man should know. Actually Bob's problems have multiplied as he has tried to follow the advice and suggestions offered and failed. Bob worries about what will happen when he gets to college because the guidance man has pointed out that there "I just can't learn everything." Often Bob wonders how he will ever establish "that dividing line" the guidance man has told him he must determine. Bob states that "schedules don't help" and neither do study methods. Knowing that his problem is "mental" ("That guidance man told me that.") does not dissipate the anxiety but rather heightens it. Is Bob better off doing "three times as much worrying but half as much studying"? The words of advice he received a year ago still echo for him and serve only to multiply the feelings he does not understand.

Yet another significant person has attempted to help Bob and the results have been the same. His mother has been telling him that he is just as good as anybody else. Unfortunately Bob, like all people, applies his own meanings to "anybody else" and to him the phrase tends to mean his brother or the person he views as popular or on top. The words offer no reassurance or solace for Bob because he constantly tries to prove that he is as good as "anybody else" in his interpretation of the words and, as he says, he tries to believe it, but "it just don't work." Again a significant person has heightened Bob's anxiety because of the way Bob has interpreted and internalized the well-meaning words.

Heightening of the problem for a person in trouble is all too easy. Advice given by one person on the basis of his own values and motives rarely is suitable for those of another. Superficial attempts to treat the symptoms, such as teaching good study habits, only too often bring about attempts to adopt methods that do not work and an increase in underlying anxiety. Words of reassurance and encouragement are often only denials of a person's feelings and such denials connote only misunderstanding. None help and all can and do multiply the problems.

Like many people, Bob finds himself unable to cope with his feelings and his problems after reasoning and advice have failed. The more he thinks about them, the greater they become until it is all a "miserable mess." He is left caught in tangles he knows he should not encounter, doing things he realizes he should not do, and feeling emotions he thinks he should not experience. Bob seems to feel that there is no solution to his dilemma, but he wants desperately to find some way out.

THE WAYS OUT

Despite half a century of guidance and advice for the "normal" individual, mental patients occupy the greatest number of hospital beds and usually live out their lives in a state of being tranquilized. Despite fifty years of testing and test interpretation, occupational information, help with jobs and career choices, and careful selection of students for college, the percentage of students now graduating from college remains roughly unchanged. Neither has the drop-out rate from high schools changed significantly. The problem of preventing severe mental illness and of helping students to develop themselves and their abilities remains. A half century of failure should be sufficient to emphasize the fundamental point that there are no simple solutions to important personal problems and conflicts.

Because they depend so directly on the internalized values, ways, and motives of an individual, his problems do not lend themselves to simple solutions. Like Bob, many people have tried the simple solutions and found they do not work. The problems and conflicts only recur and often in a form aggravated by anxiety and the failure of the simple obvious solutions. Some of the difficulty comes from the tendency of many Americans to try to solve personal problems as though they were making adjustments in machinery or relining a brake. Unfortunately in most cases, solution is merely wishful thinking and the use of the word itself obscures the real nature of problems and conflicts.

Some problems and conflicts have no solution or even resolution for some things cannot change. The youngster with a physical handicap can learn to live with that disability, but in a world where most people have the full use of two arms and legs and all five senses, he remains different without an arm or a leg or hearing or sight. The child without arms who draws pictures of people without arms is viewing society from his perspective. Artificial limbs may provide him opportunities to make his way in a society in which he is different, but they are not real arms. The boy who cannot run when he wants to, faces again and again a recurrence of conflicts and problems that cannot be solved. Similarly the person whose color is different cannot change that color. In a nation of white men, he remains black or yellow or red just as the white man remains white in a nation of yellow or red or black men. A person can learn to live with differences regardless of what they are, but his problems and conflicts are continuous. Regardless of artificial devices and theories of compensation and adjustment, the basic facts cannot be altered. The problems and conflicts recur.

Most problems and conflicts whether physically caused or not recur again and again. Bob's perfectionism extends into all areas of his life. Each hurdle he faces causes reactions of anxiety and worry. Bob's strivings for absolute popularity make each decision about a party a recurrence of similar basic conflicts. Bob's amassing of evidence about his own successes and acceptance makes each decision about being editor or president or star a replay of the same fundamental conflicts among his motives and values. He can resolve the problems temporarily by making choices and decisions, but these do not cause the problems to disappear.

Almost all important problems and conflicts recur. Man, for example, does not make a single vocational choice, but an endless series of temporary resolutions to the fundamental, personal question, What am I going to do with my life? The so-called fantasy choices of childhood become realities for some people. The conflicts along the road to advancement more often than not demand wholly new decisions and changes in kind and type of work. Often the temporary resolutions are made more difficult by the values imposed on a person, for as the youngster explores he often makes a choice that sounds "good" in terms of his parents' and counselors' value systems. Too often, he is stuck with his temporary resolution.

Time helps to heal many problems and conflicts. The youngster who is taller or shorter or brighter or duller than his classmates may eventually find that time can help. His friends may
grow taller or he himself may suddenly spurt in height. In college or in graduate school, he may be with people just as bright
or brighter than he. The youngster once viewed as dull may
develop or he may seek out the things he can do and so no
longer suffer the indignities of being the class dunce. He may
even drop out of school if the comparisons become too odious.
One way or another, as he matures, the problems and conflicts
may not be quite so poignant as they once were although elements of the earlier conflicts will remain. Bob lost weight, but
still views himself as too heavy and somehow "conspicuous and
abnormal." When no change occurs, time at least allows most
youngsters to differentiate between the ideal values by which
children and teen-agers live and judge themselves and the relaxed values through which adults find their protections.

Although time may alter some problems and conflicts, it
does not solve them. The youngster is not helped by being told
he is "going through a stage" [8] or that someday he will not be different or will value being different. The matter of living day-by-
day with the conflicts and problems remains dramatic for the
youngster living through them and can and does often determine
the kind of person he becomes. The students speaking in the
Appendix, like Bob, tell fully how immediate and large and real
these problems are. They are the important concerns of the people having them.

Resolutions of problems and conflicts can be helped by
allowing the person to look at their probable underlying causes.
As long as Bob himself holds his particular values and motives
and applies to them the meanings he has applied, his problems
will remain. What is needed is some personal, internalized
change that will allow him to shift slightly a meaning or a goal
or an aim or a motive so that he can gain satisfaction from his
endeavors and temper his perfectionism. Such a shift in mean-

[8] See Appendix, "The Group," line 120.

ings or motives will not be rapid for values do not change easily. No one changes one set of values for another.[9]

What is happening to Bob in the course of the counseling sessions supplies an indication of how a youngster can be helped to begin to make the slight shifts for himself. Bob is finding that he does not have to be perfect to please the counselor. Through this process, he is learning that he is acceptable to another person despite the way he feels and acts. He is externalizing and verbalizing his problem without having someone offer him facile, easy solutions that do not work or value judgments about his values, ways, motives, meanings, and feelings. He is beginning to see new relationships among his values and to reexamine in his own way and at his own pace the interrelatedness of his problems and the true meaning of his goals and aims. The mere fact that the counselor can accept and understand him as he is helps to symbolize for him that he is not abnormal or peculiar. He has worth in his own right.

Bob is not alone in making important learnings from the counseling process. Mike learns that he merits the counselor's time. Jim and Laura find relief in being able to discuss and examine their problems.[10] Paul finds understanding in his definition of that word, a person who is willing to discuss cars for three counseling sessions. Through this experience, Paul gains enough confidence in the counselor and in himself to be able to

[9] Interestingly, the implication of some recent volumes on changing the values of drop-outs and juvenile delinquents seems to be that a complete value shift ca˗ and does take place. Perhaps the extremist position along this line is that of Martin Katz, *Decisions and Values, A Rationale for Secondary School Guidance* (New York: College Entrance Examination Board, 1963). He discusses such patently absurd points as consistency in value systems when he talks about "changes associated with age." "One consistent values system may be replaced by another equally consistent system; that is, certain elements may change, others may continue, but each system is free from internal contradictions." Such blatant misunderstanding of motivation, problems, and conflicts certainly should not—although it may —provide a rationale for either guidance or counseling.

[10] Jim remarked to his counselor that after the second counseling session he set up his own tape recorder and tried talking into it. He concluded, "You do a lot. Without you, it just didn't work at all." The learnings from the interrelationship are extremely important.

begin to verbalize about his areas of concern. It is no accident
that in the process Paul begins to think enough of himself to care
about his appearance and to try to stop his fighting. None of
these students has been told how to change or what to change
because they themselves are the only ones who can find the
changes and shifts for themselves.

In addition to shifts in values and motives, a person can
often be helped to find his way out by learning for himself that
the feelings he has are neither abnormal nor bad. Most youngsters can understand why other people feel and act the way they
do far better than they can understand their own motives and
feelings. The understanding Mike displayed is not atypical. Paul
has to learn and is learning by the counselor's reactions that hating his father and, at times, fearing that hate do not make him
unacceptable to the human race. Laura's feelings about her sister
can be discussed openly and it is less difficult to do so with a
stranger than she had imagined. The girls in the group interview
comment about the importance of understanding and verbalizing
feelings. Feelings are acceptable; "reason" and "realism" need
not be the only bases for discussion.

Many people can find ways out when they learn to live with
the inevitability of problems and conflicts. What is needed is not
a passive acceptance, but the realization that there are no simple
solutions. The "other fellow" does not solve his problems by a
magic wand or a crystal ball. The other person does not reason
away his emotions or live without feelings. The other person is
just like everyone else, caught in the inevitable problems and
conflicts caused by his motivational system. He, too, is a dynamic human being ever striving and ever changing.

Perhaps ways out for increasing numbers of people can be
found if the real meaning of individuality, motivation, and
change becomes understood. Only in this way can counselors in
school deal with the important concerns of people, their feelings,
values, and motives. For normal people, by verbalizing their
problems, by understanding and exploring their feelings, by gaining confidence and a sense of being worthwhile human beings,

have the power to find for themselves the "right way" out of their problems and conflicts. This process in itself is a learning that makes the next period of resolution of problems easier because practice and a method are there. Since all important problems and conflicts tend to recur, this learning is essential. Without it, prevention has no meaning.

5

THE INDIVIDUAL AND HIS REALITIES

Any theory offering a new approach to motivation requires an extension to include a new or modified view of the individual himself. Any approach to the individual consistent with the theory could be valid, but one that deals with the realities of the person not only amplifies the theory, but also relates directly with some of the problems currently encountered in guidance and counseling.

An individual lives in the midst of many realities, which may or may not bear much resemblance to what an objective observer might call actual reality. Thus Bob lives with the reality of unpopularity despite the view of others that he is one of the sought-after students in the school. The individual's realities center around him and are for him the important facts of his life. His realities have emotional meaning to him and form a part of his unique self. Hence any consideration of the selfhood of the individual involves a discussion of his realities, whether explicit or implied.

Realities like motives, values, and aims change as the individual changes and assume greater or lesser importance to the individual as he and his life situations vary. Realities do not lend themselves to categorization and certainly the individual cannot separate them out or distinguish them by name or descriptive adjective. Nonetheless, clarity and organization require some such division as the varied realities and the primary reality to aid in a discussion of the totality of an individual's realities. For the individual, however, his realities are whole and indivisible.

THE VARIED REALITIES

The life of an individual is influenced by many realities, which are for him the actualities of himself and the world around him. Physical reality, temporal reality, learning and thinking reality, emotional and motivational reality, the reality of values and ways, reality of identification, reality of meaning, symbolic, behavioral, and interpersonal realities are only a few of the ways of describing and distinguishing those realities most significant to the individual. They are neither discrete nor exclusive, but their listing serves to point up some of the elements entering into every person's total reality.

Physical Reality. Physical reality for the individual consists, first, of his own physical endowment and may include such items as skin color, physical handicap, energy level, predisposition to certain diseases, physique, and appearance. For the colored person, reality may be a world in which a white skin is the ultimate. For the crippled child, reality is crutches, frustration, and well-meant attempts to help. For the low-energy person, reality means making an extra effort to do what others seem to accomplish easily and without special exertion. Whatever the "facts" of a person's physical endowment, they make up his physical reality.

Individuals can be more or less aware of their physical realities. The colored person is often made aware of his skin color as is the crippled person of his disability. On the other hand, the low-energy person tends to be less aware of the ability of some people to want to tackle big jobs and plow into difficult tasks. Most Americans are only too aware of physical reality as regards appearance, stature, and weight; and a trip to the physician, a shopping expedition, or the casual remark of a friend can often sharpen or intensify this awareness. There is a tendency, however, for each individual to feel—for here reasoning does not apply—that his physical reality, whatever it may be, is that experienced by everyone else. People can and do learn that physical realities differ, but this realization is largely intellectual and external and does not carry over into the feeling area, which governs reactions to physical reality.

Physical reality continuously changes as individuals grow, mature, and begin to degenerate. The changes of adolescence and old age are the most dramatic and apparent, but a constantly changing physical reality is a fact of living, although people are not necessarily acutely aware of the changes. The slowing down of activity in late-middle and old age is often so gradual that it is only occasionally apparent to the person experiencing it whereas the physical changes resulting from injuries in an automobile accident or a severe illness may require a radical shift in the person's way of life and so make him intensely aware of the acute alteration in his physical reality.

People seldom, if ever, have a "realistic" concept of their physical realities. The woman who claims she can lose ten pounds before the party, the teen-ager who thinks he would be handsome without his acne, or the man of fifty-five who tries to do all the things he did at twenty are probably not being "realistic" about their physical endowments. From the point of view of the impartial observer (if there is such a person), the woman probably cannot lose that weight, the teen-ager even without acne will be only acceptable in appearance, and the man who overexerts is foolishly courting a heart attack. Each of these individuals may in time experience the truth of these observations. But at the moment, their own ideas are part of their physical realities and will remain so until experience teaches otherwise. They are no less real to those individuals because an impartial observer might judge them "unrealistic."

Physical reality also incorporates what might be described as environmental, but is so closely linked to the physical that separation is undesirable. A child's physical environment, whatever it may be, is for him the right, the only way to live. Thus the youngster who grows up with his own room and bath cannot visualize life without them—for him, they are part of his physical reality. Less privileged children, on the other hand, living in crowded conditions and with little or no personal privacy find their physical reality in these conditions and cannot conceive of a more private way of life. In a large family, noise may be constant and a part of physical reality whereas other families may include quiet as part of their physical realities.[1]

Whatever the individual experiences and internalizes as part of his physical life becomes for him physical reality. This concept may change and develop as the individual changes, but one factor seems fairly constant: for the individual, his concept of physical reality is the only one and must be that of everyone else. Experience, of course, teaches the perceptive person that there are as many physical realities as there are human beings, but even he cannot experience and feel realities other than his own. The diabetic child, for example, cannot skip a meal without probable consequences to himself. His concept of physical reality includes a pattern of regular meals and he cannot conceive of a way of life that allows one to omit breakfast or lunch. The diabetic *knows* other people can skip meals, but he *feels* they cannot and is always a bit taken aback when they do. Physical reality is highly personal, individualized, and centered in the person and his learnings.

Temporal Reality. Like physical, temporal reality is a function of the individual and his experiences. Time is an extremely slippery concept for all human beings and few, if any, manage to avoid a time orientation that does not begin and end with the self. The times that an individual has lived through become the times that everyone has experienced and knows. The teacher who speaks to a class about "the war" may mean World War II and assume that his class understands the same thing by

[1] This aspect of physical reality is finding confirmation in the work of people attempting to prepare culturally deprived youngsters for the school experience. The introduction of these youngsters to such elements lacking in their environments as pictures, books, magazines, crayons, pencils, paints, and toys as well as such intangibles as routine and control is expanding their physical realities so as to enable them to profit from their school opportunities when they reach the appropriate age.

his phrase only to discover that for his students, most of whom were born during or after World War II, "the war" is the Korean or the Vietnamese conflict. The parent whose values and motives were shaped by experiences during the Depression cannot understand his child who has known only the affluent society and its vastly differing values and ways. Temporal reality differs from generation to generation and offers one explanation for some of the difficulties adults encounter in working with young people whose experiences do not cover the same time span.

Individuals also feel differently about time. For the young, the days, weeks, months, and years stretch out in a seemingly endless succession. For older people, time passes much more swiftly and a consciousness of the evanescence of time is much closer to the surface than it is with the young. Children view summer vacation as never-ending and the imminent approach of the new school year always comes as a shock whereas adults find the summer slipping away almost before they are aware of its arrival. These feelings about time constitute part of the temporal reality of the individual and enter into much that he does or plans to do.

Temporal reality provides an explanation for some of the conflicts and misunderstandings between teen-agers and guidance workers. With a view of time as interminable, many teen-agers feel no urgency about planning for the future or getting things done as soon as possible. Feeling that time is slipping away from them, adults, on the other hand, tend to be impatient with this lack of concern and try to impose their temporal realities on youngsters. When adults attempt to force teen-agers to take a long-range view of their lives, they immediately embroil themselves and the youngsters in a conflict of temporal realities and all too often fail even to recognize its existence, much less the reasons for it.

Temporal reality for the individual changes as he grows older and his view of life and the time allotted to him alters. Sometimes these changes may be abrupt as when a teen-ager decides that at nineteen he is too old to go to college or a college sophomore believes it is too late to change his major field. More often, however, changes in temporal reality are slow and insidious and only strike the individual when he reviews his accomplishments during a particular period of time and decides he cannot balance the time invested and his achievements or when he looks to the future and what he may do in the years left to him. Then he begins to feel the pressure of time and the importance of not wasting it, whatever that may mean to him. Temporal reality is, of course, affected by American values and ways concerning time, but probably no two people have exactly the same feelings about time or experience it in the same way.

Learning and Thinking Reality. What a person learns from a given experience is a function of himself, his background, and his learnings and constitutes for him his learning reality. He learns from a situation not necessarily what he is expected to learn, but what he is ready and capable of learning or what he makes a particular effort to learn. Sometimes outside help intensifies or broadens his learnings; sometimes insight, as used by the field theorists, enables him to see new relationships and make highly personal, if not original, discoveries.

Certain selective mechanisms enter into learning and influence whether or not the individual will internalize or ignore that learning. This selection process is so little understood that only its existence is evident. Why does one child learn the difference between subtraction and division while another of similar ability does not? Why does one child learn fear in a situation that teaches another self-confidence and poise? Background and past experiences as well as intelligence influence this selection, but they do not fully explain it. Nonetheless, selection is an important part of the learning process and determines for the individual his learning reality.

Each individual utilizes his learnings to think about himself and other people and to arrive at conclusions about himself and about himself in relation to others and to the things he and they do. A person assumes that everyone thinks in precisely the way he does. This assumption is not rational or even conscious, but rather stems from the fact that an individual knows only one way of thinking, his own, and cannot realize that there can be any other way. And yet, there seem to be many ways of thinking about oneself and one's way of living.

Oftentimes several people arrive at startlingly different conclusions on the basis of the same set of data. These conclusions depend, of course, on the previous experiences and learnings of the individuals involved and their various motives, values, aims, and feelings. Conclusions, however, seem also to be influenced by different processes of putting the data together. Although both seem to be present in all thinking, the admixture of emotion and intellect entailed in utilizing data seems to differ from individual to individual. The speed and completeness with which the data are used contribute to the way of thinking of the individual and tend to make his way different from those of others. Some people possess the ability to see relationships among various data while others do not and this ability also leads to differences in ways of thinking.

All too little is known about how people think and even less about how and why the ways of thinking of two individuals differ. Only in intimate contacts do these discrepancies in ways of thinking manifest themselves and intrude upon the relationship between people. Each individual assumes that everyone else learns and thinks exactly as he does and is startled and even shocked on the occasions when he discovers that his assumption is erroneous. Differences in learning and thinking realities can separate individuals and give rise to misunderstandings and conflicts.

Emotional and Motivational Reality. Enough has already been said to indicate that every person has his own highly individualized reality of motivations and emotions. What he values, what he wants and strives for, and how he feels have far more real meaning to the person than does the reality counselors so often refer to and discuss. Bob, for example, is facing the reality of his own emotions and trying to reconcile how he feels with how he thinks he should feel according to his interpretation of the "real world." He is beginning to study what he wants and strives for in comparison with what he thinks he should try to do. Reality for Bob, however, remains how he feels and what he wants despite his nascent recognition of the possibilities other people see for him.

Bob illustrates another point in connection with the reality of emotions and motivations. His own feelings and desires are for him so real that they blind him to those of others. He cannot understand why all his classmates do not want the same things he does or do not feel as he does. This emotional-motivational blindness is typical of many people who cannot understand why a particular person tries so hard to advance socially or makes such a fuss about something that would be inconsequential to them. Every individual has his own emotional and motivational reality, which obscures his vision and understanding of that of another person. What the individual wants and feels is for him real; what others want and feel has for that person a quality of unreality except when it happens to coincide with his own strivings and emotions.

Reality of Values and Ways. Values and ways of thinking and doing share the same egocentric and ethnocentric qualities as the other realities. What a youngster learns is good remains for him the "real good," the "true good," until his own learning and experience modify or change it. The things he believes are "good" and "right" are always better and truer to him than what others hold to be "good" and "right." Although age may bring with it a certain tolerance, the person continues to wonder how others can be so benighted.

Strivings to perpetuate one's culture strongly influence the reality of one's values and ways. A person may cling to time-honored ways of doing because for him these are good; the modern machinery and new-fangled ways are for him valueless or even evil, if only because they are strange. New things and ways have to acquire value for the individual before he can alter old ways to accommodate them. Strivings to perpetuate make value changes come slowly and with difficulty and necessitate a process of learning to value the new more than the old. Learning, particularly about values, takes time and requires emotional as well as intellectual exercise.

The reality of one's own values and ways persists despite one's recognition of their susceptibility to change and the existence of other values and ways different from one's own. Some people cling to their values with greater tenacity than others, but the capability for change exists in all persons as does the ability to understand the values and ways of others. Awareness of one's own values in contrast to those of others is a more difficult learning, however, and for many people this awareness seldom progresses beyond a recognition of the existence of differences and surprise or shock at those differences. Today travel, the Peace Corps, reading, television, and concern about world affairs are causing Americans to become conscious of the varied realities of values and ways among the peoples of the world. There is, as yet, relatively little awareness of the many realities of values and ways that can and do exist within a single, complex society. Of all the realities, perhaps that of the values and ways of an individual is the most consistently overlooked and misunderstood.

Reality of Identification. Identity and the search for it have long been problems for individuals in American society and a source of concern to the psychologists and psychiatrists who work with them. The search for identity is an outgrowth of the universal striving to express oneself within one's culture and seems to embody the person's attempt to express and achieve some recognition for his own peculiar uniqueness, whatever form it may take. The questions, Who am I? What do I want to be? How do I want to live? What is important to me?—all contain elements of this seeking for identity. That they also contain elements of values and motives is not surprising because the relationship between identity and one's motivational system is extremely close.

Most children obtain their first sense of identity from their parents and spend their early years as the Jones' child or son or daughter. They are what their parents are. In adolescence and early adulthood, American youngsters struggle to achieve an identity in their own right. Then they begin to question the values and ways of doing of their parents and to seek their own values and ways. Inevitably the question of identity arises as it does not arise in many other societies. As Hsu points out, the pre-Communist Chinese achieved his identity through and as a part of his family group while the Hindu found his in his search for identity with his God.[2] For most Americans the problems of identity are not so easily or automatically solved.

Americans achieve their identities through their jobs, their friends, the associations and clubs of which they are members, their churches, their civic activities, and even the recreations in which they participate. A football fan club, the N A A C P, a union, a fraternal group, a fishing crowd, a club of people with high I.Q.'s, an unusual religious sect, or a neighborhood bridge club—all may be sources of identification for certain people. The problem facing the adolescent or the young adult is which of the many groups will provide him with the kind of identity that he wants. And more important, What kind of identity does he want? Some answers to these questions are supplied by his values and the motives that direct him into certain groups and activities as well as his job and some other circumstances of his life. Even so, the individual has considerable choice as to the kind of person he wants to be and the identity he would like to build for himself and herein lie the difficulties facing many youngsters.

Identity is not merely an adolescent problem, however, for if the person is truly dynamic, he must also live with a changing identity. Certain aspects of his identification probably remain stable, but many other aspects change as he changes and matures.

[2] F. L. K. Hsu, *Clan, Caste, and Club* (New York: Van Nostrand, 1963).

The successful lawyer who abruptly leaves law and becomes a minister is not simply changing vocations, but is also changing his identity in such a way as to make it consonant with what he thinks he is and wants to be. He may always have sought identification as a "good" man and now sees the change in vocation as a further means of expressing himself. Changing identity either abruptly and drastically or slowly and undramatically seems to characterize the progress of many Americans throughout their lives.

The reality of identification thus is changing like most of the realities previously discussed. This reality alters as an individual becomes independent, decides on what he will do with his life and then changes those plans, moves from one section of the country to another, shifts from one group of friends to another, develops interests in new or different associations and activities, or makes any of the myriad possible changes in his pattern of life. Identity is no more static than any of the other aspects of the human being although it may incorporate within it some persistent factors that characterize the individual.

Who he is and what he is constitute the reality of identification for each individual. Even such confusion and indecision about identity as that shown by many adolescents are for them a reality of identification. Whatever the individual feels he particularly is makes up this reality for him. Distinctions between the identity of a person and his self-concept are probably artificial, but the idea of identity seems to represent an attempt to sort out questions of the who-am-I from those of the what-do-I-think-of-myself type. Questions about identity tend to be less judgmental in nature than those about self. Nonetheless, his identity at a particular point in time is for the individual one of his important realities.

Reality of Meaning. Each person supplies his own meanings to abstract words, ideas, and concepts. These meanings may be similar to the dictionary definitions and to those of the general populace, but personal connotations always remain. These are the individual's idiosyncratic meanings and are the reality of meaning to him.[3]

Each person has his own connotations of key words and phrases. "Heroes" to Mike are the athletes who get the dates just as "suckers" are the "heroes" who lose their money to him in a card game. Mike defines "trouble" as himself. Laura, on the other hand, defines "trouble" as the difficulties experienced by her sister when she became pregnant before marriage. Bob has his own interpretation for the phrase he keeps repeating, "You're just as good as anyone else" because the words "anyone else" have certain implications for him. The girls in the evaluation interview are seeking to find precise statements about what the counseling experience has meant to them individually.

Similarly everyone develops individual meanings for his values, ways, motives, goals, aims, and satisfactions.[4] He may distinguish among his values only vaguely by the words "good" and "bad," but simultaneously he establishes for himself a range of meaning implicit in those two words. Perhaps he can distinguish only the extremes as Paul does. In a family where the father could "get drunk all the time and come home and beat up on Mom," Paul states that "It upset me when he picked on Mom like that." (67–68) To the outsider, violence may seem to be the greatest "bad thing." To Paul, however, "the worst he ever treated me" was when "he said he didn't care what I did." (161–163) In Paul's reality of meaning, violence is not so bad as rejection, although Paul could probably not state clearly such a hierarchy.

Values especially cause conflicts among the personal realities of meaning. Who is a good student? A good patient? A good employee? A good Christian? Who is a bad teen-ager? A bad actor? A bad parent? Each person uses such phrases from his own point of view and his own system and definition of values. These comprise the realities of meaning for him whether they are

[3] For an interesting cross-cultural discussion of meaning and its psychological ramifications, see Herbert Hendin, "National Character," *Columbia University Forum*, Winter 1964, pp. 31–34.

[4] See Chapter 3.

shared by others or not. To one teacher, the "good student" may be the one who causes no trouble and does his homework promptly; to another, the one who erases the blackboards, arrives on time, and hands in neat papers; to another, the one who questions and offers new ideas. The definitions will be as individual as the value systems on the basis of which people form their meanings.

Perhaps the area of greatest multiplicity of meanings lies in the abstract words used to discuss feelings and the meanings these have for the individual. Anxiety may mean far different things in terms of degree and intensity for each person who uses the term. Love or hate may signify varied concepts for different individuals. Medical research on pain indicates that thresholds for pain differ greatly and perhaps further research will reveal similar thresholds for anxiety and conflict. The important point here is that all the words used to designate and describe feelings have individual connotations that often hamper communication and inevitably depend to a large extent on individual meanings and experiences.

Meaning is important for the individual because it supplies his framework of definition for his thoughts, actions, and feelings. These personal definitions then furnish the basis from which he describes himself, his motives, and others. They are integral to his personality and his value judgments.

Symbolic Reality. Each individual has symbols that are especially important to him and closely related to the particular meanings he holds. These symbols represent meanings and serve as goals for the individual's strivings. The tidy house or the meticulously done piece of work may serve as symbols of love and affection, prestige, authoritarianism, mastery, or any other concept which has meaning and value for him. The meanings of the symbols and the symbols themselves are his own.

Symbols are societally influenced and the members of any society tend to accept some fairly generally. In a materialistic society like that of the United States, important symbols tend to be tangible. Many youngsters grow up learning to strive for the gold stars, the merit badges, the brownie points, the trophies, and the notices in the newspaper. They learn to expect the many toys and presents that symbolize their parents' love and affection and possibly guilt. It is no wonder that many youngsters who have not internalized the more or less common symbols are puzzled by them when they enter school or that youngsters who cannot secure some of the things symbolized try to reach for them in their own, sometimes antisocial, ways. The symbols of the juvenile gang are almost an unconscious parody of those highly significant in the American society—the great number of elected officers, the jackets that identify, the implements that signify power, the group itself at a time when membership in a group is almost a necessity, and the notoriety—for how else can the members experience recognition and importance?

Important societal symbols are never static, although they may be similar. The two-car garage replaced the stable. The luxury apartment superseded the suburban dwelling. The kinds, styles, and makes of cars that are currently "in" change almost as frequently as the fashions that epitomize the current high style in dress for any given group. Even occupations fall and rise in symbolic value as peoples' views of their respective status change. Perhaps in an affluent society with intensive and extensive means of mass communication, generally accepted symbols change far more rapidly than in a relatively simple, isolated group.

Even generally accepted symbols are not all universal. Each religion, for example, establishes symbols meaningful to it and the spirit house of the Buddhist has no significance to the Christian. The smile may be a universal symbol of friendship, but not inevitably. The overweight person may symbolize to the American one who does not stay on a diet but, to the Asian, a rich man because he can afford to eat enough to gain weight. Symbols may be similar in nature, but not necessarily in meaning.

Each individual learns and attaches meaning to certain symbols. He need not accept those of his society and no two people view the same symbols in the same way or with the same degree of feeling. Not everyone strives for the large bank account, the title on the door, the college education, the high-fashion silhouette, or whatever other symbols may at the moment be in vogue. Each person strives for the things that he himself has learned to view as important and valuable.

In a subtle way, the individual learns to view certain symbols of feelings as perhaps the most essential ones for him. Such a statement as, "When he hits me, I know he loves me" may be amusing to some people, but to the individual saying it, hitting is a symbol of love. Communication can be either fostered or hindered by an understanding or misunderstanding of the symbols that have particular meaning to the individual. They are a significant and personal reality for him.

Behavioral Reality. Each person's behavioral reality is the way he sees himself behaving in any situation. This behavior is a blend of how he views himself in a situation, how he feels about it, how he expects to behave, how he judges himself as behaving, and how he feels about his behavior at the time and afterward. Whether his behavioral reality matches others' views of his behavior is immaterial in this connection because his own view is real to him.

Every individual learns ways of behaving and tends to perpetuate them. Like Bob, a student acquires a feeling of how he will approach a test and because he has learned a method, he tends to perpetuate it. A person may seek out difficult situations in order to prove to himself that he can perform in them. He may expect to flee from danger and do so. He may learn to make quick decisions and stick to them. He may work like a dynamo or postpone tasks until mañana. Whatever his behavior patterns are, he will tend to find his security in them and be motivated to continue them whether others judge them as good or bad.

Similarly a person learns feelings that influence his behavior and become a part of his behavioral reality. He can learn to be confident, to have faith in himself and others or he can learn to distrust his own abilities and the actions, beliefs, and intentions of other people. He can learn to be fearful or courageous. He can learn that he himself and his opinions are worthwhile or inadequate. He can learn to express himself readily and to believe in the value of his own ideas and feelings or he can inhibit his spontaneity and guard cautiously the expression of his opinions and feelings.

Too often behavioral reality is not discussed. Behavior itself is considered under such descriptions as "defenses for the ego" or "behavior mechanisms," which are then rarely integrated into a theory of motivation and personality. Yet behavioral reality is central to what every person does. Everyday most people engage in varying degrees of withdrawal, aggression, regression, reaction-formation, fantasy, rationalization, hypochondria, identification, and all the listed types of behavior. These are man's reactions to the situations in which in finds himself.

Some "behavior mechanisms"—and they are never as mechanical as that phrase suggests—are societally approved and tend to become popular within a particular group. In America, for example, rationalism is an accepted "good" way of thinking and consequently its behavioral adjunct, rationalization, is extremely widespread and often inseparable from the rationalism that spawns it. On the other hand, fantasy tends to be viewed as suspect and teachers reprimand students for daydreaming. Other adults speak slightingly of the dreamer and the idealist until and unless their dreams and ideas prove to be the basis for "something useful." Youngsters soon learn that illness is a socially acceptable excuse for avoiding an experience or a situation. American society tends to disapprove of the person who seeks solitary pursuits and to encourage all people from childhood on to gain some identification with groups whether formal or informal. In this manner, American society tends to foster certain "behavior mechanisms" and to discourage others. Societally approved behavior mechanisms tend to perpetuate themselves, while the less approved are hidden or disguised by the individual sometimes even from himself.

All psychological indications are that the person with a wide range of ways of reacting to situations tends to be emotionally healthy. Once again emotional problems and abnormality seem to spring from inflexibility and lack of balance. Thus some people find release from tension and are able to cope with a situation only by means that are in the long run self-defeating. They may feel they must always be with a group of people; they cannot be alone. They may take refuge in illness to avoid the unpleasant. They may know only that compulsive actions seem to release the tensions that build up within them. They may rationalize any action whether it be self-defeating or harmful to themselves and others. Their range of learned behavior is narrow and their behavioral reality permits only limited and repetitious actions.

An individual's behavioral reality is never static. Each new learning and each new experience can and does change it either toward greater flexibility or rigidity. The cases in the Appendix demonstrate how some youngsters are beginning to enlarge their behavioral realities through the experience of counseling with its acceptance of them and their behavior and its encouragement of spontaneity.

Misunderstanding often arises when the behavioral realities of individuals clash. One person may say about another, "Why doesn't he attack the problem instead of doing nothing?" "Why doesn't he do things this way and he'd be much better off?" The implication is that the other person should approach his problems from a different behavioral reality. But behavior changes slowly and the changes must be internal. Understanding can come only when one person realizes that his own behavioral reality is not and need not be that of another.

Interpersonal Reality. Closely connected with behavioral reality is interpersonal reality, which includes the individual's perception of other people and of himself in relation to them. How one gets along with other people and how one feels about them are integral parts of this reality and influence one's actions in relation to others as well as one's view of self.

The cases in the text and the Appendix illustrate some facets of the interpersonal realities of the individuals being counseled. Paul, for example, sees other people as inimical to him and, with the exception of his brother, as nonunderstanding of his interests and problems. Laura views others self-consciously and somewhat suspiciously and seems to feel that many of her relationships are colored by others' views of her sisters. The girls in the group analyze some aspects of the counseling relationship and point up how their perceptions of what a counselor does may differ from those of many counselors. Jim, who has an open receptive approach to people, shows his view of them in his attempts to understand his mother and to see things from her point of view. All these examples show some phase of the interpersonal reality of the individual involved.

Some of the values and ways that he has learned and some of the motives he has developed profoundly affect an individual's interpersonal reality. Thus Bob continually compares himself to his friends, his brother, and to the objective measures of his school work and abilities. He even compares himself emotionally when he claims to be "more miserable than anyone." Similarly Mike compares himself to the athletic heroes, but he balances his assessment by also contrasting their respective card-playing abilities. Competition as a way of behaving and of relating to other people is an extremely important factor for both these boys and provides another illustration of how values, ways, and motives underlie and affect the interpersonal reality of each individual.

Everyone's interpersonal reality is necessarily self-centered. No one can either review his own behavior in a given situation with absolute objectivity or analyze objectively the behavior of others toward him. Thus one's interpersonal reality incorporates elements of the unreal which are nevertheless very real to the individual. Laura's feeling that her friends are constantly thinking about and reminding her of her sister's misfortune has both real and unreal qualities, but for her this feeling is a concrete reality with which she must live. As time passes and memories fade, this reality may change; but for Laura, it is an important part of her interpersonal reality.

Interpersonal reality also includes the influences brought to bear on the individual by the other people in his life. Bob and his guidance man, Jim and his relatives, Paul and his not-too-acceptable friends, or any of the youngsters and their parents provide illustrations of influences upon the individual that push him in one direction or another. Many of these influences serve to make the person feel that he should do something that does not coincide with his own desires while others urge him to do something he would like to do, but sees no way of accomplishing. All, however, are incorporated in the interpersonal reality of the person and modify or strengthen his view of other people and of himself in relation to them.

People are infinitely different and the most important of these differences occurs not only in motivation but also in the important realities which each person has. These realities encompass a person's view of his physical being and place, time, learning and thinking, emotions and motivations, values and ways, identification, meanings, symbols, behavior, and interpersonal relationships. These comprise his frame of reference concerning himself and are for him the immediate and ultimate realities.

THE PRIMARY REALITY

None of the important realities is discrete. There is constant interplay among them and they merge to form a whole. For the individual, the various realities constitute his world as he sees it. Within that world, he acts and feels and thinks as a holistic being. He expresses this holism in the way he feels about himself and this feeling is his primary reality, his self-concept.

Self-concept is the inclusive collective value judgment each person makes about himself. It is his estimate of self in terms of the important realities. From this point of view, self-concept is not only the collections of value judgments each person inevitably makes about himself in relation to the varied realities, but also the pervading way he feels about himself—his judgment of himself at any point in time.

The individual may express his self-concept in many ways. One is the broad value judgment a person makes in such statements as "I'm a pretty good person" or "I'm a bad guy" or "I'm fairly satisfied with myself" or "I'm unhappy." Bob talks frequently about his self-concept when he says that he feels inferior or when he states that "I'm just about the farthest thing from being conceited that I've ever known of" or "actually I'm more miserable than anybody." Paul, too, speaks in terms of a collective value judgment of himself when he says that he would like to do something that "would just please someone sometime" or when he states, "I got nothing to be proud of. I ain't done nothing to be proud of." These are pervading value judgments that color all of Bob's and Paul's realities.

Although the person himself rarely makes distinctions among his varied realities, he tends to discuss his self-concept in terms of them, and especially in terms of the ones most important to him at the moment. Bob frequently speaks of himself in terms of his physical being, his emotions and motivations, his values and ways, and his interpersonal relations—all highly important to him. Mike makes several judgments about himself in terms of the various realities thus revealing his self-concept. About his behavior, he remarks that "I just cause trouble" and again "Trouble, that's me." He has not had much opportunity for interpersonal relations with girls because they prefer the heroes and he does not feel he is a hero. Mike feels physically ill-equipped for sports and inept at them. Cards, however, elicit different expressions about self for it "makes you feel a little bit bigger man if you can walk in and say, 'I beat them guys.'" Mike knows his emotions get away from him at times, but he is working hard to control his temper. He feels he works hard and has done a good job. Several times, he expresses a collective judgment that he is not really worth "wasting time on," but he manages to retain some kind of a balance among his judgments.

Jim, on the other hand, expresses no feeling of being unworthy of the counselor's time. Rather he says that he is clarifying his own views (and judgments) of himself by explaining them to the counselor. He feels that he is "independent" and a "fatalist." He wants to maintain his way of life and standards and motivations even though his father is dead. Interpersonally he feels he is a worthy individual and fairly popular. He tries hard not "to show what I feel" and believes that "some things bother me too much." Unlike Bob and Mike, he has no concerns about his physical being or his appearance. He enjoys being with people and being alone. He wants to have a purpose for what he does. Jim can change readily his estimate of his abilities as he does in terms of the girl who was "just nothing but smart." After being in class with her, Jim decided that "I'm no smarter or dumber than she is." The collective value judgment that emerges is that Jim feels he is a capable, worthwhile individual although he speaks of his self-concept largely in terms of the varied realities.

Regardless of the way it is expressed, self-concept is never static for the normal individual. All experiences shape it and it is, therefore, a continually evolving concept. Just as the individual shifts, modifies, and changes his varied realities so also these modifications and changes affect the collective value judgment he holds about himself. This process of change means that the development of self-concept is lifelong, continuous, and dynamic.

Change in self-concept evolves slowly and the change is usually never complete. Elements of all the realities that comprise it remain. The youngster who suffered severe rejection as a child will retain some of the feelings associated with rejection as an adult although he may learn to view himself as a worthwhile, acceptable individual. The youngster who felt himself to be unattractive as a child or too short or too tall or too heavy will carry over some of the feelings of inferiority and insecurity about his physical reality long after the cause of them may have disappeared. He may never change his feelings about his physical being, but his physical reality may no longer be as important to him. Change in self-concept is seldom instantaneous or automatic but results from a slow process of internalization.

Practically never does an individual modify and change all his varied realities at once although changes in any one of them may affect the others and his total self-concept. A person may shift slightly his temporal reality and hence affect his goals and aims. He may learn to operate on the basis of relaxed rather than ideal values and cease to judge himself so harshly in terms of them. He may find his behavior patterns acceptable in a different group and gradually evolve a different concept of himself.

Occasionally abrupt changes that profoundly affect his self-concept can occur in a person's realities. A physical illness that demands reorientation to ways of living and thinking about oneself can cause a dramatic upheaval in self-concept. Many youngsters facing severe conflicts in values go through a similar experience. The child from an underprivileged, lower-class home may have found love and acceptance among his family and friends. When he enters school, the stronghold of middle-class values, he often finds himself in an alien world of strange values and ways to which he can not really adapt. As he tries to solve his school problems in values, motives, and ways, his realities suffer a drastic shock and he willy-nilly alters, usually downward, his view of himself and his estimate of his worth. Similar changes often occur at retirement when the sudden shift from being a productive, worthwhile citizen to a "has been," and a "hanger-on" causes some individuals to make new value judgments about themselves and their realities. What constitutes an abrupt change depends upon the individual and the realities he views as most important.

At different times in his life, different realities may be more important to an individual than others. He is the only one who establishes the hierarchy among them and this hierarchy is continually changing. Although Paul's behavioral reality may seem most important to the school personnel, to Paul his interpersonal and symbolic realities are close and poignant. His feelings about his father and the symbols and meanings he has attached to cars are preeminent to him as he discusses his problems. Similarly, Laura has difficulties with respectability that are especially important to her as she talks with the counselor. To each person at a point in time, some realities are more obtrusive than others and play a predominant role in self-concept.

Every person seeks positive experiences as he and his society define them. These positive experiences and satisfactions help the individual to maintain balance among his realities and influence his self-concept in positive directions. Mike expresses this idea when he says that he feels "a bigger man" when he can win at cards and that "a guy's just got to feel important." His positive experiences at cards and on the job help Mike to balance out the shortcomings he feels he has in other areas. Bob, on the other hand, gains few real satisfactions from what he does and cannot shake the pervading value judgment of inferiority that he places on himself.

The troubled youngster has difficulty in maintaining balance among the varied realities and in achieving positive experiences that carry over into his collective judgment of himself. Certain problems and conflicts loom so large that they color everything he feels and does and so shape his self-concept. Externalizing problems in a counseling situation seems to aid the person to attain balance and to achieve positive experiences. Counseling assists troubled youngsters like Bob, Mike, Jim, Laura and many others to utilize their capabilities for making new internalizations and modifying their realities so that they can secure positive experiences and satisfactions in their lives. More severely disturbed individuals—of whom Paul may be one—have similar capabilities, but the process of aiding them is long and arduous and requires considerable reinternalization before they can function effectively in their particular milieu.

There is no such thing as a realistic self-concept as judged by outsiders. Only the person himself can make the important value judgments about himself because he believes, feels, and knows only his own judgments—they are real to him. Anyone trying to help another person must start by understanding him as he is at this point and against the background of his varied realities and primary reality, his self-concept. Any other starting point for counseling will simply multiply the youngster's difficulties as Bob's were compounded by the "guidance man." One person's realities are not those of another just as one person's emotions, values, ways, motives, goals, aims, and satisfactions are not those of another. The individual's own realities are the *sine qua non* for understanding him, how he feels, and what he does.

The individual and his realities furnish new meaning and increased emphasis to two important, much-discussed and little-applied concepts: dynamism and holism. Dynamism means simply that any individual at any point in time is different from that same individual at another point in time. Each person engages all his life in the continuous process of modifying and changing his realities. He does not stand still because he is continually internalizing new experiences and being impelled to action and feeling by the universal motivating forces and his own subsidiary motives. No person is ever static.

The second concept, holism, means that no person can be understood either in terms of some of his parts or as a simple addition of all his parts. He can be understood only *in toto* with all his realities and judgments. He is not just a thinking being or a vocational being or a personal being. He is a human being with individual values, motives, feelings, and judgments about himself. Without holism the human quality is lost and without the human quality, none of the behavioral sciences has purpose or meaning. In its purest sense, holism is paradoxically a reiteration of individual differences.

TOTAL REALITY

All the realities discussed in this chapter combine to form the total reality of the individual. This reality describes his world and how he sees it and incorporates whatever has meaning to him. It is whole, complete, and dynamic and is constantly being modified and changed as the person lives, learns, and experiences. Above all, it is his personal, idiosyncratic reality.

One question remains: Is this total reality of the individual "real"? The answer can only be: More or less. From the point of view of the objective observer, the total reality of an individual has to incorporate elements of the "real" world in order for him to function in that world. But that reality cannot and does not include the "real world" in any completely objective sense—and perhaps should not. Rather an individual's reality takes in elements of the "real world" as internalized by the individual and sieved through the amalgam of his learnings, experiences, thoughts, and feelings. It is both real and unreal and perhaps has to be that way because the real elements enable the individual to function, while the unreal insure that he will want to.

6

THE INDIVIDUAL AND THE SHIBBOLETHS

Guidance and school counseling are the means by which presumably most people today are reached and which could offer the most help in preventing mental illness. Hence the tenets and practices of these fields are especially important in the light of a new theory that attempts to explain why ordinary and not-so-ordinary people do what they do.

Currently much guidance and counseling work centers around activities that have developed in connection with particular concepts, now virtually catch-words and slogans. Diagnosis, adjustment, realism, "truth," and normality as they relate to the school-age and college-age students are such shibboleths. Most of them had their beginnings in some of the fads of school guidance and in the prevailing concepts of psychotherapy at a particular period. These shibboleths have unfortunately persisted so long in the literature and the thinking of many guidance workers that they have become an underlying theme in much of the theorizing and the practices of the field.

The persistence of and meaning given these shibboleths have many effects on the people with whom guidance practitioners and school counselors work. Furthermore, the concepts of diagnosis, adjustment, realism, "truth," and normality have never been analyzed in the light of a comprehensive theory of motivation and behavior to examine their applicability or lack of it. The purpose of this chapter is to see how the shibboleths and their application influence the counselor's work with youngsters who receive guidance and school counseling help.

DIAGNOSIS

Psychology had its origins in medicine and so adopted many medical concepts, among them that of diagnosis. In order to treat a person, the physician first has to diagnose the cause of his patient's ailment. Originally all that was done for a mentally-ill patient was to distinguish his ailment and classify his type of psychosis. Perhaps Sigmund Freud's greatest contribution was the healing emphasis he gave to psychotherapy,[1] but even this emphasis was still within the traditional medical framework. Only comparatively recently with the growth of modern psychotherapy have diagnosis and treatment gradually come to assume a more logical balance in relation to each other and the attempts to heal have taken on merited importance.

Guidance, school counseling, and school psychology arose apart from the dynamic development of modern psychology and psychoanalytic theories. The original base stressed identification of abilities, interests, and aptitudes by means of pseudo-scientific testing instruments. Gradually as psychological theory began to penetrate the field and personality inventories were developed, guidance workers paid lip-service to prevention as a function. This function has never been well defined or made explicit, but rather has continued to consist mainly of attempts to identify or diagnose problem students early. The emphasis has continued to be that of identification and diagnosis, not treatment or alleviation although increasingly diagnosis in its medical sense has become relatively less important in psychology. The fad, however, continues in guidance although the word identification cloaks the diagnostic practices.

Diagnosis is essentially a process of discovering through the use of any and all techniques and devices what is wrong with a person. It is intrinsic to medicine, probably to psychiatry, and possibly even to psychology, although here its extensive formal use is somewhat less easy to rationalize. Its use in guidance and

[1] See Gregory Zilboorg, *A History of Medical Psychology* (New York: Norton, 1941).

counseling, except in certain unusual instances, is even less easy
to explain. Diagnosis presumes the existence of a specific ailment with symptoms that can be traced and a causative factor
that can be remedied or at least alleviated. The youngsters who
consult guidance workers and counselors do not in general have
such ailments. Rather they are people who are struggling with
certain problems of living and who are perhaps not adequately
equipped or prepared to solve those problems without help.
These youngsters do not present a picture of a disease syndrome
either physical or mental; they offer an educational problem in
how to learn to live in a world that makes of life a series of
tension-causing and problem-provoking situations.

What does diagnosis mean to the individual? Usually a
battery of tests administered in order to reveal information about
the person. But such tests are not always valid or reliable and
produce at best a very limited picture of the person and his life.
What, for example, would a diagnostic battery tell about Bob
that would be more informative than what he himself tells? How
would Paul respond to a series of diagnostic tests? Test interpretation, which is the customary follow-up to such a battery can
be and frequently is a devastating experience for the individual,
especially if he is particularly impressed by tests and the results
are at variance with his own estimate of himself. Destruction of
self-confidence and lowering of feelings of worth are sometimes
the results of test interpretation to say nothing of the anxiety,
self-doubt, and fear connected with the mere taking of some
psychological tests and inventories.

Guidance workers and counselors sometimes appear to be
using diagnosis for its own sake. They seem to feel that attempting to diagnose what is wrong with a youngster is sufficient. And
yet there is no logical justification for diagnosis unless one intends
to do something to eliminate the causes of the youngster's difficulties. If one's records show that a child comes from an unstable
family of poor economic status, this knowledge may serve partially to explain why the child is caught in conflicts at school and
failing in academic work, but unless the counselor is willing and

able to act on the knowledge, he might as well not have it. Similarly a diagnostic reading test can be an informative and useful instrument in working with the child who is retarded in reading, but, unless the counselor can relate it to the person and will do something constructive with the results of such a test, there is no point in giving it. Diagnosis for the sake of diagnosis is never justified because no one can predict the effects of the diagnostic procedures on the individual.

Diagnosis, more often than not by dubious devices, may have an even more far-reaching effect for the individual. If the results of such diagnostic procedures as pencil-and-paper personality inventories are frightening to the guidance worker (who may frighten easily), he may start a youngster on a round-robin of referral that runs the gamut of psychological and psychiatric consultants. By and large, the problems of children and adolescents do not require or merit the attention of a psychiatrist or even a clinician, but are the rightful province of guidance workers and counselors who should and must be willing to interpret broadly the problems that fall into their domain and be competent to deal with them. A discussion of dreams, an attempt to talk about emotions and values, a score indicative of maladjustment on a personality inventory, or a statement such as "I hate my father" are not in and of themselves sufficient justification for starting a youngster on the referral round-robin. Such a trek for him can mean tremendous anxiety, considerable self-doubt and confusion, and more often than not little help, for the consultants frequently offer only further diagnosis.

The current diagnostic emphasis has also an indirect, but extremely important, effect on youngsters. Guidance workers and counselors who subscribe to extensive diagnosis tend to look for *the* cause of a youngster's behavior and to think and act as though difficulties arise from a single source, which when ferreted out and changed would eliminate the problems. This idea that behavior has a single cause can be extremely misleading for the counselor and detrimental for his counselee. Behavior has many causes and no one problem can or should be singled out as the causative factor.

Diagnosis has some uses as in the sorting out of learning difficulties, but even here it should be used cautiously for many learning problems stem from problems in the youngster's life other than the inability or failure to learn certain skills. Diagnostic techniques can sometimes provide some clues to a youngster's difficulties, but these clues can often be acquired by other surer means and in ways less traumatic to the individual. Essentially diagnosis should not be as important to the person working with so-called normal individuals as it is to the person who customarily deals with the abnormal for the need to track down the difficulties is less. School children need help with the developmental problems that are troubling them at the moment, not a complete reexamination and restructuring of their entire experience. In this kind of relationship, diagnosis should play a minor role.

ADJUSTMENT

For years guidance workers and counselors have wrangled about what they mean by adjustment and where the concept fits into their philosophies. The questions of adjustment to what and for what have been raised but never satisfactorily answered in terms of the modern world. And yet, the concept of adjustment persists both in the thinking and activities of individual counselors and in the theorizing of writers in the field.

In the light of the theory presented here, adjustment is virtually a sterile concept. In a dynamic society, what is there for the changing, developing individual to adjust to? He can learn to live with and to accept change, but this process is not the same as adjusting to change. Essentially adjustment is a post facto concept in the sense that change takes place and then the individual adjusts to it while presumably everything else stands still until he catches up. Such an approach to adjustment will not stand up in terms of this or any other dynamic theory or the modern world.

Adjustment is a counselor-focused concept. Guidance workers and counselors would like to see every youngster well-adjusted to the school environment, but their aim may or may not coincide with the youngster's own aims. Individuals seldom, if ever, strive for adjustment in the sense in which guidance people use the word. The first three universal motivating forces may direct individual strivings toward some facets of adjustment, but the strivings to express oneself and to achieve positive experiences are frequently in direct conflict with the idea of adjustment. When school personnel speak of adjustment as an aim, they usually mean that they would like to see every child behaving in school as they think he should behave and learning those things that they think he should learn in the way they think he should learn them. Learning and living in a school or college community elicit all kinds of behavior from the individuals involved, not all of which could be labeled well-adjusted but much of which seems to be a necessary part of learning. School administration and discipline might be easier if every child were "well-adjusted," but the learning process would also be duller and more rigid and stultifying than it already is.

Judgments about adjustment are, of course, value judgments and stem from the learnings, background, and experiences of the judge whether he is a trained psychologist or an unqualified layman. Such judgments seem to divide into two types: first, an over-all judgment of a youngster in terms of how he gets along at home, in school, and among his peers; second, a series of less sweeping judgments incorporating any facet of personality pleasing or offensive to the judge. Judgments about adjustment are subjective even when they are based on presumably objective measures like tests, for someone has to make up, score, and interpret the tests and many subjective elements enter.[2] The

[2] Anne Roe suggests that one reason why many psychologists score well on personality instruments is because they devised them as well as the concept of what good adjustment is. *The Psychology of Occupations* (New York: John Wiley, 1954), p. 220.

judges of adjustment define it personally and no two persons' judgments will precisely coincide.

Even those youngsters who are labeled maladjusted may actually not be if the factors in their environment are fully taken into account. The juvenile delinquent may react with hostility to a hostile environment and, while society as a whole may view his reaction as maladjusted, it may represent for the youngster his own best adjustment.[3] Judges of adjustment have for too long been too glib and facile in their statements about what good adjustment is. For the individual, it cannot be represented by an ideal or a standard set by some group or other, but has to be to a particular set of circumstances that should be all-important in any judgment about its quality.

The popularity of the idea of "good adjustment" has had a profound effect on individual students. High school youngsters, for example, try to impress college admissions officers with the excellence of their adjustment. Some plan their high school careers with the precision of generals on the brink of a battle. They take the usual array of courses plus anything unusual or difficult that their school offers to show broad and unusual interests; a team sport to demonstrate their ability to play in a group; an individual sport to show individual capability and lack of group domination; band as evidence of love of music; debate as proof of verbal interests, poise, and ability to think on their feet; and various other school activities chosen to show popularity and well-roundedness. Outside school such youngsters may engage in church work to show moral character and religious training and jobs to indicate appreciation of the importance and worth of work.[4] The immediate striving of these youngsters is not toward adjustment, but toward the *appearance* of "good adjustment" as they understand its definition. Regardless of how

[3] See Chapter 1, footnote 9.

[4] This listing is a paraphrase of the remarks of a counselee who was explaining to his counselor why he was doing what he was doing. He thought he was doing too much, but he could not bear to give up any of his activities lest it have an adverse effect on how his record would look to a college admissions officer.

one views adjustment as a concept, striving for the appearance of it seems a sterile activity unrelated to the universal motives or value orientation of the individual.

The concept of adjustment has also done disservice to guidance workers and counselors in their attempts to help culturally deprived youngsters. The aim here has been to adjust the individual youngster to the school and to the social environment. Work has been directed toward modifying his behavior rather than toward helping him to restructure his values and ways and to reshape his motives in accord with these values. There is a tendency to regard the culturally deprived individual as being maladjusted and to use external means to "adjust him" rather than to try to understand his adjustment in terms of his frame of reference and help him to understand his own motives and values. When such a youngster is labeled maladjusted, he is merely being given another tag that fails to describe him and can mislead those who want sincerely to help him.

Finally, adjustment is a dangerous concept to the individual because it carries with it the implication that he is the one to be adjusted. When an individual gets out of step with other people, guidance workers and counselors tend to assume almost automatically that he needs to learn to adjust to the group, the rules of the school, or the mores of society. But is it always the individual who is wrong and must make the adjustment? Some things in American society perhaps should be changed rather than changing the individual to fit them. Unless guidance workers and counselors recognize and implement this fact, they run the risk of limiting the spontaneity and creativity of the youngsters with whom they work and of attempting to make them "well-adjusted" conformists who will not be able to work for social improvement or even to see the need for it.

In terms of this theory as it relates to the individual, adjustment is an alien concept. Self-expression and the search for positive experiences are antithetical to a concept of adjustment. Despite the shaping of the person by the society in which he grows up, his strivings along these lines are not always in accord with the dictates of that society. Some individual freedom (not license) exists and should exist so that the person may have some leeway in his idiosyncratic strivings. To a considerable extent, the idea of adjustment eliminates this leeway and encourages conformity. Modern society needs constructive, healthful individualism in its members; they need to be afforded the leeway for its expression in order to contribute creatively to society and to seek their own fulfillment.

REALISM

Realism is currently a major aim for many guidance workers who seem to believe that students must be realistic in their planning, about their capabilities and interests, and particularly in their concepts of self. Presumably students must not be allowed to set their sights too high or too low, to ignore the practicalities in their thinking, or to take into account their own feelings about themselves. Realism, whatever it may mean to the individual guidance worker, is rapidly becoming a major area of concentration.

And yet, what is realistic? This adjective merely describes one person's value judgment of another's behavior, thinking, or dreaming. As a value judgment, any statement about realism incorporates the values, learnings, and experiences of the person using the word. Some things like chairs, airplanes, and atomic bombs are presumably real although scientists and philosophers might claim that even these objects are less real and less substantial than many people would like to think. In the areas of human behavior, thinking, and feeling, realism becomes even more indefinite and more subject to idiosyncratic interpretation. Is it unrealistic to want to be the first man on the moon, to plan to travel at five times the speed of sound, to envision the establishment of a Negro state within the United States, or to anticipate the ethical problems related to growing human beings in test tubes?

The concept of realism and judgments about it fail to take

into account the varied realities of the individual. How he feels, what he wants, and what he believes he is are his realities and outside judgments about their realism have relatively little meaning for him. Certainly a person has to be able to live and function in the world around him and his realities, therefore, must incorporate aspects of that world, but this is hardly realism in the sense that it is used today. An adolescent's realities need not and will not include all the hard cold "facts" of life as adults have learned them. Some of these "facts" he may never have to learn and he may face others far harder and colder. In a womb-to-tomb society, adolescents will probably never have to experience the insecurities of their depression-reared parents, but they are learning to face the possibility of the extinction of their species.

Guidance workers are only too ready to agree that students should be realistic, but they have never examined to what extent this realism should be carried. How realistic should people be? How realistic can they be and still be happy, creative, productive individuals? It seems likely that some balance of realism and unrealism is a necessary part of living for every one if he is to find outlets for his talents, expression of his uniqueness, and satisfying positive experiences and if his society is to prosper. People seem to use their illusions, their dreams, and their unrealities to maintain their striving, to strengthen their aims, and to have something of worth for which to strive.[5]

A concept of realism can lead counselors to attempt some dangerous tampering with the aims of youngsters. Aims include

[5] Eugene O'Neill's *The Iceman Cometh* should be required reading for all counselors dedicated to the validity of their own value judgments of realism. After the "iceman" has stripped away everyone's illusions, O'Neill has one of his characters cry out to the depressed, listless group: "By rights you should be contented now, without a single damned hope or lying dream left to torment you! But here you are, acting like a lot of stiffs cheating the undertaker! . . . Can't you appreciate what you've got, for God's sake? Don't you know you're free now to be yourselves, without having to feel remorse or guilt, or lie to yourselves about reforming tomorrow? Can't you see there is no tomorrow now? You're rid of it forever! You've killed it! You don't have to care a damn about anything anymore!" *The Iceman Cometh* (New York: Vintage Books, 1946), p. 225.

ideas of what one wants to be, how one wants to live, and what
one wants to live for and these are uniquely the individual's.
These ideas do not have to be identical with those of the greater
society so long as they are not in conflict with the laws and fundamental customs of that society. More importantly, youngsters'
aims are not those of their counselors and they should not be.
When a guidance person judges the aims of a youngster as
realistic or unrealistic he is actually judging them in terms of
his own values and aims and his statement can only be interpreted as a judgment of how well the youngster's aims reflect
his own.[6] Judgments about realism tend to narrow, restrict, and
limit the aims of the individual and to force him into a mold
created out of the value judgments of others.

A concept of realism has the further disadvantage that it
tries to eliminate the dreams of the young. Much has been
written about the harmful effects of fantasy and dreaming and
of their close relationship to creativity and productive thinking.
Dreams and fantasies can be aims, values, and motives in other
guises; they can even be planning. And they are not necessarily
bad or destructive or even unrealistic. Yet there is a tendency
to label the dreams and fantasies of youth as lacking in realism.
Many of those dreams will, of course, come to nothing, but others
may lead to important contributions to human society.

"TRUTH"

The concepts of realism and "truth" are closely related as they
are used in attempts to help youngsters with their problems of
growing up. Just as guidance workers strive to make youngsters
realistic in their thinking and planning, so also they seek to find
out the "truth" about those youngsters. And like realism, truth
is not understood in objective, impersonal terms, but rather includes the values, aims, and motives of the person seeking it.

[6] For a full discussion of realism as one of the myths of vocational
guidance, see Ruth Barry and Beverly Wolf, An Epitaph for Vocational
Guidance (New York: Bureau of Publications, Teachers College, Columbia
University, 1962), pp. 90–102.

Truth is a misleading word in and of itself for people tend to think of it as something absolute, definite, and determinable. And some truths are. Boyle's Law in physics embodies a truth about the behavior of gases under certain conditions and it is absolute, definite, and determinable. But the truth about a human individual is not so easily reached or definite and it is seldom, if ever, absolute. Since human beings are dynamic, constantly changing entities, truths about them cannot be as static as the laws of physics or as absolute as some of the dictates of religious belief.

School personnel and guidance people have long sought information about students and have regarded that information as the truth. And certainly some of it is. The individual's name, birth date, and place of birth are relatively fixed truths although he may change his name if he so desires. An individual's place of residence might be termed a temporary truth for it is subject to frequent change in American society. School grades and test scores might be called tentative truths for they incorporate not only clerical and statistical errors, but also personal values, subjective opinions, and biases of all kinds. The judgments of school personnel about a particular individual are, of course, not truths at all but judgments embodying the opinions and prejudices of one individual about another at a point in time. Much of the data collected in the schools is at best only partially true in nature and some of it is or becomes false.

When one moves into the area of human personality, the truth is even less easy to pin down than in the more objective areas. Some facets of a person's personality may show themselves only in particular situations and in relation to certain other people. Thus the teacher who finds Joe intolerable in class may find others who consider him well-behaved and cooperative. Similarly the child who has trouble in relating with his peers or in accepting authority may learn to do so as he grows older and gains experience. The capability for change inherent in every human being makes the truth about personality difficult, if not impossible, to establish. School personnel may do individual youngsters a great disservice, even considerable damage, when they attempt to describe and delineate the "truth" about them as people.

Truth as a concept enters guidance and counseling in another way. Telling the truth is a great American value to which youngsters are expected to adhere absolutely while adults receive greater latitude in their interpretations of it. Parents and school people expect children to tell the truth and are alarmed and concerned when children seemingly lie. Often they fail to recognize that what they believe is a lie is, from the child's point of view, the truth. The preschool child who squirts whipped topping over the sofa and answers the inevitable question of why with "I don't know" is very likely telling the truth—he does not know why he did it. If he is pressured long enough, he may present some relatively acceptable reason and in the process learn a bit about the value attached to rationalism in his society. He may also make a start toward adding rationalization to his behavioral repertoire.

In their anxiety to teach youngsters to tell the truth, adults often fail to recognize it when it is offered to them. The boy who tells his counselor, "I'm failing everything" is telling the truth as he sees it at that moment. The counselor may know that the boy's grades are three C's, one D, and an F, but from the boy's point of view of this moment he is a total and complete failure. Hence his statement contains the truth about the things of importance to him, his feelings and self-concept, as well as a possible amount of exaggeration and self-dramatization. Truth about feelings, realities, and self inhere even in the "lies" students tell.

Thanks to scientific ways of thinking and the importance of numbers, there is currently an unfortunate tendency to discount what people say about themselves as a useful source of data and understanding. Guidance workers and counselors seem to think that they can find out more about a person through tests, structured interviews, and questionnaires than they can by merely allowing the person to talk about himself and the things important to him. These instruments are presumed to elicit more

truthful information than one can obtain through the non-
structured interview. And yet do they? A student can lie on a
test as easily as he can to a counselor—perhaps more easily.
Moreover, personality measures and checklists are validated in
the final analysis against interview materials so one must assume
some veracity in the materials coming out of counseling interviews. Truth as it relates to human beings is not a tidy entity
that can be neatly stated, but is an amorphous, changing,
developing thing that is equivalent to personality itself.

When a student is asked to tell the truth about himself, he
is being given an impossible task. By and large he does not know
the truth about himself anymore than the counselor does. He
can and usually does tell his counselor the truth in terms of his
realities as he sees it and knows it at the moment. If his counselor understands this fact, then counseling can become for the
student a process of discovering for himself some of the truth
about himself. If, however, the counselor is looking for the kind
of data he can organize on a record card, he will not get it and
he will eventually come to believe that students are liars. What
this belief can do to their self-concepts hardly needs iterating.
Truth has to be considered against the background of the various
realities of the individual. It can only be defined for him in terms
of what is real to him, what is meaningful and significant.

One question remains: Why has the "truth" become so important to guidance workers and counselors? Partly, of course,
because of their values about telling the truth and the "badness"
of untruths. But partly, too, because the truth provides a rationalization for doing what they are doing in the way in which they
are doing it. If one assumes that the most truthful data can be
acquired only by objective means, then one has a rationale for
dealing with people in an impersonal, detached manner and on
a mass basis. If one believes that the discovery of the truth about
a person is an individual, highly personal process, then one is at
a loss to explain many of the things being done in the schools
today. If one subscribes to the former view, the assurance that

one knows or is finding out the "truth" becomes an important justification of what one is doing. But the search for "truth" as justification leaves out of consideration the student himself and the importance to him of seeking and discovering for himself the meaningful truth about himself.

NORMALITY

Who are normal youngsters? Or adults for that matter? Normality generally means conforming to a certain standard or norm. In psychology this definition has been particularized to mean in addition free of mental defect or disease. But the word normality contains nothing to designate what standards are to be used in judging it. Nor does it contain limitations on the areas of human life or behavior that may be considered under the rubric normal. Thus anything from dress to human behavior can be judged in terms of its normality and more importantly the standard against which the judgment is made can be general and societal or personal and idiosyncratic. Normality can be as various and as variable as reality or truth.

Any discussion of normality entails automatically a consideration of abnormality. If something is not immediately classifiable as normal, is it therefore abnormal? The normal child is physically whole. Is the child without an arm or a hand to be described as abnormal? Certainly he does not measure up to the norm in physical terms, but does he consequently merit the inclusive designation of abnormality? Is the adolescent who rebels against parental supervision and authority abnormal? Is the youngster who reacts aggressively to a hostile environment abnormal? The questions are many and the answers are equally varied.

Essentially questions about normality and abnormality can only be answered against the background of the society in which they are posed and then only in relatively limited terms. Styles of dress, kinds of food, patterns of living, and varieties of behavior are normal or abnormal only as judged against the standards of a particular society or even those of a subgroup of a larger society.[7] Wearing a nose ornament is normal in some parts of India and New Guinea, but not so normal in New York City or Decatur, Illinois. Eating insects and grubs is normal for some people in Africa, but definitely abnormal to the American mother who sees her toddler chewing a grasshopper. Many Americans view life without indoor plumbing as abnormal and cannot feel that existence without bathrooms is a normal way of life.

In the realm of behavior, the standards by which normality or lack of it is judged vary more widely and more subtly from society to society than do other forms. Adolescent rebellion generally regarded as typical behavior for American teen-agers is far from the norm in other societies. Withdrawal from mundane society is definitely abnormal for most Americans, but quite normal for nuns, monks, Hindu ascetics, and other religious devotees. Mistreatment of animals is the norm in some parts of the world, but distinctly abnormal for Americans, even for the very young. Normal behavior has to be defined in terms of the society in which it occurs.

Most societies can tolerate a wide range of behavior, some of which may deviate sharply from the societally defined norm. Thus the Arapesh do not exclude the choleric man even though they may deplore his anger. Americans deride the man who is seemingly uninterested in material things, but they permit him to continue his participation in the group. Some societies either honor or expel the person who is different. The man who is subject to seizures or hallucinations may become the shaman or priest of his group; in the United States, he would probably be institutionalized or, at least, put on tranquilizers. Albinos who are commonly expelled or even killed in primitive societies are fully accepted in most civilized groups. Standards of normality differ widely as does the rigidity with which people are required to meet them.

[7] In this connection, see Ruth Benedict, "Anthropology and the Abnormal," *The Journal of General Psychology*, 10:59–79, 1934.

Normality in its broadest sense seems to describe behavior that is accepted or at least tolerated by a particular society. The youngster who fights continually with his classmates may be viewed as abnormal because his behavior is intolerable in the school setting. The pilot who sets records for planes shot down, however, is considered normal, even patriotic. Normality depends on setting, time, appropriateness of behavior, and acceptability to society. Americans can tolerate the man clad in flowing robes and sandals who wanders around town urging sinners to repent because he is "harmless" and does not radically interfere with their freedom of action or cherished beliefs. The boy who expresses strong interests in art, music, literature, and dancing frequently receives less tolerant treatment from adults and his peers even though he is equally, if not more, "harmless."

Normality is a highly relative concept that depends for its definition on the society in which it is considered. In a complex society, it has as many specific definitions as there are subgroups using the term. The child who sits quietly in school doing his work and asking an occasional undisturbing question is evincing normal behavior. Such behavior is not normal for the business executive taking part in a group conference designed to elicit new ideas for creative business practices. Like most concepts dealing with human beings, normality is dynamic and changes as the individual, his situation, and his society change.

When guidance workers and school personnel adopted the concept of normality, it lost much of its flexibility and breadth of interpretation. It also ceased to be applied with the caution characteristic of practitioners in psychological areas. Normality took on a rigid quality that seemed to imply that there was one fixed standard of normality for everyone and everything. It lost the implication that there are many possible standards by which to consider normality in various ways. One illustration of this trend is found in the repeated requests of guidance people for a theory of normal personality. In a complex society with many subgroups whose standards of normality change as values and ways change, no one can define *the* normal personality, and without this definition no theory is possible. There is no such thing as *the normal* personality; there are only many varied different personalities who are members of, maintain, contribute to, function in, and change their society.

The guidance worker's search should not be for the impossible theory of normal personality but for a comprehensive theory of motivation and behavior that allows room for differences. The emphasis on normal personality has served as a protection and rationalization for many guidance practitioners. It has permitted them to ignore dynamic theories of personality because these apply only to the "abnormal," to continue their current practices unquestioningly because there is no theory of normal personality by which they can be examined and judged, and to rationalize or to ignore lack of progress because they are waiting for the theory. In the meantime, the separation between guidance and psychology grows increasingly broad as members of both groups concentrate either on normality or abnormality and forget that a theory of behavior should serve both groups equally well.

Normality as a concept has had some dubious effects on individuals to whom it has been applied or who have tried to apply it to themselves. The brilliant student who questions whether he can have a "normal" life if he becomes an atomic physicist demonstrates just one aspect of the concern of the individual with normality. The high school student who plans his school career with the college admissions officer in mind is seeking to present at least the picture of what he considers to be normality. Bob wants to be average, does not think he is, and guesses maybe he is not and so exhibits his concern and ambivalence about a concept he does not understand. The stress on normality in recent years has led individuals to question their own normality whenever they differ even in unimportant ways from the standards described in the popular press or portrayed on television. Youngsters wonder whether they are not a little odd when they occasionally want to be alone or whether it is not abnormal to disagree with a group of peers. The late-maturing boy may never lose his doubts about his masculinity engendered when other boys matured before he did and he viewed himself as "abnormal." Regardless of how the individual interprets normality, his concerns and fears about it may trouble him all his life.

Implicit in the concept of normality is one of conformity. A definition might almost read: to be normal one must do, think, and feel what everyone else does, thinks, and feels. Whether or not such a definition is correct is irrelevant because this is the way in which many people—and most young people—think and feel about normality. Stress on normality constitutes a pressure for conformity that is contrary to the theory presented here and to many of the known facts about human beings. People are different and they should be. From their differences have come all the significant developments of civilization.

The important forgotten feature of the opposition between normality and abnormality or conformity and nonconformity seems to be balance. In the process of living, internalizing, and perpetuating his culture, a child acquires enough of the attributes of a typical member of his society to enable him to function in his group, and his society constantly presses him to take on more. If he cannot or does not acquire these attributes, then he may perhaps be judged abnormal in terms of his group at that point in time. Society also forces the individual to conform to certain rules and standards and those who cannot are sometimes judged abnormal. Against these pressures, the person strives to express himself and to achieve positive experiences within the limits imposed by society. The individual who maintains a balance among these pressures, however precarious and at whatever personal cost, is probably the only one who deserves to be called normal regardless of how he differs from the stereotypes of his society.

In stressing normality, guidance workers and counselors have forgotten one of the starting points of psychological thinking, individual differences. Concern with the mirage of normality has tended in their thinking to minimize the fact of difference. Youngsters are and should be different one from another. Any theory that attempts to explain why people behave as they do should incorporate an emphasis on difference, not similarity, and a recognition that the encouragement of difference, not normality, is an aim of work with human beings.

THE SHIBBOLETHS

Diagnosis, adjustment, realism, "truth," and normality have become catch-words of guidance thinking and theorizing. They are convenient words to use in summarizing what guidance people want to do to and for the students with whom they work. Insufficiently defined and analyzed, they serve to camouflage a lack of clear definition and purpose as well as a failure to implement some of the basic precepts of psychology. Furthermore, they embody an idea of what the guidance person is going to do: namely, he will diagnose; he will adjust the student; he will impose realism; he will discover the "truth"; and he will force conformance to standards of normality. All of which, of course, leaves the student with no responsibility for himself and, even worse, no choice.

All these concepts have some worth both to the guidance person and the student when they are temperately and cautiously used. Diagnosis can be extremely helpful if done with a purpose and with the intention of using the results in a constructive fashion; normality can provide standards that suggest, not determine, ways of viewing and understanding human beings. Unfortunately, guidance workers have tended to regard these concepts as absolutes and to judge, not understand, their students in terms of them.

Any of these concepts applied rigidly to the individual can harm rather than help him. And herein lies a significant failure of guidance workers for they have never examined their concepts from the point of view of the students and how those concepts affect them. Diagnosis is not an aim of the students nor is adjustment or realism. Truth is something most people spend their lives searching for and normality is so elusive and multifaceted that most people would seldom consider it if great prominence were not given it in the popular and scientific press. These five concepts have relatively little meaning to the individual except as they are forced into his awareness by circumstances or other people. He wants a good, happy life, however he defines that phrase, and his concern lies in the struggle for it, not in the shibboleths that outsiders attempt to impose on him.

Somewhere in the course of sixty years, guidance has lost some of its humanitarian purpose. Instead of seeking to help people that aim has been buried under a welter of scientific and pseudo-scientific appurtenances that entail a mechanistic approach of doing things to people to improve them rather than a personalized one of helping them to improve themselves. The five concepts underlie some of this loss of humanity and undergird a lack of faith in the human individual to improve himself, his lot, and his society.

7

IMPLICATIONS

Any theory of motivation is one of human behavior because a concept of why man does what he does is essential to an understanding of what he does and the kind of person he is. Any such theory has many implications not only for understanding the individual but also for working with him. If, for example, one believes in an economic theory of motivation, he will concentrate on economic means to try to motivate people. He will try to keep students in school by emphasizing the economic loss they will incur from leaving. His theory will stress economic factors and values and his practices reflect the theory on which they are built. On the other hand, if he believes that early severe conditioning experiences are most instrumental in shaping behavior and personality, he will seek full knowledge of these experiences as essential in understanding motivation. The practitioner will then consider it necessary to probe for full recall of these often repressed experiences to bring them to the level of awareness in order to facilitate a change in behavior. There is no starting point for practice other than the theory on the basis of which one operates.

The reverse of the coin is also true. Every practice or set of practices implies a theory—or even theories—whether the practitioner acknowledges the basis formally or not. Much guidance work with normal individuals today demonstrates practice-implied theory. Essentially guidance practice emphasizes information-giving and information-gathering. Obviously the only theory that supports this practice is one that states that information about self and society can motivate the individual and produce understanding. Such a theory obviously takes a rationalistic view of man, emphasizes reason to the exclusion of emotion, and ignores the holistic approaches to personality long advocated by behavioral scientists. The fact that most guidance workers are either seeking or awaiting a theory of "normal personality" that will support their work does not eliminate the implied theory on which it already rests—one that finds its roots in nineteenth-century faculty psychology. Practice has a base of operation, a theory, whether acknowledged or not.

Implied theory is far more dangerous than overt. The latter can be analyzed and examined openly. Not the least of Sigmund Freud's contributions to psychology was the definite outline of a theory with its accompanying practices that could be tried, questioned, and qualified. Implied theory unfortunately is seldom examined, analyzed, or criticized. Evaluation is practically impossible because the practices are be-alls and end-alls in and of themselves and there is no comprehensive, clearly stated theory against which they can be judged. There is no basis for questioning.

Contrary to the hopes of practitioners, real theory cannot develop from a potpourri of practices, many of which were originally improvisations. Trying to devise theory from practice always results in a rationalization of what exists, a justification of what is. In the 1930s, college personnel workers tried to write a theory supporting the work they had been doing for over half a century. Their results clearly indicate the dangers of the backward approach to theory. They justified what had evolved into college personnel work and today their practices continue relatively unchanged without a theory against which they can be judged. The same difficulties that plagued those workers in the 1930s are multiplied today and their field has not benefited from the fresh surge of development that inevitably follows new theorizing. Rationalization and justification are not theory.

Attempts to modernize outmoded or inexplicit theory by the application of a whitewash of new jargon are perhaps the most dangerous of all. Neither the theory nor the practices change, but the new finish serves to mislead both the theorists and the practitioners. Basic vocational guidance practices have not changed since the 1920s. They were then and essentially are now reflec-

tions of Parsonian economic theory dating from 1908. Both theory
and practice, however, have now taken on the coloration of the
modern behavioral sciences and are discussed in such inapt terms
as relativism, existentialism, cognitive dissonance, self-concept,
identity, and realism. The whitewash serves only further to obfuscate the implied theory and to confuse both critics and practitioners.

Today, there are many slightly different theories of human
behavior supporting psychotherapeutic practices with disturbed
individuals, but no explicit theories underlying the myriad information-giving and advice-giving practices used with the normal
individual. If a theory is sound, it should be applicable to all
people, however categorized. It must take into account deviant
behavior of all kinds and support practices that might prove useful in working with all people. The contrast between current
psychotherapy and guidance practices leads to an absurd conclusion: one group is irrational and the other, rational; one has
emotions and the other does not. Actually this absurdity results
from the lack of comprehensive theory.

Theory is basic and necessary. Without theory, there is no
profession. There are simply endless practices and improvisations concocted and carried on because they might do some good
and, hopefully, do no harm. Only theory that makes room for
modern developments in the behavioral sciences can spark a
spontaneity of ideas and a development of new approaches that
characterize professional work. Theory is essential for only from
it can practices be molded that support rather than defeat the
aims they are supposed to implement. Only theory makes practitioners professionals instead of technicians.

Theory essentially provides an understanding of what causes
something to happen. In behavioral terms, theory means explaining why a person does what he does in the way that he does it
—offering an explanation of motivation. Only such a theory when
applied can furnish indications for methods of preventing aberrant behavior and helping people to cope with their problems and
conflicts.

This book has outlined a theory of motivation with the normal individual as its focus of concentration. Its importance, if any, lies in the fact that the theory can supply a base for work with functioning individuals within a school and college environment. It can supply a foundation for the work done by guidance-personnel people and, in addition, have implications for psychotherapy. The implications drawn in this chapter, however, are those important to guidance-personnel people and apply to the essential ingredients that should comprise the basis for any work with human beings: focus, view of the individual, view of society, and methods. The theory has special implications for dynamic, developmental counseling.

FOCUS

The theory implies only one focus: the individual. This focus means that the starting point is the person and what is important to him. It is the individual as he is at that moment from his own frame of reference, not as other people hope he is, not as his test scores reveal him to be, not as the value judgments of others report that he is, not as people have grouped him, not as the information gathered about him implies that he is. Only the individual in terms of his own perceptions, values, ways, motives, feelings, and realities can supply the focus, for without this focus there can be no beginning to understanding him.

Every theory implies a focus as do practices even when carried on without a specified supporting theory. Focus in counseling, for example, is most commonly revealed by whatever a counselor spends most of his time doing or views as most important. If he concentrates on testing groups and individuals, his focus is on the tests and usually the diagnosis of the individual or group. Every program for helping people has an emphasis that highlights what its focus really is.

The theory presented here and the focus it implies raise a fundamental question about guidance practices, presumably the chief source of help for most young people: Can individual focus be maintained within a mélange of mass techniques? The question is paramount for all guidance counselors today.

Guidance counselors have long attempted to help the individual while the focus of their practices has belied their alleged emphasis. The literature of the past twenty years implies a focus on the refinement and completeness of the cumulative record, the mass administration and interpretation of increasing numbers of tests and inventories, the handling of personal problems through a kind of classroom or homeroom guidance, and the mass dissemination of information. Such means touch large groups of people and reveal much information (both valid and invalid) about *groups,* but their value to the *individual* has yet to be determined.

Even more subtly, guidance has acquired several peripheral emphases apart from the individual. The first of these might be termed "blanket" focus. Many guidance workers list as one of their greatest concerns the question, How do I interpret tests?, as though a "blanket" rule would cover all interpretations regardless of the particular individual. Similarly, many counselors concentrate on what they feel to be the commonest teen-age problems as though the greatest number of people could be helped through an emphasis on the "blanket" problems. Most counselors feel that what is done for one must be done for all—an overly conscientious interpretation of American values about democracy. This "blanket" version of equality often serves to divorce the work from the individual because it negates what essentially makes him an individual, his differences.

The second focus could be called "diagnostic categorization." Here the guidance worker seeks to "identify" the individual in various terms. The possible ways and classifications are many: underachiever or overachiever; reader or nonreader; gifted, average, or dull; mature or immature; drop-out, potential drop-out, or potential graduate; college or noncollege; trouble-maker or nontrouble-maker; and that most popular of all, a vocational, social, educational, or personal problem. Often the possible help offered the individual through this focus is further minimized by

the fact that nothing is done beyond the mere process of diagnosing and categorizing.

The third focus is "gimmick." Many counselors snatch at
all extraneous devices that they feel may improve and enlarge
their programs. They quickly put into practice all the new gim-
micks and emphasize the acquisition of new informational material, the new test, the new audio-visual instrument, the new reading machine, the new technique. Here the focus is certainly not
on the individual, but rests squarely on the current gimmick.

The fourth and often the subtlest emphasis might be termed
"penchant." This focus means that the counselor, not the counselee, is central. Whatever the counselor likes and feels he can
do best constitutes the heart of his program. Even within the
counseling interview, he concentrates on what he thinks should
concern the individual and program planning, employment, test
interpretation, advice-giving and information-giving are often his
favorites for these topics allow him to remain detached from the
individual and his concerns. Many counselors use their penchants
as protections and their discussions with students are often limited to, as Betty states so pointedly, "school, school, school." [1]
Whether a counselee can be helped while the counselor focuses
on his own penchants is not even a moot point. Inevitably such
a focus prevents all understanding.

Unfortunately blanket, diagnostic categorization, gimmick,
and penchant focuses are growing more popular as the number
of students increases because none of them demands a focus on
the individual. Yet at a time when population, depersonalization,[2] misunderstanding among cultures and peoples, and personal problems and conflicts are all multiplying, nothing is more

[1] Appendix, "The Group," lines 251–252.

[2] Depersonalization is most interesting in its subtle forms. During the
past ten years, for example, Americans seem to have discarded the use of
the personal relative pronoun. Whether in news reports, conversations, or
elsewhere, the construction "the person that" or even "which" has largely
replaced "the person who." This usage not only reflects weak teaching of
grammar but a subtle change in a way of thinking. People are *"thats"*—not
even *"its."*

needed than a focus on the individual and a theory that necessitates such a focus. Whether helped or not, the individual is and will remain an individual, and his problems will increase, not decrease, as his civilization becomes more complex.

VIEW OF THE INDIVIDUAL

A focus on the individual can serve to guide practices, but the theory of motivation presented here implies also a particular view of the individual integral to that theory. This particular view stresses many of the intangible facets of human personality, similarities and differences, and individual motivation.

The individual is ever-striving. He seeks continuously in his own way and in the ways of his society for some satisfaction of the universal motivating forces—to live, to internalize a culture, to perpetuate that culture, to express himself, and to find positive experiences. He groups around these universals the subsidiary motives growing out of the universals and the values and ways important to him. The result is a person who finds at best only temporary satisfaction of his ever-shifting goals and aims, who discovers the happiness, spontaneity, and challenge of living through the continuing pursuit, and who experiences every day the power and strength of his internal motivation.

The individual is also continuously learning from his varied experiences and internalizing new values and ways. These learnings are idiosyncratic, but commonalities are more frequent among members of one society than among members of different cultures. These learnings are total and internalized totally. No man learns intellectually and not emotionally, for internalization demands an emotional commitment. The learning process is never terminal because the strivings to internalize a culture and to express oneself are lifelong. Regardless of his abilities, the individual begins learning at birth—some would say before—and ceases only at death.

Conflicts are inevitable for the individual because they exist among the universal motivating forces and are compounded by discrepancies and inconsistencies among his values and ways. The individual can almost never find lasting solutions to his problems and conflicts because he is constantly faced with different values, motives, and internalizations and attendant recurring or new difficulties. He has, however, the ability to learn to live productively with his conflicts even when the complexity of his society intensifies them.

Although similar to other men, each person is unique in certain essentials aside from the many physical differences. Psychologically, these individual differences exist in internalizations, values, ways, meanings, goals, aims, and all the realities that are integral to the personality. These essential differences mean that every man has his own motivational system and his own problems and conflicts. Each man establishes his own hierarchies and relationships, which are outgrowths of his particular differences.

Each person has his own physical endowments, which he can be helped to use. Modern research is rapidly unfolding greater knowledge than ever before about the physical make-up of the human being, his inheritance, and the importance of his body chemistry. These findings contribute to the behavioral sciences and to an understanding of physical development and what can be done to help or to hinder it. Regardless of physical ability, each person seems able to develop within his own limits as long as he is afforded opportunities to do so and methods are available to aid him.

Fundamental to any helping science is the basic concept that the individual can and does change. Like learning, such change is personal and internal, but it takes place. External means, however, do not produce internal changes because only the individual can change his values, motivations, and realities. What is needed are additional means by which the individual can be helped to make such changes for himself when he wishes to make them and when he deems such changes desirable. Past learnings will never disappear entirely, but the individual is constantly developing, internalizing, and relearning. Change is part of being human.

The theory also presents a picture of the individual as both a product of his culture and a contributor to it. He internalizes what he has the opportunity to learn. His idiosyncratic internalizations and combinations create the change and the development in cultures. Hence each person must be viewed as the essential means by which both continuity and change come to characterize societies.

Fundamentally, the theory implies a view of the individual not only as an individual and unique but also as holistic and dynamic. Because of the growth of the behavioral sciences as separate entities, difficulties often arise in taking a holistic approach to the individual. In the modern world, however, no proponent of the behavioral sciences can afford to see the individual predominantly as an economic, sociological, psychological, or anthropological entity. Such singularity of view only distorts the interrelatedness of motivation and fragments the holism of personality. Man neither lives by bread alone nor strives only for economic gain nor learns solely as a product of his environment and his culture nor develops a realization of self apart from the factors creating it. He is a total human being and can be understood only in terms of all the external and internal forces that create his unique personality.

A holistic view is not achieved by adding the parts of the person like a set of numbers in arithmetic. It cannot be reached simply by pooling the resources of a coterie of experts each of whom reports on one aspect of a person and may dilute the results by his own perceptions, values, and motives. This combination approach minimizes and sometimes ignores what the individual knows about himself. Holism cannot exist where the divisions of the individual are preestablished for administrative reasons that have no relationship to human personality. Dividing an individual into vocational, educational, personal, and social units or into housing, personal counseling, financial, moral, social, and disciplinary units can only multiply distortion and misunderstanding. Holism is essential and new means must be found that do not negate this starting point.

Individual dynamism is as important as holism and as easily overlooked. The current emphasis on prediction implies a belief in the static qualities of the human being and more time and money are now devoted to finding the "stable" qualities of human personality, the constants, than to coping with the undeniable differences. Testing instruments that seem to predict for the group cannot predict for the individual and do not take into account his dynamic qualities. The dynamic view of the person is lost in a welter of attempts at prediction.

The theory presented here denies a static approach to personality and implies one that emphasizes the important dynamic qualities of people. This dynamic view means that the individual must be understood in terms of the very things that make him an individual—his values, ways, motives, and realities. Only thus can he and his society benefit from their mutual relationship.

VIEW OF SOCIETY

To a certain extent, view of individual determines view of society. Philosophers over the centuries have either started with a view of the individual and constructed society around him or started with the ideal society and had the individual fit into it. More recently, behavioral scientists have taken over this philosophical function and talked about society either as it envelops the individual and influences his behavior, or as the individual molds society, or as specific aspects of it, whether economic or sociological, appear to them all-important. Willy-nilly, a view of society is implicit in any theory.

If the view of the individual is unique, dynamic, and holistic, the accompanying view of society must take on these same characteristics. The uniqueness of the individual allows him to initiate and contribute to the changes in his society. Because man is dynamic, the societies he builds are dynamic. Occasionally a society can lose its dynamism by curbing the self-expression of its members, but such repression is never complete or continuous and so self-expression and new internalizations either rapidly or slowly cause society to change. The individual and his ability to see new relationships create the wheel or the machine or the formula or the space craft. Hence uniqueness and dynamism go hand-in-hand. Society is never static but ever-changing.

Holism is as important a concept applied to society as to the individual. American society is not just materialistic or affluent, but pluralistic in the full connotations of that word. Its individuals have different values, motives, goals, aims, meanings, and realities and so does the society they create. Many of the common values have been codified as laws and others are expressed as taboos. On the other hand, certain common values emphasize the freedom to be different in speech, belief, religion, ways of thinking and doing. Only holism can supply an adequate view of a pluralistic nation.

Uniqueness, dynamism, holism—all have practical implications for those engaged in trying to help the individual within his society. The first implication is that a practitioner cannot afford to take a limited view of society. School guidance workers have long been concerned with a narrow view of society as either a "world of education" or as a "world of work." [3] Each of these views delimits the understanding and possible help the guidance practitioner can offer because individuals do not live either in a world of education or a world of or at work. Such "worlds" do not exist. Attempts to solve educational problems or employment problems fractionally and apart from society as a whole are futile. They lead only to myopic distortions of the motives and values of individuals and to misleading and false information about something that does not exist.

Society in the present and in the future is not the world of the counselor who deals with, for example, teen-agers. The counselor's world as he feels it is not the world of the present-day youth. His experiences in his world may or may not have the

[3] Interestingly, a 1964 publication sponsored by the National Vocational Guidance Association shows a feeble attempt to break out of this confining structure by speaking not of a "world of work" but rather of *Man in a World at Work.* Whether real progress can be made *mutato nomine* is questionable.

same relationship to the present as do those of young people. Society today is undergoing such rapid fundamental changes that one generation swiftly loses touch with another. Exploration of space is not and cannot be as meaningful to the adult who remembers clearly his first airplane ride as it is to the youth to whom jet flights are a little passé. Neither can the counselor who spent his formative years during the Depression expect to find the concerns he remembers in the youths who are products of affluence. His concerns and his world are not theirs. As Betty states, "He's got to sort of forget the good old days when he walked three miles to school, you know." [4]

Fundamental to the counselor is not only a dynamic and holistic view of society but also an enlarged and modern view of community. The majority of people in the United States no longer spend their lives in the place where they were born. During the past fifteen years, television and other methods of communication have brought the entire world into the living rooms of 98 per cent of the population. Jet airplanes have made most stops in the world a matter of a day's journey. The proliferation of automobiles has literally placed the American population on wheels. As small businesses decrease in number, even the "job" has lost its set geographical boundaries. The old demarcations of community no longer exist.

The views of society and community implied by the theory mean that the counselor or any adult working with modern youth must attempt dynamic and holistic approaches. He must make room for a total view of society and make certain that even his informational programs are not geared to the past, for the world of today is not the world of tomorrow.[5] He must extend his realities and make room for change. He must take a view of society that stresses wide exploration and allows for individual differences in values and motives.

For the counselor, however, even a view of society as dynamic and holistic is not enough. In order to understand the

[4] Appendix, "The Group," lines 167–168.

[5] Paul Gardner, "Theory into Practice," *Guidance: Critical Issues* (Columbus, Ohio: Ohio State University Press, 1963), Vol. II, p. 52.

societies and the worlds of his counselees, he must be able to recognize at least partially their important realities, which comprise the framework of their intimate "worlds." Society for each person differs just as the realities concerning self and others vary. The counselor must have the breadth of perception and sensitivity to shed his own realities and temporarily to take on those of another.

Because subsidiary motives are culturally determined, understanding of society and culture underlies a real understanding of the individual. A general knowledge of sociology, for example, is not enough. Sociological materials should and must be so integrated into those of the other behavioral sciences that understanding of and feeling for the individual results, not merely information about social caste and class and how the other half lives. Understanding differences in values, ways, and subsidiary motives demands a knowledge of the culture that produced them.

The theory presented in this book has implications for other cultures and societies. In order to understand the motives of other peoples, the American has first to recognize the different values and ways that give rise to those motives. The American cannot apply his values to another culture and use them as a focal point for understanding its people. Each society has its own values and ways that are the sources of the subsidiary motives of its people. Cross-cultural understanding depends on a realization of the differences in values and ways, for these help to determine the difference in cultures and societies.

METHODS

Nothing is more needed today than methods that will prevent mental illness and assist those who are disturbed. As societies grow more complex, people face increasing problems in conflicting values and ways. Closer contact among individuals in a single society or in several societies brings with it different concepts of community and the world and greater possibilities either for understanding or misunderstanding. Cultural exchange entails the intangibles of values as well as the tangibles of movies, *outré* foods, and technical imports and such exchanges are not without tensions. As tensions mount, men desperately need ways of learning to live constructively with emotions, conflicts, and differences. The true purpose of the helping sciences is to aid men in this pursuit.

Present methods of helping individuals with their problems and conflicts are confused and confusing. In general, there is psychotherapy for the severely disturbed and guidance for the normal, whatever those terms may mean. Their usual meaning is that the person whose problems are so severe that bizarre behavior results is likely to receive more individual attention and help than the person whose problems are troubling and handicapping to him, but not markedly detrimental or annoying to others. Despite a half century of development, psychotherapy continues to be reserved for the "irrational"; guidance, for the "rational." [6]

The sharp distinction between therapeutic and advisory-informational services literally leaves without help the "normal" person with his "normal" problems and conflicts in emotional understanding, motives, and values. If he goes to a psychiatrist or psychotherapist, he is likely to be told that he can cope with his problems and that they are not dramatic or startling or severe enough for long-term treatment. In a sense, these experts, already overworked and overbusy with severely disturbed patients, push the "boredom button." If he approaches a guidance counselor, this troubled person is likely to find himself either limited to peripheral educational or vocational topics, given advice or information about what he should do, and/or referred to a psychologist when he attempts to discuss the things that really disturb him, his emotions and values. Because of self-defined limits, the guidance worker tends to push the "panic button" on many normal problem areas. The loser is the individual who cannot

[6] See Chapter 2, pp. 58–59.

find the help he seeks from anyone, for he is left in the no man's land between the territories marked out by the "boredom" and "panic" signs.

The no man's land exists thanks to limitations of theory. Psychotherapy operates from dynamic theories of personality that apply to the abnormal and focus upon the aberrant personality. Guidance, on the other hand, reflects vestigial economic-vocational theory and eschews abnormal theory. Functioning in a school setting, it tends to accent educational-vocational problems as though they were discrete entities. Without dynamic theories of normal behavior, guidance workers rely on a strange kind of "eclecticism" that allows each worker to justify what he is doing in terms of an amalgam of theories. The result is either rationalization or cacophony. Theoretically and actually, the people who suffer are all the normal individuals who, like the students in the text and the Appendix, are growing up in a complex society and not finding help in dealing with their motives, values, emotions, aims, realities, problems, and conflicts.

The theory of motivation and personality presented here has implications for methods of helping the normal individual and preventing mental illness. The first of these stresses the areas that tend in later life to create trouble for the individual because the theory indicates where and how mental difficulties may begin. These areas include learning to live with and to accept emotions as facts of life; to withstand the inevitable stresses and tensions that come from motivational and value conflicts; to practice a wide variety of ways of reacting to situations; to develop many ways of seeking and securing moments of satisfaction however temporary; to reach some understanding of differences in values and ways; and to arrive at some degree of externalization of personal values and realities so that self-understanding becomes possible. Basically the starting point for method has to be the implications of theory because only then can help for the individual be concentrated on what is important to him and what will keep him healthy.

Second, the theory implies that every individual must in his own way be able to find some satisfactions for his universal motives. American civilization has done much to aid people in satisfying the first motive, to live. Standards of living are higher now than ever before in history and life expectancy indicates the success of the many attempts to prolong man's life. For most Americans, there are unlimited opportunities to internalize the culture and to perpetuate it; for some, these opportunities are still minimal, but continuing efforts are being made to expand and extend them. In general, American society tends to do and to offer more in the areas of the first three universal motivating forces than in those of the last two. Self-expression is still possible, but the concerns about conformity and the organization man expressed by many behavioral scientists are not idle. Self-expression can rapidly become a neglected right of the individual—even a dangerous one. American society—built as it is on Puritan values and accenting the other values and ways as it does—often tends to scoff at or to curb the spontaneity and joy of positive experiences and to delimit possible sources of satisfactions. The age-old split between work and pleasure is as sharp and handicapping as that between the emotional and the rational. Methods of helping the individual must acknowledge the universal motives and their importance, as well as how the subsidiary motives fostered by society either help or deter the individual in his never-ending search to satisfy the universals.

The theory certainly has implications for today's guidance methods. The concern with diagnosis, categorization, and prediction far overshadows all others in guidance work with students. Unfortunately, these three areas do not help the individual with what is important to him. They may contribute to fuller school records and administrative practices, but whether these "benefits" justify the time and money spent on them is a moot point. That they do and can harm the individual student is the point largely left undiscussed. How, when, and why they should or should not be used is a fertile ground for analysis.

Certainly there is little harm in the dissemination of information unless it is done in a limited, rigid fashion designed to force early, unnecessary decisions on students. The dangers in informational programs are that they are selective and that they often usurp or replace other activities such as counseling that might be of real assistance to the student by focusing on what is important to him. Information is supplemental, not basic.

Group guidance classes have grown in popularity over the past few years as a means of handling increased numbers of students. There are vast differences that need to be examined between handling personal problems in a classroom and in a group counseling session. The girls in "The Group" in the Appendix highlight the points they consider essential and these are the very points that often are ignored in a group guidance class. A better concentration might be on group counseling rather than group guidance. One is individual and internal; the other group-oriented and external.

Counseling is perhaps today the best method available for really helping the individual with what is important to him. It offers the means of aiding such students as Bob, Mike, Jim, Paul, and Laura. Such counseling cannot be informational or advisory, but rather must arise from the principles of comprehensive theory based on the modern behavioral sciences.

DYNAMIC DEVELOPMENTAL COUNSELING

Modern counseling has to be holistic, dynamic, and developmental. Only thus can it be the most practical way of helping the normal individual cope with his problems and conflicts. Counseling can be of assistance because it implements, not negates, the theory from which it arises and maintains the focus, view of the individual, and view of society implied by that theory.

Certain principles basic to the theory of motivation presented here form the groundwork for dynamic developmental counseling. The first of these is that no subject is taboo in the counseling session. The counselee can discuss whatever is of importance to him without the counselor intruding by changing the subject, bringing in his own experiences and thus shifting the focus, establishing limits to subject matter, and pushing the "panic button." Each individual establishes his own hierarchies and he alone can determine what they are at any given point. Only the counselee really can attempt to know what is troubling him and he must have the freedom to discuss whatever he wants to discuss.

The girls in "The Group" return time and time again to this first principle as they evaluate their counseling experience. Dot, for example, remarks that "Some kids have obvious problems. Like maybe one parent or no money." She then makes an interesting comment about hierarchies of problems when she says, "They're real problems, but our problems are just as important to us as theirs." (86–88) The undramatic, personal problems can be as troubling as the dramatic or the obvious. The girls are also grateful for the opportunity to discuss what they wanted to discuss—"we brought up our own problems." (252) They were able to discuss them openly because the counselor avoided doing what they feel shuts off counseling: "talking and talking" (116); "telling me I'm going through another stage" (120); reminiscing about "the good old days when he walked three miles to school" (167–168); "monopolizing" (166); setting limits around the topics such as "school, school, school" (251–252); and getting "all shook" (163).

The second tenet of dynamic, developmental counseling is that it offers the individual a chance to discuss what is important to him—his values, motives, feelings, aims, realities—in an absence of value judgments. Perhaps no point is so little understood as this second principle. Most school counselors feel that they must go on record as pointing out errors in a youngster's values when and if they occur (from the counselor's point of view) and must stand up and be counted on the side of school values. Perhaps they should, but *never* in the counseling interview. All such judgments accomplish is a fatal shift in focus from the youngster to the counselor that cuts off discussion and often ends the counseling. Value judgments negate understanding and symbolize to the counselee that here is just one more judgmental adult who will not allow him to examine his own values.

The interviews with Paul illustrate how counseling can progress through the application of the first two principles. In the first interviews, Paul discussed what he chose to discuss and through the symbolism cars have for him begins to view the counselor as a person who can understand them and thus him. Tentatively in the fourth interview (included in the Appendix), he begins to talk about some of the things he has done and felt that he knows or thinks he should not have done and felt and he continues to find acceptance as a person through the absence of value judgments. The counselor does not have to tell Paul that he should not make brass knuckles in his shop or must not fight on the playground or ought to struggle to make passing grades. Plenty of people have undoubtedly issued and are continuously issuing these value judgments about his behavior, his motives, and his values. With a youngster like Paul, one ill-considered value judgment from the counselor could relegate him to the category of human beings who do not understand and so end his contact with Paul.

Values and value judgments in counseling cause controversy and difficulty because counselors working with school students have never clearly distinguished between teaching and counseling functions. Both the classroom and the counseling room are areas of learning for the individual, but the means by which the learning takes place differ radically. The teacher's lecturing, informational and advisory techniques are antithetical to the counselor's role; the counselor "teaches" in another way and "teaches" other values. He "teaches" acceptance, understanding, and faith in the individual by living them in the counseling room.

Everyone teaches values directly and indirectly. In American society, the direct teaching of values is the right and proper function of parents, teachers, clergymen, and all those who help the youngster to internalize his culture. The function of the counselor is important because he does not duplicate or usurp these duties, which rightfully belong to others. Rather he allows the youngster to examine his own values in the absence of the value judgments that are a necessary and sometimes too constant factor in other settings and situations. No counselor should or need try to be a teacher, parent, or clergyman. He has a difficult and important enough job being a counselor.

The third essential ingredient of dynamic, developmental counseling is understanding. When the counselor asks the group of girls what kind of counseling they want, they respond with one word—"understanding" (126). Without understanding, there is no counseling. As the theory implies, this understanding has to be so complete that the counselor can know and feel the values, motives, aims, and emotions of the counselee. The counselor must be able, at least partially, to go outside his own frame of reference and view the world and the self from the background of the counselee's realities. He can accomplish these difficult tasks only by recognizing his own values and where they intrude and by projecting himself into the inner situation of the other person so that he can feel and think with him while at the same time retaining an analytic detachment. There is no more difficult task.

The girls in "The Group" attempt to explain what such understanding entails. "Looking understanding" is not enough; the counselor has to "know." (145–148) The counselor has "to know what to say at the right time" (136), and what he says cannot "shatter what we were trying to say" or "tell us what to do" or "how to do it." (132–135) Rather it must convey understanding, which means that the counselor must recognize not only the problems and the feelings about the problems, but also "catch every little thing . . . because lots of times we don't know what we're talking about and then again we do." (157–159) The counselor has to understand not only what is said, but also "what the kid is trying to say. I mean, maybe they'll just mention it once, but they're thinking about it so hard inside that you don't know what you've said and what you're thinking so you just sort—and you've got to be able to fit the pieces together." (152–155) The counselor has to understand and respond to the stated, the felt, the implied, and the unstated. Such understanding is an essential of counseling.

The fourth principle is that the counselee be allowed to travel at his own pace. Paul needed three interviews to build his faith and trust in the counselor's ability to understand him because his past experiences with adults had taught him anything but faith and trust. Bob, on the other hand, was ready to pour out his problems in the hope of finding some kind of help. All youngsters, examining and discussing values and emotions often for the first time, have to find their own pace. Such an examination involves constant relooking from a different angle, repetition, and retracking ground covered before. These are necessary for the learning that takes place because each person learns and internalizes in his own way and at his own rate of speed. The counselor has to be sensitive to the counselee's pace.

Time seems to be a bugaboo for many school counselors. They defend their informational-advisory activities by the amount of time they presumably save and reject real counseling because it is "too time-consuming." Obviously they confuse counseling with the "normal" individual with psychotherapy or psychiatry. The cases included in the Appendix are not long-term counseling, except for Paul who had over fifteen sessions. If, however, one balances the amount of time spent on Paul by all school personnel before counseling began against the time spent by the counselor, the only conclusion possible is that even relatively long-term counseling saves time—that important American fetish.

Essentially the question is more often one of whether to help or not to help the individual. Even four sessions of counseling with Paul produced more effect than had years of advice and reprimand. Furthermore, counseling can be efficient if the counselor eliminates all the practices that waste everyone's time —the artificial means by which he tries to establish rapport and wastes half the interview; the time he spends on reminiscence and facile advice-giving; the number of times he selects the topics of the interview and the student goes away unhelped and puzzled. These are the real time-wasters. Counseling that really helps the student is never a waste of time.

The fifth essential of dynamic, developmental counseling is that the counselee be allowed to cope with his own problems by means of the new learnings that result from the self-understanding and confidence he gains. Without exception, the youngsters in the cases are seeking ways of coping with their own problems and conflicts. In evaluating their counseling, the girls feel that confidence and ability to cope grow out of their increased understanding of themselves and other people. The counseling has made them aware of the nature of their problems and conflicts and given them greater perspective. The process of externalization and verbalization has allowed them to see for themselves what they might do.

Enough has already been said about the futility and uselessness of advice. The girls emphasize this point when they say that "we don't like people always telling us how to do it. We have to sort of solve it ourselves, but you have to help us." (134–136) The help that the counselor supplies is not telling them what to do or suggesting possible solutions, but rather acting as a catalyst for their own examination of their problems and conflicts. As Dot says, the essential step is "facing the reality of problems," admitting they exist, and "then you're on your way to solving them" (71, 81) or at least learning to live with them.

Counseling based on these five premises is consonant with the theory outlined in this book. A forthcoming volume, *Dynamic Developmental Counseling*, will present in detail the techniques and processes by which the counselor can help the student to help himself. Such counseling is, of course, dependent on the skills of the counselor for he provides the setting, creates the atmosphere, and willy-nilly directs the progress of the interview. He and he alone can offer the counselee the freedom to discuss all subjects or limit the topics to those acceptable to him. He can hinder the progress by value judgments or further it by understanding. The counselor can be alert to the counselee's pace and try to understand his frame of reference, motives, and emotions or the counselor can make fallacious assumptions about problems and conflicts and hand out advice and suggestions. He can accept the counselee as a person, recognizing his capacity for growth, or attempt to reform him and so ruin the relationship. Only the counselor can make of the counseling session a positive learning experience in which the counselee can gain self-understanding, awareness of himself, and confidence to cope with his own problems or the counselor can demonstrate no belief in the capabilities of his counselee. The choices are all the counselor's and rest on his knowledge of his profession, the behavioral sciences, and how textbook learnings apply to live people.

Behind the principles and the process is the theory, for without theory there is only confusion and chaos. The theory offers a means by which understanding of all peoples can come about because it emphasizes what makes the human being human and challenging: his motives, values, ways, emotions, aims, and realities. It supplies a starting point for realizing the singular importance of individual differences, uniqueness, dynamism, and holism. From its tenets can come means by which prevention of mental illness can be a reality and by which each individual can be helped to gain at least a small portion of that dream each of us has "dreaming us."

APPENDIX

The appendix contains protocols of interviews with four students and one group-counseling evaluation session. In all these interviews—as in any interview, where they are allowed to do so—the students talk about the things most important to them, their motives, values, and feelings. These students are neither typical nor atypical because they are all individuals facing their own problems and conflicts.

The students themselves come from various sections of the United States. They vary in abilities, learnings, age, social class, sex, interests—in all the countless factors that make each a unique individual. What they say about themselves provides a basis for recognizing these important differences.

Each of the individual interviews and the group session, too, provide the reader the opportunity to analyze what the students are saying about themselves. The same framework and method used to analyze Bob's remarks in Chapter 4 can serve equally well for these interviews. What the counselor really has to understand about the student he sees is, What are his motives and values? What are his aims and goals? How does he believe he should think and feel? How does he feel about himself and others? What is the broad gamut of problems facing him? What can he from his own framework do about these problems and conflicts? Fundamentally, the counselor can understand his counselee only in the light of a motivational theory that is comprehensive.

The group session included is not a counseling interview. The counselor structured the session in order to find out how the five girls felt about their counseling experiences. Their freely given comments express what they feel should be the values inherent in school counseling. As such, this protocol offers the reader the opportunity to draw his own implications from what the students say.

The interviews as printed differ in only two ways from the original protocols. Certain changes have been made to protect the identity of the participants, but such necessary changes have been done so as to preserve as nearly as possible the spirit of the original. Some of the protocols have been cut to make their inclusion possible. Where these cuts occur, they are indicated in the introductions to the interviews.

The counselors range from trainees to experienced professionals. They share a basic approach and some important values concerning counseling and people—that the range of the normal is broad; that each individual is unique; that each individual has the right to shape his own values; that only the individual can find his own way out of difficulties; and that, given the opportunity to discuss the things most important to him, the normal individual can benefit from the process and find his own way, the right way for him, in adult society.

MIKE

A teacher referred Mike, a senior, to the counselor. Throughout his high school years, the school staff has viewed him as a trouble-maker, a poor student, and a potential drop-out. The interview is the first between Mike and the new school counselor.

Mike enters the counselor's room hesitantly and slouches over to a chair. He is about five feet nine inches in height and slender in build. He looks at the counselor, shrugs, and comments, "Well, I'm here. You can bawl me out now." The counselor recognizes these feelings and Mike goes on to talk about school. The interview starts at the fifth exchange between Mike and the counselor.

MIKE: I'm doing a little better than I was at the first of the year. But I don't know yet how much or how good this last semester of work is. I guess I just don't have the will power or

whatever it is to work harder in school. If you goof off the
5   last semester, why—you don't care too much about it.

COUNSELOR: How do you feel about it?

MIKE: I'm not sure. (*Pause.*) I got to study a little fourth
period. Some of us got activities. Some of them, like me, we
just sit around.

10   COUNSELOR: Sit around during this hour?

MIKE: I just do what I want to do. Nobody cares. This one
teacher—she's my history teacher—she doesn't care. If I want
to, I just get up and walk out.

COUNSELOR: You don't think she cares whether you stay or
15   not.

MIKE: She doesn't really. I cause a ruckus—well, pretty easy.
I just cause trouble.

COUNSELOR: Bring trouble along with you.

MIKE: Yeah. Pretty much. I don't study and I suppose I
20   cause most of it myself pretty much. I just—before I came
down here a kid started chucking some rubber bands and he
hit me. So naturally I had to fling some back. I got in trouble
for that. There's really no reason for me doing it, but—that's
me. Goofing off and causing trouble. The other kid didn't have
25   to do anything. I think that's a little unfair 'cause he's a real
trouble starter, but he never gets caught. But whenever a group
gets in a room—well, like we had an election. One of the girls
running was in our room and this guy kept saying embarrassing
crazy things to her and she didn't like it. So I hit him. The
30   teacher didn't say anything to him.

COUNSELOR: You don't like fellows saying crazy things to
girls.

MIKE: I haven't had much experience with girls. Just around
town here, messing around a little. Picking them up after the
35   show or something. Casual date now and then. That's all. Just
haven't found one I really like in this town. This town's kind
of different, I guess. The girls we got—why they're going steady
mostly with the guys who wear the athletic jackets so that kind
of leaves me out.

40   COUNSELOR: They'd rather go with the athletic heroes than
with you.

MIKE: They do definitely around here. With the letter-jacket
guys. The guys on the teams, they're all going steady and the
rest of us just have to take a chance. Try to pick up a girl
45   without a date after the show or something. A couple of them
might be walking along and if you're with a guy who's got an
in with one of the girls, then you can pick one up—once in a
while. So I would say that the letter-jacket guys just got the
jump on you. Like this other guy, if he'd call a girl then you'd
50   get that outside edge because they run around pretty much
together, kind of a closed circle. I know one or two but I just
ain't got that letter jacket. They'd rather have someone who'd
be more of a hero than me. (Pause) They're not really
heroes, not the way they think anyway. They're about half
55   what they're cracked up to be. They—well, if you look at the
records for the school for the past few years—well, the last few
years the team ain't done too good. It's more the coaches' fault
than anything else I guess. We've had some pretty good guys
the past few years. We'll have three guys back next year who
60   lettered this year. They're all good. Same thing last year. We
had three or four real good guys coming back. But nothing
comes of it. Last year in one game we went thirteen minutes of
the first half and only scored one point.

COUNSELOR: Basketball?

65   MIKE: Yeah. Our coach didn't help us too much. Pretty
good player and all that, but he just don't know how to get it
across. Some of the players think so anyway.

COUNSELOR: You play basketball?

MIKE: No. I work after school. That's my excuse. I say I
70   work after school, but I wouldn't be any good at it anyway.
Just not coordinated good enough for that stuff. Oh, I play
around with the guys. Play around a little on the tennis court.
Played with this one guy who's six feet two and with another
guy who's a starting forward and another guy who's second
75   team who might start next year and then this other boy who's
in college. Boy, it didn't take long before I was pretty well
winded. First two or three times down the court. They were
still going strong. I ain't done any working out or running steady
like they have with their football and basketball and track.

80 They're really in shape. All I do is work after school and that
don't compare with running up and down a basketball court.

COUNSELOR: Work can't get you in shape.

MIKE: Not like that. Might strengthen your arms or wrists
carrying things, but it don't compare with real workouts. Run-
85 ning gets muscles you don't use ordinarily.

COUNSELOR: Kind of tough having to work.

MIKE: Yeah. In a way it's kind of a cover-up for me. I'd hate
to go out and be beat up by freshmen. That'd probably be the
end of it. There's no point in wasting the coach's time if you
90 know already that you're no good at it and you know there's
lots better than you are. Just don't make sense to be going out
wasting your time. Play football and go running around there
when it's hot in the summer before school starts and get
pounded all the time. Don't get anything for it. Like me. I
95 wouldn't even get in a play maybe. Well, like this summer, me
and them three guys. They started last year, too. I'd work all
day and they'd practice football. They'd be a lot tireder than
I'd be. Sort of laughed at them. Made fun of them and all
that stuff, but I wished I were out there with them. But—
100 (laugh)

COUNSELOR: You didn't feel you ought to try it.

MIKE: Yeah. (Pause) Oh, I suppose I could have played
this year if I went out and really tried. But I never get into
nothing or do anything but I pull some boner or something.
105 Probably cause them to lose a game or something. Whatever I
do, I always goof it up someplace along the line. Trouble, that's
me. Somebody once said, some poet or something, that everyone's good at one thing but—like someone's good at sports, why
you're better than he is at something. Well, I must be better
110 than them guys at something else because they're all better than
me at sports.

COUNSELOR: What are you good at?

MIKE: Seems kind of funny, but playing cards. I like playing
cards. I don't know. Those guys play with me and I win a lot
115 of money from them. They always get beat. (Laugh) They're
good at showing their muscles around, but they don't think so
fast.

COUNSELOR: Cards give you a chance to be a winner.

MIKE: Yeah. They're okay, but they—oh, I don't know. I
120 learnt from a guy who taught me to play "Smear" and then he
taught me to play poker. Playing with those bigger guys, you
had to learn fast. I guess I take more chances than they do.
They like their money. I like my money, too, but I'm not afraid
to lose it.

125 COUNSELOR: Heroes can be cowards at times.

MIKE: It's not easy for them. They're afraid of losing. Played
with them not long ago. Won about thirty-two dollars in three
days. It was just a way to pass the time at noon waiting for
school to open. All the kids know I play cards. I guess I'm
130 always lucky. That's what they call me, "Lucky." What I can
do if I want to—I can draw any card I want to. Makes you
feel a little bit bigger man if you can walk in and say, "I beat
them guys." It isn't the money. Of course, sometimes you feel
kind of like a heel doing that. I hate taking—some of the guys
135 I play with they think they're good, but they're really no good
at all. I hate playing a guy for a sucker like that. But then I
tell myself he thinks he's good, why then that's his worry.

COUNSELOR: You'd rather play against people on pretty even
terms.

140 MIKE: It's more fun if you play against someone equal to you.
It's more of a challenge. If I play with some people and I
know I can beat them, why, I just mess around more. Doesn't
interest me then. There's just a few of us who can really play.
Most of those kids who thought they were really good found
145 out they're not so good. They don't want to play with us. They
call us card sharks—I don't know why. They can't stand to
lose. They win once in a while. They get lucky. There's just
a few of us left to play. We're friends. Pretty good game when
we get together. We're all of us pretty good at playing. Well,
150 there's really not much else to do. The show's not over till 9:30
and the pool hall's not open. I suppose we could go sit in one
of the drive-ins all night or we could hang out on the streets or
just sit and talk somewhere or play the pinball machines. We
got to have something to do so we play cards. Cards is as good
155 as anything.

COUNSELOR: At least it gives you something to do.

MIKE: Yeah. Television's no good. Besides most of the guys are like me, can hardly stand to stay home. I'd rather get out and just do anything. Even just walk up and down the street.

160 COUNSELOR: You don't like to stay home.

MIKE: I had to sit there quite a while. Stayed in bed there quite some time. Since then the idea of staying in one spot too long just don't appeal to me. I had to be in for about three months and I got a little tired of it. Actually it was over four

165 months I was laid up. Back in the seventh grade. Since then I keep running around. (*Laugh*) Maybe if it weren't for that I wouldn't be running around so much. Funny how you go back to something like that—like a sickness and you can't stand staying in one place too long.

170 COUNSELOR: Get pretty restless.

MIKE: Yeah. It's funny though. If I'm doing something interesting or got a good play going on television or got a radio going or something like that, then I don't mind. But if there's something going on television I don't like or something where

175 I get bored, I just gotta go somewhere. (*Pause*) My dad's on the road five days a week. When he comes home, he says that I go on the road for two. It's about the truth. We hardly ever see each other. He's on the road five days a week, comes home late Friday night, and leaves early Monday morning. I get up

180 about six-thirty and leave, come home about six at night, and then go out and come back about one or later. I sleep late the next morning. Get up about two or so. I get so tired I can hardly drag myself out. Then I go out again that night. Dad leaves the car and he don't say nothing. I just take the car and

185 nothing's said. I just walk in and pick the keys up off the dresser and say I'm going and that's all that's said. Sometimes something about keeping the paint on the fenders or some wise remark like "You're the guy the keys follow around" or something like that. But Dad doesn't care. I generally win. Dad's

190 a pretty good egg that way. Makes me feel pretty good to be driving around in a pretty good car. Especially on Sunday. If it's a nice day out, there'll be a lot of fellows wanting to go riding around.

COUNSELOR: Makes you feel pretty good to have your dad trust

195 you with the car.

MIKE: Yeah. I'm probably one of the luckiest guys in this town—that way. If something important is coming up for me on a Friday night, no matter how far away he'll be, he'll always try to make it home early enough so that I can have the car. He'll go along with almost anything. Drop everything and come home like that. He probably isn't doing his business exceptionally good but—

COUNSELOR: Your dad knows this is important to you.

MIKE: Uh-huh. He probably feels that—well, he's been in his job about five years now. Before that he worked in a store and almost had a nervous wreck on account of that. He was never home then. He was assistant manager and had to be there all the time. Even then he tried to spend time with me. Now I think he feels he's kinda left me out, him never being home. Feels like he owes it to me.

COUNSELOR: You agree.

MIKE: I don't think he owes me anything. He gives me the car and all the money I need. Whenever I run short from when I get paid, he gives me money. Whenever I want the car for something special or just driving around over the weekend, I can. And, of course, that's important to him. If his car should break down, he couldn't go anywhere or make any money. If he trusts me with that—why, he trusts me pretty well.

COUNSELOR: You'd like to have more time with him.

MIKE: Yeah. I got a little brother and he plays around with him. Mostly he just sits and watches television. You drive the car all week and it's pretty tiresome. He gets pretty tired during the week and he'd just not like to drive the car or do anything during the weekend. Ma can't even get him to take her for a ride. He says he doesn't want to go anywhere. He gets real tired during the week. He doesn't even want to go to the grocery store.

COUNSELOR: You take Mom to the grocery store?

MIKE: The store where I work. I mean I take her to the store on Saturdays. Then I just stay up front and help sack up groceries. The help they get on Saturdays, the girls up front don't like too well and neither do I. So I just sorta help out. They just stand there like posts and don't do anything. I think

I work a little harder than they do. You see I work during the
235 week. I like to see people come in because then I can work
harder. I help out in the back, too, stacking groceries. Mom
does most of her shopping on Saturday. Sometimes she'll call
in during the week and then I bring things home to her. I like
to eat. I eat like a horse. There's not much doubt about that.
240 But it doesn't seem to do much good. I suppose it's all the
running around I do. I've always had a car. First, I had a fifty
Ford, but it don't work so good now. We were always out at
the drive-ins. I ate three times as much as everybody else did.
This one kid, he'll be a senior next year, he weighs about 200
245 pounds and I'd make him look like a baby eating. He's still
about 200 and I just stay about 135.

COUNSELOR: Just doesn't seem to stick.

MIKE: Well, I eat a big breakfast and then go to school. Then
Mom likes me to pick up my little brother and she's got a pretty
250 good meal prepared and I eat all of that. Then when I go down
to the store I eat anything I want. I eat up to three candy bars
in an afternoon. Bananas, grapes, apples, and everything. Go
home and eat. Go out to the drive-ins and eat. I put away a
lot of food I think. I just don't grow very good. Maybe it's the
255 food I eat. Maybe it's not the right kinds, but I eat all kinds.
It seems with all the food I put away I ought to gain a little
weight. After I was sick, when I got up that next summer—
while I was sick I weighed about seventy pounds. That summer
I gained about twenty-four pounds and grew about six inches.
260 I shot up real good that one summer. The doctor couldn't
hardly believe it. Well, I swore I got all the poison out of my
system and that was what was keeping me back. I worked
myself up this far. Maybe these hamburgers and malts at the
drive-in—maybe they don't do you much good, but I eat
265 enough of them. I keep telling this lady who runs this one
drive-in out here—she comes into the store and buys groceries—
that that's my money right there she's buying with. It's about
the truth too. Between me and the rest of the guys who go
there with me, why we probably make about nine-tenths of her
270 business. Her food's okay, but mostly we just go to play the
pinball machines and listen to the records. Just something to
do. If we're in there about 10:00, we just stay there till about
twelve o'clock playing the pinball machines and eating food.
She doesn't care. She's glad to have us because we—well,

275   there's a gang of kids who come around to the drive-ins and
       make a real mess of them. Knocking furniture around and that
       sort of thing. That's not us. She'd just as soon see us in there.
       As long as we're in there, the other kids stay out. She doesn't
       want that gang in there. They cause trouble and we don't so
280   she doesn't complain too much.

       COUNSELOR: She likes to have you then.

       MIKE: She'd rather have us than have them bums cluttering
       up her place. They just cause trouble. (*Pause*) Maybe I'm just
       nervous. It must be that. I keep trying to find something that's
285   wrong. I know I don't work the weight off. I don't work that
       hard. When I first went to work there a couple of years ago, it
       seemed like a lot, but now it's just the same old grind. You
       learn to take it in stride, but it's no work really. This summer
       I worked there all day long all summer, but I can't say it's that
290   either. And then when I work, I'll have a candy bar in my
       pocket and get a bottle of pop from the freezer and drink it.
       Then when the bakery deliveries come in, you can take pastries
       out of the pan and eat them. I eat pretty good up there so I
       don't think I work too hard. Lot of these guys who come around
295   are pretty good guys, salesmen like my dad, but some of them
       are pretty stuck on themselves, too. Most of these bread guys
       are pretty good guys. They seem to keep their jobs. Most of
       these salesmen change jobs about five or six times a year. At
       least the guys who come in there do. Can't be pretty good jobs.
300   The fellows who work in the grocery stores don't get much
       either. They don't have really good jobs. Most of the deliveries
       come in on Tuesdays and Fridays and about the only time I
       could say I worked real hard was then. Unload the truck and
       carry it in—that's about all. I carry it in and stack it and load
305   the shelves. That's about it. The first three weeks I was there,
       I just stacked and then I got more work than I ever thought I
       would. I suppose I really do more work though than a couple of
       other guys who work there all the time. I do a lot—well, each
       guy has a section that is supposed to be reserved, that he takes
310   care of. There's this guy who keeps care of the meat counter
       and then the fellow who keeps care of the vegetable rack—
       well, I keep care of most of the rest of it. All the canned stuff.
       I tried to do the best I could.

       COUNSELOR: That work you're doing down there really makes
315   you feel you're an important part of the team.

MIKE: Yeah. I was just working there after school and then the summer came, it made me feel kind of important when he asked me to work full-time during the summer. And I did it and he said I did a good job. Makes a guy feel pretty proud
320   that you were able to do it, get it done, do it right.

COUNSELOR: It's pretty necessary to feel important.

MIKE: Yes, it is. A guy's just got to feel important. You feel important and you're going to do a better job, I think. If you like the job and the people you work with—I can't complain.
325   I like the fellows up and down. And the cashiers are nice to me. They'd do about anything for me. I got one problem though. I lose my temper pretty easy. (*Laugh*)

COUNSELOR: Get mad easily?

MIKE: I've blown off at a few customers. Can't help it at
330   times. (*Pause*)

COUNSELOR: Helps you to blow off now and then.

MIKE: Yeah. It helps, but then I feel sorry afterward. This summer I've learned a little not to blow. I still get mad, but I keep it inside. I take it out on my car afterwards. After work
335   —well, I feel like—well, sometimes I'd take it out at home. I'd come home to eat and my little brother would come in and I'd tell him to shut up or get lost. Sort of take it out on someone who it wouldn't hurt. I've got so I can sort of store it up for a while. I still get mad occasionally. At some of the customers.
340   Especially, I think, at the stupid questions. And then sacking up groceries. Nobody appreciates it. You get it put in three great big sacks and someone wants a box. You put in a box and they want it in sacks. Take Friday. That's a pretty busy day. We unload the trucks and put it out for the customers.
345   About four-thirty or so, I get pretty tired about then. Whatever a customer says seems to get on my nerves about then. Whatever a customer says, I get mad and feel like blowing off right then. Then they generally got some answer for you. Get mad and say they're going to tell your boss and all that. It
350   doesn't really bother me too much 'cause I'm not worried about getting fired. If he fires me why then—why—I figure I do a real good job around there and if he don't think enough of me to—well, to see why I can get mad once in a while, why—but it's okay. So far he's defended me all the way. He must

355   think I'm right doing it. I know some lady—well, somehow—
well, I don't know whether I did it or not, but—well, some
canned goods fell off on her basket and one of her milk cartons
got broke and she called me and bawled me out for that. She
was nasty and I got mad so I told her there was just one solution
360   for that, "Don't buy so damn many groceries." But I guess the
boss knows what I'm up against. (*Pause*) He's been here for
over thirty years so he's pretty well accustomed to the complaints of the customers. He don't say much. He kinda just
sits back and lets everyone else run the store. I suppose you
365   could say he runs the store, but take those guys who are in
charge of the sections of the store, they do their own ordering
and all that. He just sort of sits back and—why if there's
anything important or that, he takes part. He don't say anything though. Mostly he just lets you go about what you're
370   doing. Anything special he wants done or something like that,
he'll tell you, but mostly he's just around—that's all. If he
wants something done or something important has to be done—
well, he has a lot of faith in you. I guess he feels that if you've
been around there a while and you don't know what to do, you
375   must be pretty dumb or something because you can't work in
a store every day without getting used to what has to be done.
That's why I hate to get mad.

COUNSELOR: But there are times when you feel you've taken
all you can.

380   MIKE: Yeah. It isn't the work in the store—that's not bad.
It's the customers more than anything else. Sometimes you
think you don't deserve those things. The public's pretty bad
people. You learn you can't please everybody. Boy, someone's
always got to complain about something. Why some people if
385   they can't complain about someone, they don't know what to
do. The women are the worst. (*Nervous laugh*) They really
complain. There's some old ladies I even hate to see come
around. Boy, I think—when they come in I just head for the
backroom. I can hardly stand them. (*Nervous laugh*) Just so
390   long. They have the same complaint every time. The same
little thing. You're always out of something. Some little
canned good or something. Nobody's gonna die just because
you're out of it. Why, they can blow that up into the biggest
thing you've ever seen. A man comes in—why, he's got that
395   list and if he can't find something or we ain't got that canned

goods—why he don't say anything. Those women—some of them can complain for half an hour.

COUNSELOR: Women make you real uneasy then.

400   MIKE: Yeah. (*Pause*) Just as soon get out of the store as deal with women. Oh, there's a few—but not many—just a few who are real busybodies. They cause you trouble. You don't know where this is or you ain't got no avocados and you try to explain why—well, one time we got short on one kind of cake and every time I walked down the store some woman or another
405   would ask, "Why?"

The counselor's summary of the rest of the interview follows: Mike had been tapping the tape recorder and I did not turn it off because it was near the end of the tape. The tape ran out and, therefore, the sudden halt to the recorded interview. Shortly after this happened, the English teacher came into my office where we were conducting the interview and hastily backed out. Mike commented, "That was our English teacher. He's leaving after this year. We really gave him a hard time. He knows English, but he doesn't know how to teach it. We're on literature now. That's not so bad. But we sure ran him off. A lot of others, too. We'll have to get a lot of new teachers next year." Then he returned to general comments about his importance as king of the poker players and a recognized worker. Finally, he began to sum up some of the things he had been discussing and to explore some ways in which he might make some changes in his own behavior. The bell rang and Mike bolted for the door, but he stood in the doorway. As I got out of my chair and began to walk to the door, he said, "Well, it's been real nice talking to you, but I know you'd rather talk to some of the other kids. I'm a senior this year so you can't help me much, but there's a lot of kids I know in the lower grades who ought to see you about their problems. You're good at making me see things. So good luck with someone else." He continued to stand in the doorway, however, and I said that I would be glad to see him again if he felt like coming in to discuss anything with me. As I

said this, a look of complete bewilderment or perhaps incredu-
lousness came over his face and he said, "Well, other kids need
your help and you've taken too much time with me already.
Nobody in school ever spent this much time with me." I told
him I would take as much time as he cared to take and would
be glad to talk with him as long as he would like to talk. At that
point, he said, "Really? I bet you have to see some other kids."
I said again that I would be glad to see him if he wanted to see
me. We made an appointment for the following week. This
seemed to make him very happy and he shouted, "See you next
week," as he dashed out the door, and added, going down the
hall, "Okay. It's a deal."

JIM

When Jim, a high school senior, entered his office, the counselor
saw a tall, poised, smiling student. Jim said that he was not sure
what counseling was, but thought that he might like to try it.
During the first interview, Jim discussed his plans for college and
his feelings of responsibility for his mother and sister. He then
asked the counselor if he might come again. The materials included are from the second and third interviews.

Second Interview

COUNSELOR: You like to make your own decisions on things
pretty much.

JIM: I do. I just feel sort of independent or something. I don't
know. I guess I just like to solve things myself. I think that's
5   best. I'm going to have to do it later on anyway. There's not
always going to be someone to fall back on so I think it's a
good idea. Like your parents. I mean, it's real easy to run
home to the folks and say, "Gee whiz, what do I do now?" but
if you can work it out yourself then that's good. Of course, you
10   shouldn't depend entirely upon yourself. You should be able
to get some advice from your parents, and other people who are
smarter than myself. I think that's important, too.

COUNSELOR: But there are still these things you don't feel like talking over even with your mother.

15 JIM: Yeah. It just seems that some things—to me some things are personal and they'll work themselves out, but if they don't, then is the time to ask for help from your parents or something of that effect. Do you think this is right? Do you think I depend on myself too much? Is that a good trait? Am I right
20 in that?

COUNSELOR: You're wondering if the way you feel is the right way.

JIM: Is that the correct way of feeling about personal problems and things—that you should try to work them out yourself?
25 Is that the wrong attitude to take? Well, the wrong way to feel? About personal problems or any problems, trying to work them out yourself—or asking for help or leaning on someone. I'd just rather not lean on somebody. I suppose I like to be a little bit independent. Is that a right way of feeling? I suppose all teen-
30 agers are prone to be independent at times. Is that just an age that I'm at or is it some little idiosyncracy that I have? I just want to know if that's a correct way of feeling. If I should share more things and not try to do so much for myself.

COUNSELOR: You have doubts. Sometimes you feel you should
35 talk to someone about different things.

JIM: Yeah. Course now my father's gone. I used to talk to him about everything. I was always closer to my father than to my mother. I suppose that's normal. Boys are always closer to their fathers. Now I've become quite close to my mother,
40 of course. I just don't—didn't feel as close talking about every-thing with my mother as I did with my father. I suppose that's possibly why I've become a little more independent. I suppose it's a good idea to have someone whom you can really talk to, but I don't have anyone anymore except for my mother. I
45 wouldn't go down to a good friend or one of the good friends of the family and confide in him. I wouldn't do that. I don't know why, but I wouldn't confide in just a friend of the family. I'd rather—unless that was the last possibility—I'd rather just try to make it on my own. In my case, I think that's best any-
50 way. We, of course—well, even the relatives. After Dad died, all the relatives were trying to tell us what to do and—and, of

course, my mother didn't appreciate that because they don't know all the problems. They told us to sell the house and—oh—well, send the kid to work. Mom didn't pay too much
55   attention to it. They thought—well, send the kid to work. He's going to have to learn to make a living. He's got to make a living some day. She thought school would be more important. I feel the same way. Of course, the relatives always feel you should do some things and you shouldn't do other things. Well,
60   we haven't sold the house and things like that and they get kind of peeved that we don't do as they say. But they don't understand everything that goes on either. They don't see all the areas. So I don't feel that I could confide in any one of them. They've given some bum advice on other things. We have an
65   excellent standard of living, which we couldn't have, if we'd sold the house and moved into an apartment. Yet that's what they want us to do. They think that big house we have is too much for us. We don't.

COUNSELOR: You'd like someone whom you feel you could
70   confide in.

JIM: Yes. Well, I don't know if I would like someone now. Now that I'm getting older—I think that stage passes, but—well, like my father. I used to talk to him a lot about anything and I thought that was really good. I really liked that. Of
75   course, all kids do. Any young person has to find someone. Maybe that was a stage of my life that I suppose just sort of died and made me more independent than it need have. Also I'm just getting a little older and a little wiser and I don't really need someone to lean on anymore. I'm not self-sufficient
80   by any means. I don't mean that but I have a pretty good outlook on life, I feel. Of course, they always say pride cometh before a fall so I suppose I feel I have a pretty good outlook and it'll fall to pieces some time, but I feel fairly confident in my judgment and wisdom, so to say. (Chuckle) So maybe outside
85   of my mother, I don't really need someone to tell my detailed problems, which I have few of probably.

COUNSELOR: But possibly it'd clear up things a little to—

JIM: (Interrupting) Oh, yes. I think I spend a lot of time just thinking. Instead of doing my homework sometimes, I just
90   think things over. How things are going for us and for me. What am I doing? What am I going to try to do? What kind

of a person am I? Things usually work themselves out. Of
course, I have to help them along, sometimes quite a bit. But
things usually turn out one way or the other. I'm just general-
95   izing now. I can't think of any—any big problem except that—
the only one—the one that kind of bothers me most, of course—
now it wasn't too long ago that my father passed away and my
mother misses him, of course. When she gets in a bad mood
and starts thinking about it, then it gets me in a bad mood and
100   I like to keep my mind and her mind off from it as much as I
can. That's about the only big problem. That's the only thing
that worries me.

COUNSELOR: Worries you?

JIM: Well, sometimes a husband and wife die within a short
105   time of each other. I'd sure hate to have that happen to Mother.
I'm sure she's not because she isn't—well—that overcome by
the thing. She's awful sad, but she knows that she has to raise
my little sister. She's only twelve. She's got a long way to go
yet. Mom at least has to put her through college before she
110   can let up. So it doesn't bother me terrifically, but I'd like to
keep her young and spry after that, too. That's probably one
of the main things that worries me. She doesn't know that.
That bothers me quite a bit sometimes. I just try to be nice and
cheerful and keep things as much normal as I can. I think it
115   helps. I know it helps. (Pause) I know I'm doing the right
thing there, too, because someone has to. She wouldn't listen to
anyone else as much as she would listen to me. I am her son
and she respects my judgment, too. We talk things over about
our income and things like that and she respects my judgment
120   just as I respect hers. The things I can do or say to make her
cheerful seem to help—help quite a bit. That's the only one
that really worries me and I get along pretty well. I don't think
I'm going to crack up under the load. I have other things to
worry about, too, and one thing sort of offsets the other. Well,
125   school and stuff like that and athletics—I'm very interested in
athletics. Well, I worry about doing well, you know, and stuff
like that. That's minor—very minor, but I worry about that, too.
Oh, I can't say I actually worry about it, but I just hope I
make it. Things like that go along with other things. They're
130   really trivial things. They'll never count for anything except
maybe a little personal pride, I suppose. Well, I just don't
worry all the time. It seems to me that it sounds as though I

worry all the time and that's far from the truth. I go out a lot
and I have a lot of fun with the kids and I have a girl and
135 stuff like that. I have as much fun as any other kid. I just sometimes think about these things.

COUNSELOR: You still wonder once in a while about the lack
of someone to confide in.

JIM: Sure. I'd like sometimes—when I'm in a poor mood, you
140 know, and things aren't going right—like if I'm worrying about
my homework or things like that, then I'll start worrying about
everything else, too. Then it'd be nice to have someone to talk
to, but then I just—well, I have an advantage over my mother
on things like that because I can just go out and find some of
145 the kids and have a good time and that usually lightens things
up and you can find some kind of an answer sometimes that way.
Of course, Mom—she can't just go out and have a riot. She
isn't a kid anymore. She can have the ladies in for tea and
things like that, but by no means can she get rid of as much
150 steam as I can. That's for sure. I don't know whether I want
anyone to confide in or not. I really don't know. Sometimes
it'd be nice and then other times I don't feel that it's real necessary. I know that—I personally feel that that's the wrong way
to think, but that's just the way I think. That's just me, I
155 guess. (Pause) Of course, Dad's death had a terrific effect on
our lives. That was just recent. That was only a year ago. No,
not exactly a year ago. One of the things that really bothered
me about it was that it was on Thanksgiving and for some
reason that rubbed me the wrong way. I don't know, but that
160 —for some reason that seemed to mean something and I don't
know what it is. It's too much of a holiday or something for
something like that to happen. I don't know. That kind of bugs
me. I don't know if that should or anything. It would have
been nicer if it had been the day before or the day after, but
165 Thanksgiving—that kind of bothered me. It's too easy to
remember—that's one thing. Here you have a big holiday—
and, of course, I never knew how sick my Dad really was until
after he died. I thought he was going to get well and get up
again, but when he went to the hospital they gave him five or
170 six months to live. I never knew that. After he came home, he
started getting well again. I thought so anyway. It looked like
it. He could get up and walk again and everything. Then he
got sicker. I always figured though that he would make it and

we always talked about how he would go back to work. Well,
175 it came as kind of a shock to me. Well, in the back of my mind,
I didn't really believe it, I think, but—that he was going to live,
I mean. It looked pretty hopeless to me. I just convinced myself that he was and there was no reason for me not to think so.
So it came—it was kind of a shock, I guess. I—I really don't
180 know the difference between—I really don't know how I'm trying to distinguish between problems and things I worry about—
if they're the same. If a problem is something you worry about,
then I have some problems, but—well, everything's gone pretty
well for me. What I call problems are probably something I
185 worry about. It's probably the definition there, I guess. So just
keep in mind that I mean one and the same thing when I say
problem and worry.

COUNSELOR: You felt you probably should have known about
this beforehand.

190 JIM: No, I don't think so. I wouldn't want that. No, that
would have—well, I really can't say. But—well, I know—well,
I knew something was wrong on Thanksgiving. I just knew it.
I could feel it. In fact, I went up to my room and cried in the
morning and he wasn't even really sick then. I went up in
195 my room and I cried because I just suddenly thought, What
if Dad died? I just knew there was something wrong and I had
never cried about it before—very much. I could just feel there
was something wrong and then I thought, Aw, heck, that's kind
of farfetched. Nobody in our family had ever died before and
200 I kind of thought that was just something that happened to
other people. You know, it could never happen to me and—
but—but I could just feel it on that day. We came back—the
relatives knew what was going on, of course, so they took me
out to dinner. I came back to the house and—well, there was
205 nothing on the outside that looked unusual. I went into the
house and Dad's bed was empty. His bed was empty and I
thought—well, I was hoping that they'd taken him to the
hospital for something because he'd been in and out of the
hospital sometimes, too. There wasn't anybody in the house
210 then. Well, then I realized that what I had hoped hadn't
happened had happened. I was kind of glad I was alone because I didn't want to see anybody at the time or talk to anybody or anything and I cried all by myself for a while and then
my mother came over and found me and I was kind of half-

215 resigned and half—I was still awful sad, of course. I knew it had
happened and I was still sort of half-shocked, I suppose. I—
I—I'd known all day there was something wrong and it didn't
come as a—as a complete shock, I don't suppose I can say. I
think I'd really known for a long time that there was something
220 really wrong, that shouldn't be and so I—well, I guess I'd really
known deep in my mind that he was going to die, but I didn't
want to think about it. So I didn't. (*Pause*) But I think it was
by the grace of God that he did die because he—well, if he'd
gone along for six more months for some reason that would have
225 been no kind of life to lead. It must have been kind of terrible
for him so I—well, it was probably kind of good for him that
he did die when he did. He saw everybody he wanted to see
again. All the relatives came at one time or another. All his
friends—they came in every day. I'm sure he was resigned to
230 the fact himself. (*Pause*) Of course he couldn't feel anything
or anything like that, but I suppose it was terrible. He got all
skinny and puny—of course, he would, but I didn't like to see
that. He had been the athletic type and—and he liked—he
liked to play tennis and everything like that and he didn't have
235 much time for it, but he sure liked to fool around at it. I didn't
like to see him wasting away like that either. When he got
down—when he got down so far I just seemed to feel that it
would be better—well, if the end came and that's the way I felt
after he died and that's still the way I feel. (*Pause*) He just
240 went, I guess, when the time was—well, due, I guess. I
couldn't—couldn't see anything more in life for him. As far as
I could see, it was all done. From my point of view it would
have been. I probably wouldn't have lasted as long as he did.
Naturally—(*Pause*) I suppose you have some idea of what I
245 feel like now. (*Pause*) Kind of a touchy subject though. I've
never talked about it before. (*Pause*) I'm kind of glad I could
come here and say some of these things. It's kind of—well, I
feel miserable after I come out of here, but still I feel glad I
could say it sometimes. It helps a lot. (*Pause*) You think I let
250 these things bother me too much? I try not to. I try not to let
them affect me. Try to let them affect me as little as they can.

COUNSELOR: You think they may bother you more—

JIM: (*Interrupting*) I don't want them to bother me more than
they should and I don't know how much they should bother

255   me. I mean they bother me, but I don't want them to bother
       me too much. I worry sometimes about becoming mentally ill.
       A friend of mine had a psychology course and he was always
       telling me about how these guys go nuts or something because
       of something that happened in their childhood. Boy, that
260   bothers me. That worries me. So that's why I don't want to
       let anything be—well, too traumatic or anything like that. I
       don't want to show what I feel. Maybe that makes me hard or
       something, but I have a heart. I just don't want to have too soft
       a heart. Some things bother me too much. That's not too good
265   either, I suppose. That's kind of a silly thing to worry about, I
       suppose, but that still worries me. Look how many people
       become mentally ill. I don't know enough about it, of course,
       but this guy used to tell me about how these guys go insane
       for one reason or another. My uncle had a nervous breakdown.
270   My gosh, it can happen to anybody. He was a pretty good
       businessman and stuff like that and—gee whiz—boy, I couldn't
       —well, I wouldn't want that to happen to me particularly. I
       don't think it would, but I'd sure hate to have that happen.
       That's kind of a dumb thing to say.

275   COUNSELOR: But it worries you some.

       JIM: Some. I don't worry about that every day, but it's a thing
       that crops up now and then like when I talk about this now. It
       just kind of enters my mind. Any other time it happens, I just
       try to pass it off—like—well, I'm so well aware of it, I don't
280   see how it could happen to me. Maybe—maybe that's how
       they go, but I'm just—I'm aware of it enough so that I don't
       really think there's any cause to worry really. Gosh, I don't
       know why I started on that one really. That's an eerie one. But
       that just enters my mind every now and then.

                          *   *   *

285   I just don't feel like talking about everything to my mother who
       —well, there's only one thing. I said this before. There's only
       one thing I won't talk about to my mother and that's my father.
       I wouldn't just sit down with her and talk about that. That
       I won't do. I don't think that's too good, but—I think I men-
290   tioned sex last time, too. (Chuckle) That's kind of a—well,
       I don't know—I don't know what's touchy about it really, but
       it just is for some reason. It's just something that you don't

know everything about and something that's kept kind of
shielded and—I don't know—that's something that I just kind
295 of keep to myself.

COUNSELOR: You're a little left out on information you—

JIM: (*Interrupting*) Oh, no. That's why I don't wonder
about anything. You see—you know—when I was about eleven
years old—well, I was pretty well educated by then. Just from
300 the kids, you know. I got some wrong things, of course, that I
found out later on when I was thirteen, let's say, and I—well,
I wouldn't care to compete with someone on what I know, but
—but I don't know everything. I'm not that experienced. That's
for darned sure. I mean I—there's nothing that's deep and
305 dark about it like there used to be. You know kids really talk
about things like that when they're little and that's how—well,
that, of course, and my father told me what was going on long
before I knew much about anything. He kind of judged the
right time to tell me, I think, but—and—I mean—there's not
310 a problem there, you know. There just never seemed to be.
Why I'm not going to get anyone in any trouble before I get
married and—well—I mean you shall honor womanhood and
—well, I kind of believe in that. A lot of the kids don't but—
well, I think there's just something about that that should be
315 upheld. Lots of things are out of place otherwise so I don't think
there's really any problem there. That's the way I feel and I've
got the right attitude toward the thing and so that's it.

COUNSELOR: You—

JIM: (*Interrupting*) Unless I'm wrong. I don't need a lecture
320 on sex. (*Chuckle*) Here I sit unloading, but—but I don't
know. If there's any big thing that I don't know about sex, I'd
like to know what it is because—well, I know what's going on
now. Boy, if I don't, why I really missed something somewhere
if there's something I don't know because, you know, boys get
325 together and talk and your parents talk about it and there's
dirty magazines and all sorts of things. You can learn a lot that
way—well, about sex because there's a lot of that flying around
and it's—well, I would say that there isn't a kid in—well, there
isn't a popular kid in junior high school who isn't pretty well
330 educated. One that runs around with a group. I'd—I'd venture
to say that. I'd venture to say that there isn't hardly any kids
anymore that—well, girls are a little slower to learn, I guess,

but boys are just that way. They get together and shoot the
bull and guess what happens and guess what I found out and
335   all that stuff. They pick it up. Course they—they get a lot of
wrong ideas but there's nothing deep and dark about it anymore.
And I'm in those groups. Now I'm going to say something that
may sound conceited, but I'm a fairly popular kid. Most people
like me. I get along with everybody. You can kind of feel
340   when some of the underclassmen are looking up at you. A lot
of that comes through athletics, of course. If you're pretty fair
in sports and—well, I'm pretty fair. Some of the littler guys
and some of the older guys, too, look up to you and you can
feel that. I don't let it—I don't let it affect me because I know
345   I look up to a lot of people. I try to be humble about it, of
course. It doesn't give me any feelings of conceit or that I'm
pretty good or anything like that. I've got a lot of room to
improve, but—but I get along with everybody. Well, of course,
I've got enemies, but who doesn't? Everybody knows me and
350   I make friends pretty easily—fairly easily. Now. I didn't used
to, but I do now. I can run around with about anybody I feel
like if I want to. But I pick out the people I want to run with
and I run with them. Oh, there's some guys, a lot of creeps,
that have—oh, they're just living from day to day. Lot of guys
355   like that—well, I don't even bother to talk to them because
they're so far out that we just don't run around together. I get
along with just about everybody, but those kind because I can't
see any point to what they're doing and the way they live. I
just can't. So we haven't got anything in common so why
360   should I run with them. They don't think the way I think and
I don't think the way they think. Why fool with them? Once
in a while, when you meet someone face to face and you know
he doesn't like me, that bothers me. That would bother anyone.
I just feel there's gonna be people like that all through my life
365   so—so what the heck? There's always going to be people you
don't agree with. I don't agree with them so that's just something that happens. (End of tape)

Third Interview

JIM: I enjoy learning something that I don't have to learn.
It's more something I'm doing because I want to. I have more
370   fun doing something I want to do rather than have a teacher
say—well, I don't mind high school a bit or school. But it's

something you're gonna do and you know you're gonna go.
It's not a personal decision. It's just something you do that
everyone does. You don't have your whole mind in it some-
375   times.

COUNSELOR: You'd rather do things you decide for yourself
to do than things you have to do.

JIM: If it's your own idea, you like to do it better. That's
how people are I guess. I'd just rather feel it was my idea
380   because then it's more fun. If it's not any fun, you got no one
to blame but yourself. I think that's why I'll enjoy college more
than high school. I enjoy high school mainly because of athletics and—oh, you know, you just get to see the kids and shoot
the bull and it's kind of a social club—for me, I study, too, but
385   it's more of a social function, you know. It's good fun—athletics
—I love those. You can do them after school and if you weren't
in school, you couldn't do those things. You're around all the
kids and I like that.

COUNSELOR: Being around a lot of people is something you
390   really—

JIM: (Interrupting) Sure. I like people I think. I don't know
if I can make a flat statement and say I like people because
sometimes I'd just rather be left alone. Sometimes—most of the
time—I'd rather be around a lot of people, but sometimes when
395   I'm—when I just want to think, then I'd rather be by myself.
But I guess I generally like people—that is, I guess I like
people more often than I don't like people.

COUNSELOR: Except when you feel you want to think.

JIM: Yeah. When I—well, when I'm in a poor mood or some-
400   thing like that, then I would rather be by myself. Then I sleep.
When I'm in a poor mood, then I'm tired. I just sleep. I can't
sleep when someone's making a lot of noise or fooling around
in my room or something like that. The same thing I can't—
no one can bring me out of a poor mood, I have to come out
405   of it by myself. So the only way to do it is to get off by yourself
and buck up. Well, like if there's nothing to do, if there's just
absolutely nothing to do and I can't find any kids to do anything
with, even just to talk to, then I get—oh, owly and grouchy
and then I just lay around and do nothing and get in a poor
410   mood and—oh, I don't know—just sort of bog down. I just

don't feel like doing anything. When I get bored, then I start
getting grouchy and I just have to be on the go all the time.
I don't know. When I'm home, I'm not really home very much
when there's a lot to do. Fly in and out the door and sleep at
415 home and that sort of stuff. There's something to do, I'll do it.
If there isn't, then I'll just lay around and do nothing.

COUNSELOR: Sometimes then you find it difficult to find something to do to occupy your time and your mind.

JIM: Uh-huh. Oh, I read and stuff like that, but when there
420 just isn't anything to do then I just do nothing, just lay
around. Then I get tired and I just get grouchy and sleep a lot.
I guess I just have to do something or nothing. I like to be busy.
I like to have some purpose. At least, something to think about
that I'm going to get done. Even like studying or something.
425 Something to look forward to. Then your mind's occupied.

COUNSELOR: You like things to do. You always want a feeling
of achievement.

JIM: Well, I don't know. I'm not sure that it's always a feeling
of having achieved anything, but maybe. I can feel good with-
430 out any achievement. Of course any achievement always makes
me feel good. It's just—it's just doing something. Just something to fill up my unoccupied time. Sports, now. Sports really
takes the sap out of you so that when you go home, you don't
—you don't have any extra energy to—to use except for study-
435 ing so you don't—don't feel bored at that. Like during the
summer, there isn't really anything to do—well, I mean, there
just isn't something to do every day—something that really
poops me out and makes me—well, you know. Aw, I go out in
the field and throw a ball around and fool around with tennis
440 and run a little bit and something like that and that kind of
helps. I mean I just gotta get tired because if I go to bed at
night without being tired, I just don't sleep. I'm so used to
being active—I don't know, I just don't get tired too easy.
When I don't get tired, I get bored and, if there's nothing to do,
445 I just get bored and kind of lazy. It's kind of hard to explain,
but if I don't have anything to do, why it just seems, What the
heck? I don't know. I feel—well, I don't do anything that I
don't want to do. Athletically and that doesn't leave out much.
But if there's a kind of game and I don't like to play, I just don't
450 play it. But if there's something I enjoy doing, I don't care if

there's anyone else who likes it, I just do it. The achievement I get out of it, I suppose is just the enjoyment of doing it. That's all. I don't play anything just to win. Oh, I play to win, but that isn't the only thing I play for. I play it for the 455 sake of the game as much as for winning. It's good training and it's good for you and it's just playing the game. That's as much fun as winning.

COUNSELOR: When you do something you consider worth while and you don't achieve—

460 JIM: (*Interrupting*) Oh, that. Sure, that bothers me. If I— if I do something it's with the idea of achieving something. I don't really do anything important without a purpose. I suppose there's some things, but not many. As far as if I want to do something, there has to be a purpose for it. If it's personal 465 satisfaction or anything, I don't care what it is. It has to have a purpose to it to be interesting and then when I fall short of the purpose—when I fall short of my goal or what I want done, then it seems sort of futile. If I don't get out of something what I think I should, then it seems kind of futile. If I decided 470 to do something or go into some profession or some field and found I was a miserable flop, why then that would bother me. I'd hate to go through college and train for something and find out I didn't like it or that I wasn't really so good at it after all, that would kind of bother me. Because then it'd seem kind of 475 worthless and I probably never would make a go of it and never be any good. So I better watch what I do and make sure I like it. I'd just as soon be successful as unsuccessful. (*Chuckle*)

COUNSELOR: Success is important to you.

JIM: I suppose I worry sometimes about being successful. 480 That's one of those things—you either make or break. You shoot for something, some goal or something, and you don't make it, you're disappointed. If you don't shoot for anything, I suppose you can't really be disappointed when you don't make it. I'm going to try for something. It's survival of the 485 fittest, I guess. You aren't going to get something for nothing so you have to put something into it. I'd hate to think that I had gone through college and didn't get something out of it. Well, like I said, I don't do anything for no reason at all. If going to college is a means to an end and I have to do it, I'll 490 do it. I like learning.

COUNSELOR: You sometimes experience the big build-up for the big let-down sort of thing.

JIM: Oh, yeah. I'm glad you thought of that because that's the most discouraging thing. Well, especially during sports this
495 year. Sometimes I'd just feel I was going to have a great day, you know. But then I knew that, since I felt so good, I might not and probably would not. I'd know both sides of this thing and not know what was going to happen. I'd just have a feeling that something was either going to go right or go wrong
500 and—sure enough, if I'd feel great, I just wouldn't meet my expectations. Sometimes when I'd feel poor and I'd know this just wasn't my day, I'd uncork a good performance. But I can never get away from these feelings that I'm either going to make it or I'm not going to make it. I always kind of know
505 whether I'm going to do well or not. I don't know what it is, but I just never know. I wish I could tell if I were going to have a good day. I think most of my trouble—in individual events is that—well, it must be psychological. I can warm up and do everything just right, I think, and then have a poor day
510 —just don't do a thing. I can come out and think this is just going to be a normal day, I'm not going to do any better or any worse than usual and just—well, when I'm not expecting something great or anything out of the ordinary, then anything over my expectations is pretty good. But I just hate to feel that
515 I'm going to have a good day or a bad day or something's going to happen one way or another. It's just going to happen and I know that. I just wish I wasn't going to have a feeling as to which one was going to happen sometimes. I'd hate to come out with a defeatist attitude or something like that. I'd hate to
520 be a fatalist, too. It's just kind of hard to explain.

COUNSELOR: This carries over into other things.

JIM: Oh, sure. Well, I'm not exactly the smartest person in the world. In some of my classes, I kind of felt that I was going to be kind of snowed. I just knew I was. Knowing myself
525 and knowing how smart some people are 'cause I see it all the time. Well, there's a girl in one of my classes and she's just nothing but smart—just psychic. Way and above my capabilities. She's just plain smart, that's all. I thought, my gosh, I'm going to goof this whole thing up. Then I got in there and
530 found it wasn't as difficult as I thought. It's no harder for me than for her and I'm no smarter or dumber than she is. That's

another time when my feeling was wrong so I don't know. It's revolting, that's what it is. Just disgusting. I guess I wish I could set my mind to doing something and then just be able to
535   do it. But it doesn't seem to work out that way. So I suppose that's why I figure it's just going to happen one way or the other regardless. I guess that's the way I think about some things. Something's going to happen one way and no matter what I do, it's going to turn out one way or the other.

540   COUNSELOR: You feel you may not have any control over it after all.

JIM: Yeah. That makes me a fatalist, I guess, and you're not supposed to be that way, but it happens every time. You either got it or you don't some days, I guess. That's the way I feel—
545   that's the way I think. I suppose I shouldn't, but it just seems that I can't—well, I must not be a great champion or something. When they want to do something, they just fire up and do it, but I don't know—it's beyond me sometimes. Sometimes I can control what is going to happen but—I must be a fatalist.

After the fourth interview, Jim thanked the counselor and said, "I've straightened out a lot of things for myself explaining them to you." Jim decided that he would see the counselor again if "things don't go well."

LAURA

Laura, a high school sophomore, made an appointment to see the counselor. She hesitated before she opened the door and then walked in quickly. She sat down carefully and straightened her skirt. She wore a pastel-colored skirt and blouse and very little make-up. She was about five feet five inches in height and weighed about 130 pounds. Her hair was cut short and curled at the ends. She appeared calm, but sat rubbing her hands together and, as the interview began, she looked at her hands, not at the counselor. The interview, which is the first of three, starts at the beginning.

COUNSELOR: Laura, you can talk about anything you wish.

LAURA: Well, suppose I start with my family. I have two sisters and one of them is married and the other one is a year younger than I am. My sister that's just a little younger, we're
5 really very close. We're—lots of people mistake us for twins, but we really don't look alike, I think. Anyway we have fun wearing the same type of clothes. She resembles my dad's relations and I resemble my mother's. Actually I can't see a bit of resemblance there (*laugh*) and neither can my folks. We
10 don't really look alike at all. (*Slight pause*) I'm a sophomore. I think the sophomore class is the nicest one here, 'cause it seems that there's always in most of the classes girls especially who are stuck-up or think they're better than others. Our class isn't like that. As far as I'm concerned it's one of the nicest
15 classes.

COUNSELOR: You like school.

LAURA: Oh, yes. I've—we've got—our class ranges from quite intelligent people and then we've got some who are really good mentally and then some who are pretty low. We've got quite a
20 range, a lot of different people, all sorts. But—the only thing I don't—well, one of the prejudices I have against my classmates is that some of the boys just ride the breeze and they don't care and they just—half the time they don't have their assignments done and, as far as I'm concerned, that's what
25 lowers the standards of the school. If everyone would study harder, our assignments would probably be harder and that way I think we'd probably get a better education, but it's a good high school and I like it here. I live outside the city and I like it. I'd rather live there than in the city. Most of the people in
30 my class—well, I have a couple of girl friends who used to live outside, but they live in the city now—they think they have more fun living in town, but as far as I'm concerned, I think it seems like you're more free if you live outside and there's lots more you can do. It just seems like when you live in town, you
35 get kind of lazy and—well, it seems you have more of a character. You can do more things if you live outside. I know I have a girl friend who—all she ever does is wash the dishes. Her mother cleans up everything and slaves after her. Well, my mother always—she makes us iron all our own clothes and I
40 help with the washing except during school, of course. We

have to keep up the house while Mother and Dad work and my
sister and I have to keep the house clean and—I forgot to tell
you, I've got a little brother too. My youngest sister was nine
when he was born and everybody spoiled him. He's really cute
45   and he's not so spoiled now as he used to be. When he was
born, we were always around his baby bed 'cause we thought
that was really something. Before he was born I was—well, I
know when my mother first told me, I was—I didn't really like
it too well. I felt that it was rather odd that we'd have another
50   baby in the family—just so many years. But after we got him
home I think—I think he's been the center of attention all the
time. We're quite a close family. (Pause) I have several hob-
bies. I like to play the piano. I'm not real good at it, but I like
to play the piano. In all my spare time, that's usually what I'm
55   doing. I know, right after dinner, first thing I do when my
mother and father are still at the table is to go bang at the piano
awhile. I know when I feel just—well, sometimes when I've got
so many things to do and I know I'll just never get them done
—if I go in and play the piano, it just seems to relax me.
60   People who don't play the piano sometimes just can't understand why or what it can do for you. They just can't see how
music—well, how music just seems to sort of reach your nerves.
It just relaxes me. And I like to sew. I sew most of my own
clothes and a lot of times I like to sew without a pattern and
65   design them myself. My mother—I guess I got that skill from
my mother. My mother makes—before we were able to sew, my
mother made all our clothes. She never uses a pattern. She just
takes a piece of material and folds it and she will cut it and
it'll fit. I don't know how she does it, but it'll fit. But I always
70   have to draw my patterns on paper before. But I like to sew
and I'm now beginning to collect stamps and write to other
stamp collectors.

COUNSELOR: You mentioned you have so many things to do
and then when you play the piano it relaxes you.

75   LAURA: Well, I used to be president of our youth group in
church, but I'm not any more. But it just seemed to take so
much time and it's really just a small group and then there are
a lot fewer to do all the work because there are so many who
just think they can't do it and are not willing to help and think
80   someone else should do it. So many times it's just the better—
the ones they think are the better—people are just doing the

same things over and over and, oh, it just took so much time. And in school, I'm in almost every extracurricular activity. It really takes a lot of time.

85   COUNSELOR: You like to keep busy though.

LAURA: Yes, it just seems that, if I don't, I feel so useless I just have to do something. I know in the summertime sometimes if I just sit around the house and don't have anything to do, then I just have to do something so I eat. Or else if I really
90   don't have anything else to do I'll watch television, but I don't really care for television. As far as I'm concerned, I wouldn't care if it went on the blink or something because I hardly ever watch it. I just have to have something to do or else I feel— I don't know, it just bothers me. I'm in girls' chorus and mixed
95   chorus. I've been working on the yearbook. I'm not in the band, but I'm usually the accompanist for the trios and that sort of thing. And—I can't think right now—whenever there's something to do usually somebody asks me to do it. Typing or something like that. It seems that every hour of the day is filled
100   with doing something and yet I don't mind it. Oh, at times I wonder now why did I ever get into this. I know I knew biology was going to be quite hard because I have more ability in other subjects than in sciences—they're my low points—but I wanted to take it to improve my sciences and then I didn't
105   want to pass up geometry and I had to take history and English and I wanted to take typing. So when I knew I was going to take five subjects I told myself that this year I'm not going to play the piano for everything. I told myself that I wasn't going to, but they ask me and I do. And that's the way it goes. I
110   always tell myself I'm not going to get into this and I'm not going to get into that, but I end up being in everything anyway.

COUNSELOR: You regret it after you do it.

LAURA: Not usually. Oh, occasionally at times, when I have so many things to do, then I'll think—oh, if I'd stuck to what
115   I was going to do then I wouldn't be in this—but then I don't regret it—there are very few times. I usually just—I still have time to sew or read or play the piano. I play it by ear. I didn't recognize that ability until—well, I took piano lessons for five years and then I stopped when I started going to high school
120   and then I was—I went to camp one year and there was this girl who could just play the piano beautifully and they'd just

mention a song or a chorus and just like that she'd know how
to play it. I thought that was just magnificent and I wished I
could do it. I tried it and found out that I could do it, too,
125   that I could play by ear. Now if we need a song or a chorus
in our youth meetings, why I don't need a book, I can just play
it by ear. Sometimes it'll take me awhile to figure out the keys
and things and I have to play it over a couple of times, but
usually when I play it over, then I can remember it. I know
130   when I listen to the radio and hear a popular song, I can't play
all of them—that's certain—but if I like one real well—I have
to know it, of course—I have to know exactly how it goes—why
then I can sit down and usually play it on the piano. One thing
I don't like to do is to play the same piece over and over. Then
135   I'll usually play one song once and then I'll play out of a certain hymn book and then I'll put it away and play out of some
different ones so I don't get tired of the same songs and so I'll
continue to like them.

COUNSELOR: You like variety.

140   LAURA: Yes. It seems to get monotonous if the same things
happen over and over. (*Pause*) Like I certainly want to go to
college. I was—when I was little, I always wanted to be a
nurse. I know I could never be a nurse because even the sight
of blood really makes me sick. I know—I went to the show a
145   couple of weeks ago and in this one scene, a girl got slapped in
the face and the blood started running down her face and it
just made me sick. I couldn't watch it. I just could never stand
the sight of blood. So when I got to high school, I really took
an interest in freshman algebra. Ever since then, I've really
150   been interested in math. In grade school, I never did care much
for arithmetic. I didn't like it very well. But I really like math.
I like geometry. I really enjoy it and I think when I go to
college that's what I'll be majoring in—math. I'm not certain
what I'm going to do. In a way I'd like to be a math teacher in
155   a high school and yet in another way I think I'd like to be a
mathematician who works in a—an aeronautical agency, for
instance, and with rocket propulsion and things like that. Trying to figure out how to make better and faster airplanes, I
think I'd find that real fascinating. Perhaps I'd work for a
160   government agency of some sort, down at Cape Kennedy, for
example. I have my highest ability in math of anything as far
as I know from all the tests we've taken in school. And it is

my favorite subject although really—well, I don't—as far as all the subjects are concerned—really I don't have any one favorite.
165 I like English and biology real well, but yet as far as all the years are stretched out I guess I've liked math more consistently than all the others, but—well, I suppose I'll be majoring in math, but what I'm going to do, I'm not very certain. Naturally I want to go to college. I think my mother has a great deal to
170 do with my—I mean—ever since I was in grade school—ever since I was real little, I know one of my main goals was that when I got to high school, I was going to be on the honor roll and so I worked and I got there. She's always—I come home with a stack of books that high—encyclopedias and all kinds of
175 reference books. I usually have every book in my desk home every night. When I was studying for a test, for a week before the test every night I'd have my desk completely cleaned out. And I'd come home and say, "Oh, my gosh, I've got a lot to do tonight" and she'd say that all I had to do was the dishes and
180 she'd clean up the house and Helen and I could sit down and do our schoolwork. I know a lot of parents wouldn't do that.

COUNSELOR: You admire your mother.

LAURA: (*Long pause*)

COUNSELOR: You and your sister do a lot of things together.

185 LAURA: Yes, now. She's more of a tomboy than I am. I know she's—I know when we were little—well, we fought a lot. We weren't close like we are now. I know we'd fight and we'd always be in scrapes and Mom was always spanking us and everything. But it wasn't until my older sister got married and
190 everything that we got close like sisters. Like we are now. Oh, we've got different views on certain subjects. I know she doesn't care about schoolwork the way I do, but—(*pause*)—she's got a marvellous sense of humor and she's always making me laugh. Oh, she's just that way and we have a lot of fun. Whenever we
195 do the dishes, it takes so long. She'll start talking about something and then she'll get a real stupid mood and then she'll make me laugh and laugh and laugh. We really have a good time together. Whenever we—well, we always double-date with our boy friends. They just—well, I guess everybody knows
200 it because when I go out with different people, it seems the boys always get together anyway 'cause they just know that—well, it's just a habit—really. Go together—(*pause*) Oh, I was

wondering, I was going to ask you—well, it seems to me—well,
it really isn't anything—exaggerated or anything—but it seems
205   that my parents seem to be favoring me rather than Helen.
I was wondering if there's anything I can do about that.

COUNSELOR: Your parents favor you more.

LAURA: Well, if we'd come home late, after 10:00 or 10:30
or whenever my mother told us to come home—if we'd be just
210   a few minutes late—why it seems she'd scold Helen more than
I although I'm a year older. Just a few minutes late and she'd
always ask her where we were or what took us so long or something. It just seems like—oh, I don't know—it just—it's just in
little things it seems like—it's not in anything big. I know it's
215   slightly noticeable and I know Helen just—well, it's noticeable
if we have little scrapes or something, she'll say something about
it, that I'm my mother's pet.

COUNSELOR: You'd like to understand why this is.

LAURA: Oh, yes. (*Pause*) I guess it's because I get higher
220   grades in school and I'm—I'm assocated with more people and
—oh, I don't know. I don't know what it is. It seems Helen's
more of a tomboy and more or less mischievous and she'll poke
fun at things. It seems—well, sometimes it'll just bother my
folks. Just little things.

225   COUNSELOR: You'd rather have it different.

LAURA: Oh, yes. (*Pause*) I know—well, occasionally—well,
there's a hang-out in town. It's—it's where some of the kids
hang out—a lot of them in fact. I don't care much for it myself.
I have been in there real seldom because—well, there's nothing
230   in there for me, just sitting there and the kids smoke—it's not
my crowd and they drive like crazy. Well, Helen has a girl
friend—(*sob in voice*)—she's kind of—well, she's a nice kid,
but you know they run with that crowd. Helen doesn't want to
be different and so she'll go along. Mom and Daddy don't want
235   her to go in there, but she will anyway. (*Sob*) One time they
found out about it and they scolded her terribly. Then I went
in there once, too, and she came in there. I was in there with
a girl friend. Just went in there to visit some kids who were
there. Helen came in and she looked at me kind of funny and
240   asked, "Do you know where you are or did you fall on your
head or something or do you know where you're at?" And—it

just seemed like—oh, it just—oh, as far as I'm concerned, I'm certainly not any better than she is. Oh, it just seems like—it just seems like—oh, if Helen—well, we always both bring
245 schoolwork home, but it seems I always have more than she does. Then my mother'll make her do something while she lets me do my schoolwork. Things like that. (*Sobbing*) I'm concerned I think because my mother starts criticizing her—(*sob*) because her boy friend is from that crowd and my boy friend
250 is like us—(*sob*) and my married sister is married to an Italian and they have so many problems and—he won't go to church with her and she won't go to church with him and then they stay home and—(*sob*) it bothers my mother terribly. (*Pause for crying*) I'm sorry, I didn't mean to cry.

255 COUNSELOR: Go right ahead.

LAURA: (*Sobbing*) You see, my older sister had to get married and I guess—it was after that that—well, my folks are—religion means a great deal to them. We're quite a religious family. They just couldn't understand how she could do something like
260 that. Her boy friend got drunk and—but still they just—they took it nice and—Mother took it just terrible, but she helped and all. They moved away, but Mother went over there and helped. Getting the house ready and all. But I know the difference in background and religion makes a great—means a
265 great deal—poses a great problem. I guess that's why she's afraid—well, if Helen and I go—well, we'll have—Helen's been going steady for over a year now and she's afraid she'll always go with him and—well, they'll get the same kind of problems and all. (*Sobbing*)

270 COUNSELOR: Does the situation with your older sister worry you?

LAURA: Yes, dreadfully. (*Sobbing*) Perhaps more than anyone else I know. I know I just—I didn't go with a boy at all until just recently. I just couldn't relax myself. I just had a
275 great deal of trouble forgetting. I know it wasn't her fault really, but—I tried and tried—I suppose I've forgiven her now —but it's—it's the forgetting part that's so hard. I thought I'd forgotten and then—it was just a few months ago, I was going with this boy and—from a different town and he came down—
280 he brought some friends down—and he saw my girl friend and wanted to give her a ride home—a whole bunch came down

and gave a program at our church. And then we had lunch and this one guy who was a friend of my boy friend—wanted my girl friend to come along and we'd just go driving around
285 for a while. She said she would and she didn't—and, well, the next day in school she told an untruth to this girl friend of mine and she made a big story about it—and she said that she was afraid to go with boys and things like that and it got back to my girl friend and she called me up that night. Then—then
290 she blamed it all on me—I didn't know what to say. (*Sobbing*) Then just before she hung up, she said, "Just don't forget that when Barbara had to get married, I stuck up for her." (*Long pause for crying*)

COUNSELOR: You find it coming back more than just this one
295 time.

LAURA: I don't know really. It seems just that—well, I know when my sister had to get married—shortly afterwards in her class, there were five other girls who had to get married and they got married in a radius of four months just after Barbara
300 did. It seems like whenever anyone would discuss it—well, it seems like—well, it was a popular topic of conversation—why, it just used to—it used to bother me terribly. Every time something like that comes up, it is always what I think of— (*sobbing*) and I wish I could get it out of my system, but I just
305 can't.

COUNSELOR: You're afraid your sister is going the same way.

LAURA: Oh, no, never. I know Helen'd never do anything like that. (*Pause*) I know shortly after Barbara did get married and I wasn't going with anyone, then Helen was going with
310 Tom, seeing him occasionally. Then Mother'd say to her, "You'd better be careful. You'll get into the same kind of trouble Barbara did." It just seems that there'll be certain things that just keep bringing it back. (*Sobbing*) My mother—she's such a big person and it seems a terrible thing to be done to a mother
315 who tried so hard to raise her daughters in the proper way.

COUNSELOR: Boys make you uneasy now.

LAURA: Well, it all depends. Like I know when they start telling dirty stories or something like that, then I feel real out of place. I enjoy someone with a sense of humor more than
320 anyone else and if they don't have a sense of humor, they don't

appeal to me much. Yes, I think I feel at ease, more or less, but as soon as—well, like as if—well, this one boy I went out with—I just went out with him once—oh, he wasn't much fun and he wasn't of any decent character or anything like that—
325   that was about the only time I really ever felt ill at ease with a boy. (*Pause*) I really feel better about it already. It's probably just because I kept everything wrapped up inside of me for so long. (*Loud sob*) I don't think it really bothers Helen much. But I know my mother's much more strict about the hours we
330   come in than she was when Barbara went out with boys and things like that. She's much more strict with us. She always has to know what—who we're with and all that, what we did, what we're going to do. Occasionally she won't let us go certain places. But whenever my girl friends start talking about things
335   like girls having to get married or some of the things they do, it always seems to me that they are sort of referring back to Barbara. I don't think they really are, but that's just what I think when they say it.

PAUL

Paul, an eighth-grader, was sent to the counselor because of failing grades, disruptive classroom behavior, and frequent fist-fights with fellow students. Paul is small for his age, frail-appearing, and speaks in a high-pitched, flat, expressionless voice. The excerpt is from the fourth in a series of interviews. During the first three, Paul has discussed cars and only cars. One or two attempts by the counselor to relate statements about cars to Paul as a person have produced silence. At the beginning of the second interview, Paul showed the counselor a drawing of a car titled the "Terror" and equipped with guns, rockets, spiders, and "an evil eye." Each time Paul has brought the counselor a drawing of a car and progressively throughout the series the car begins more closely to resemble an ordinary model. When Paul enters for the fourth interview, the counselor notes a change in his appearance. Paul is wearing a clean shirt, his hands are not grimy, and his long, shaggy hair is now in short crew-cut. The boy again begins to talk about cars and his technical knowledge is extensive. After about twenty minutes, the interview takes a different turn. The excerpt contains the last forty minutes of the counseling session.

COUNSELOR: You'd like to know more about cars.

PAUL: Soon as I get out of school I want to go to General Motors Elect—Elect—Mechanical Engineering School. My chances for that aren't too good now. My grades—my grades 5 are not too good. (*Pause*) That school teaches people all about cars and you can get a high paying job when you finish. It's all mechanical work. Those are the books I don't mind reading.

COUNSELOR: You like to read those.

PAUL: Uh-huh.

10   COUNSELOR: Much better than school.

PAUL: Yeah. (*Pause*)

COUNSELOR: What have you been doing about cars recently?

PAUL: Well, we started sort of a club to go flying around with them. We elected a president. He's got sort of a place we can 15 have the meetings. Haven't had any. He just got out of jail last night. He was running around with some guys he works with and they run him in. He was in the car with them and they was drunk. He had to go on trial for cutting holes in car tops. But the club won't last long. Oh, it might. We've just got 20 eight members. If we could get about four more, it might be something. But now we can't even get a chance to join.

COUNSELOR: Takes twelve?

PAUL: Takes more than what we got. We've got three for a club project. It's our '52 sedan—(*Paul plunges back into a* 25 *discussion of cars, comparing them and using much technical terminology. He again voices the belief that the club will end in fighting and will get nowhere.*)

COUNSELOR: You spend most of your spare time on cars.

PAUL: Yup.

30   COUNSELOR: Not much else you do?

PAUL: Nope.

COUNSELOR: This gets you into trouble once in a while.

PAUL: Yeah. With my mother. My big brother, he doesn't care too much about it, but he doesn't like it too much either.

35 COUNSELOR: Your mother's afraid—

PAUL: I might get pinned under a drive-shaft or something. That ain't very likely to happen. When she brings it up, I just walk out. She gets mad. (*Pause*)

COUNSELOR: This bothers you.

40 PAUL: Yeah. It bothers me when she gets mad. But there's nothing else to do. (*Pause*) I just walk away. (*Pause*)

COUNSELOR: But then there's the problem of coming back.

PAUL: Yeah. (*Pause*) It don't happen too often. Just happens when I get in a car and she finds out. She gets all nervous.
45 (*Pause*)

COUNSELOR: You can't understand why she doesn't like cars.

PAUL: Well, she never did especially like them. (*Pause*) A few years ago, my father was teaching her to drive. She was doing all right. Then he put his foot over and pushed the
50 accelerator down and she yelled and wouldn't let go of the steering wheel and she ditched it. She don't like cars since then. (*Pause*)

COUNSELOR: Kind of annoys you that she doesn't like them.

PAUL: Yeah. (*Pause*)

55 COUNSELOR: Your father like cars?

PAUL: Uh-huh. He always helped my brother Luke with his. He and Luke always worked on our cars. He helped get the Ford running and helped get the Pontiac running and he worked a lot with Luke on the Caddy, too.

60 COUNSELOR: He never had time for you.

PAUL: Oh—he always had time enough. (*Pause*) I never did enjoy my father much. I never did get along with him.

COUNSELOR: Lot of trouble.

PAUL: Yeah. All the time.

65   COUNSELOR: Care to tell me about it?

PAUL: Nothing to tell. He'd get drunk all the time and come home and beat up on Mom and we had to throw him out. It upset me when he picked on Mom like that. (*Pause*) He's been gone a while now. I'm scared he's going to come back.

70   COUNSELOR: You don't know what to expect.

PAUL: Yeah, and it worries me. If he gets married I might have to go live with him. (*Pause*) If I get into any more trouble, I'll have to go up and live with them. (*Pause*) But they couldn't keep me very long with them up there. I'd just
75   light out and be gone.

COUNSELOR: You dislike him.

PAUL: I hate him. (*Pause*)

COUNSELOR: And you're afraid you'll have to go to him.

PAUL: Yeah. (*Sob in voice*) Then I wouldn't have any fun.
80   (*Pause*)

COUNSELOR: He's made things unhappy for you.

PAUL: Yeah. (*Pause*) And then when we don't hear from him, we figure he's probably on his way back up here. It's awful not hearing. He might come.

85   COUNSELOR: And take you back with him.

PAUL: He wouldn't want me, but if Mother sent me, he'd take me and I'd have to go. (*Pause*) He never helped any of us kids anyway. (*Pause*) Then Mom gets mad. My brother Harry, she gets pretty mad at him, too. She's threatened to put
90   him into a home or a school if he don't behave. Neither of us can talk to her. She threatened to put us both in reform school last year. But she ain't done nothing yet. (*Pause*)

COUNSELOR: You'd like your mother to think highly of you.

PAUL: Yes. (*Pause*) But that will never be.

95   COUNSELOR: Never be?

PAUL: No. I got nothing to be proud of. (*Pause*) I ain't done nothing to be proud of. (*Pause*) Maybe someday I'll think of something to do to be proud of and then maybe I'll do it. Or make someone else do it.

100   COUNSELOR: You'd like your mother to approve of the things you do.

PAUL: Yeah. I'd like to have her approve of cars.

COUNSELOR: It hurts you that she doesn't.

PAUL: Yeah. I've wanted a car since I was ten years old. She
105 tells me I should wait till I'm old enough to own one myself.
(*Pause*)

COUNSELOR: That causes you to get angry with her.

PAUL: That's something I don't do. I've never got mad at her
yet. I just leave. She treats us real nice.

110 COUNSELOR: If she'd just understand cars.

PAUL: Yeah. (*Pause*)

COUNSELOR: She just doesn't understand you.

PAUL: Hardly nobody does except my brother Harry. We
got our squabbles, but I don't know what I'd do without him.
115 I think plenty of him.

COUNSELOR: He's a good friend.

PAUL: Yeah. He hits me once in a while. He tries hard.

COUNSELOR: Nobody else seems to understand.

PAUL: Mostly. Not so bad when I'm working on cars.

120 COUNSELOR: But you just can't seem to please anybody, no
matter how hard you try.

PAUL: Yeah. (*Paul hits the microphone—sound of choked-off
sobs.*) Most everything I do causes trouble. Even set up a little
shop. Then I found out the kids were sharpening their knives
125 there and making brass knuckles. (*Pause*)

COUNSELOR: Nothing you do turns out any good.

PAUL: That's the way it is. (*Pause*)

COUNSELOR: You like to do something that—

PAUL: Would just please someone sometime. (*Pause. Violent
130 tapping of microphone*) Just once. Oh, it doesn't bother me
too much. Just once in a while. (*Pause*)

COUNSELOR: More than anything you'd probably rather have your mother understand you.

PAUL: Yeah. But more than anything I'd rather have a car.
135 (*Pause and much tapping of mike*)

COUNSELOR: There's no way you see of getting one at present.

PAUL: Oh, I could probably get one if I bothered my mother enough. Probably get it if I went up and lived with my father. But that would be worse than anything else.

140 COUNSELOR: It isn't that important.

PAUL: I'd rather be with my mother than have a car.

COUNSELOR: You really hate your father.

PAUL: When he was beating my mother up, I was thinking of how I'd kill him. (*Pause*) When I'm mad I don't know what
145 I do or what I think. That's why I don't like to get mad.

COUNSELOR: It scares you.

PAUL: A lot. I got mad at a kid yesterday and I hit him. First time I've hit anybody in a long time.

COUNSELOR: You're afraid you'll do something.

150 PAUL: Yes. Whenever someone does something and I get real mad.

COUNSELOR: Just like with your father.

PAUL: Yeah.

COUNSELOR: Just the thought of it scares you.

155 PAUL: Yeah.

COUNSELOR: Even to the point where you hope your father won't return so it won't come true.

PAUL: Yeah. (*Pause*) It scares me a lot. I never mentioned it before. (*Pause*) Since he's been gone, she's a lot happier.
160 She's got a lot of new friends and all. (*Pause*) Dad never treated me too bad. The worst he ever treated me was when I got in trouble. Then he said he didn't care what I did. He said he didn't care. I could just do what I wanted and maybe someday I'd end up in a reformatory. Then our house would

165   be a better place to live in. (*Pause*) He's got into trouble
plenty of times himself and Ma's got him out of it. (*Pause*)
He said he'd never claim me.

COUNSELOR: This hurt.

PAUL: Not too much. I've never claimed him so I don't see
170   why he should claim me. (*Violent tapping of microphone*)

COUNSELOR: And you're afraid sometime you might like to get
even with him.

PAUL: Yeah. I'd like to get even with him for a lot of stuff. He
can be really nice sometimes, but sometimes he can be real hate-
175   ful. Most of the times he's hateful. The only time he's nice to us
kids is when he's drunk and then he hits Mom. (*Pause*) Mostly
it's trouble. (*Pause*) When I was eight years old, I started
around with the wrong crowd. That's the first time I got in
trouble. With the law and all. I haven't got into any serious
180   trouble since except for the brass knuckles. That wasn't my fault.

COUNSELOR: The only way you can get away from all these
feelings is to go into cars.

PAUL: Yup. I like cars with power and speed. (*Pause*) But
power and speed's not all. I like them with a nice body. Lots
185   of cars got power and speed, but they look like old junk.
(*Pause*) But it frightens me quite a bit. I don't fear nothing
I could do to my mother 'cause I know I couldn't do nothing.
I couldn't hurt her. (*Pause*) I've always liked her.

COUNSELOR: She's always been the one who's understood you.

190   PAUL: Except about cars. When I was working with bicycles,
she thought that was pretty good. I started making them myself.
Just junk parts. I'd put them together and ride them around.
But then, too, she was scared they'd fall apart in the middle of
the street or something and I'd get myself killed. But nothing
195   ever happened. One I built I had wrecked in two weeks. I just
tore it apart and sold it to another junker.

COUNSELOR: She didn't approve of that.

PAUL: No. (*Pause*) I liked to make my own though. Then
I knew what to expect. A new one, someone might miss on
200   putting it together and it might be even more dangerous.
Bicycles she didn't mind so much. When I started running

around with guys—some of my friends got cars. Pete and some of them. We used to take Pete's car out in our backyard and work on it. She didn't like that. (*Pause*) Well, she said if we

205   owned a bigger place I could have one, but she keeps saying that and I think we got plenty of room out where we live. I just think she don't like them.

COUNSELOR: This hurts you because you want to please her and work on cars, too.

210   PAUL: I want to prove to her one of these days that I know enough about them not to get hurt. But she won't understand. I just can't get her to see it. (*Pause*) I'd give anything to have her understand. (*Taps tape recorder*) I wonder how many parts one of these has got.

215   COUNSELOR: I don't know.

PAUL: (*More expression in the voice from here to the end*) How come there's a big reel and a small reel and it goes so slow? Usually on a car you put a smaller wheel on the front and a bigger one on the back to get more speed, but maybe that

220   doesn't apply to this machine. (*Pause*)

COUNSELOR: Harry understands you better than your mother.

PAUL: Yeah. (*Pause*) He's different than me. He runs a motorcycle in a race. And that's even more dangerous than working with cars. He's had one accident already. He was on

225   a road and he had tires with big spikes coming through. One of the spikes broke off and he slid. It didn't hurt him much cause he sort of slid the bike over. (*Pause*) She doesn't know about it. (*Laugh*) Well, Harry and I—he does something and he doesn't want her to know about it and he's gotta tell some-

230   one, he tells me. I do something and I gotta tell someone, and I don't want Ma to find out about it, I tell him. (*Pause*) I want something to mess with. Bicycles are for squirrels.

COUNSELOR: They're for juveniles.

PAUL: Just for younger kids. I don't like to work on them
235   anymore.

COUNSELOR: It doesn't excite you.

PAUL: Naw. I think the reason Ma doesn't understand cars is she always rides in the back seat of them and she gets car-

240 sick and I got it from her. I like cars a lot, but whenever I'm
riding in the back seat of one and not going too fast—but not
slow—I get carsick. But then she likes some cars. She
likes Bill's car—at least she goes riding a lot in it. That's the
one I'd like to get hold of. It's a nice one. (*Pause*) He's a guy
she's known for a long time. He's a few years younger than she
245 is. She's known him now for about six years. (*Pause*) Ever
since my mother divorced my father, he's been trying to blame
it on him that he—that Bill broke them up. But he should—
he knows it quite well that he did it himself. All the things he
did. (*Pause*) That's about three years ago now. Be three years
250 in May.

COUNSELOR: You like Bill.

PAUL: Quite a bit. I wouldn't mind if Mother married him.
He's got money and he knows a lot about cars and he's interested
in them.

255 COUNSELOR: He talks to you about them.

PAUL: Sometimes when he takes Mom home, we sit up till
even two o'clock talking. He's got his own car and he's fixed
it all up. He's a plumber though. (*Pause*) But he knows more
about everything else than he does about plumbing. He's an
260 all-purpose guy mostly. He can help with a car and he can do
a lot of things. We didn't have any light in the kitchen so he
fixed the light switch. And he fixed the one in the bathroom.
And he fixed the roof once.

COUNSELOR: He shows a lot of concern for you.

265 PAUL: Yeah. (*Pause*)

COUNSELOR: Getting kind of tired, Paul?

PAUL: Yeah. We've talked about a lot of things. (*Pause*)
I stayed up and watched the wrestling matches last night. I
like the Crusher. Last night he fought some guy from Texas.
270 Some big guy. He's a real nice guy, the Crusher. He just
picked up this guy and set him outside the ring. He didn't hurt
him until the kid started fighting dirty. Then he just grabbed
ahold of him around the waist and the kid fainted. That's why
he's called the Crusher. He's a real nice guy. He said after he
275 fought him that he didn't want to hurt him, but when he started
playing dirty, he couldn't help it.

COUNSELOR: You like to see the Crusher win.

PAUL: Yeah. I like him.

COUNSELOR: Paul, I didn't say anything before, but I like your
280   haircut.

PAUL: (*Laugh*) I don't. I freeze. (Pause) I'm glad somebody
likes it. Aw, I like it all right, but everyone calls me Yul or
Baldy. I can't stand that.

COUNSELOR: That'll stop soon. Well, maybe we'd better stop
285   for today. Would you like to talk with me again?

PAUL: Yes, I would.

THE GROUP

The protocol covers the evaluation session of a group of five
senior high school girls who had been meeting with the counselor
for many weeks. Group membership was voluntary and the
meetings had continued at the request of the participants. This
meeting was not a counseling session, but a discussion during
which the girls tried to examine the group experience and put
into words what it meant to them and what they derived from it.

All five girls are above-average students and frequent par-
ticipators in school and outside activities. The counselor felt that
this group of volunteers was representative of those students who
seldom are sent and tend to be reluctant to bother the counselor.
The girls said that they had four reasons for joining the group:
they wanted to understand themselves and others; they wanted
to work on common problems; they thought "it would be a relief"
to talk with others of their own age; and they believed it would
be a new and different experience.

At the first session, the girls made a list of the problems
they wanted to discuss. This included teachers, pressure for
grades, homework, scholarships, friendship patterns, number of
outside activities, student government, parents, dating, relations
with siblings, values and value conflicts, getting along in social
and school groups, cliques, school spirit, occupations, popularity,

and personality. Of these, the girls discussed parents, dating, cliques, and values at considerable length. Friendship patterns, outside activities, and siblings also received a good deal of attention. Other items on the list were either not mentioned or merely touched on in connection with the seven major topics.

Throughout the series of interviews, the girls were free to discuss whatever was important to them. The evaluation, on the other hand, is a structured interview in which the counselor suggests the topics to be covered—allowing, of course, complete freedom within that structure. As the counselor explained to the girls, this interview "meets my desire to have your evaluation of your experiences." The interview starts with the girls studying their original list of topics and commenting on them. The following excerpt picks up at the point where the girls are finishing their study of the list and turning to general evaluation.

BETTY: I've been thinking about some of that stuff and I think counseling sort of helps you to realize that the problems exist, but you can just sort of overcome them. That list covers so much.

5   CONNIE: I'm in a good mood today so I feel I have fewer problems.

DOT: All that stuff seems to—I don't know—hit home.

BETTY: Somebody shouldn't think we come in here and we overcome a lot of problems and we go walking out of here—
10   you know—perfect people.

ELINOR: Well, we don't come in here just to say that—well, we're going to solve our problems, but it helps us see—see the problem and see it maybe in two different lights—like say from our parents' point of view and ours—and analyze the situation
15   and—well, just help solve our own problems.

FRAN: I was going to say that—well, I don't think this was a place where we just come and leave our problems here and then go out and think about them all week and then come back with more problems. I think it's helped us to better understand
20   other people, too, as well as ourselves.

BETTY: Like our parents. I mean, at home my parents can't
—they don't realize that I'm turning over a new leaf. I mean,
lately I've been trying hard to be a good kid. There's a new me,
but nobody can see it.

25   COUNSELOR: Some of you are saying that our goal has been to
gain greater understanding and the ability to see things from
many points of view.

FRAN: You know how people feel about things.

CONNIE: Yeah. I mean you can see two sides to the story then.

30   ELINOR: I think it helped me because I know that other girls
have the same problems I do and you're not all by yourself.

BETTY: I agree with the other girls—I think I can understand
people a little bit better, too. I feel the same way, but another
thing—I think this is valuable because—you know, like last Sep-
35   tember—all of a sudden, we'd get all shook and we could always
think—well, we'll just wait until Wednesday and we can come
here and really—you know, figure it out and stuff. It's saved us
a lot of pain and stuff. You can't measure it with a cup or anything.

40   DOT: I think we're more sensitive to feelings.

CONNIE: I don't think I have all these problems—well, maybe
—I don't know.

FRAN: Yeah, but now you can understand a little bit better.

DOT: And it doesn't seem like they're such a burden.

45   CONNIE: Well, it's helped me a lot to understand my whole
family. It seems so funny, but when my brother comes home,
I kind of dreaded it because we—I hadn't gotten along with
him all year. But when he comes home now, we have a real
good relationship and we've done things for each other and
50   we've gone to things together and everything else and it's helped
me to better understand my own brother and—I don't know,
but—but I don't feel I have all those problems any more.

COUNSELOR: Anybody want to add to that? (*Pause*) What is
this group counseling anyway?

55   CONNIE: Well, we come here and bring up problems or things
that are troubling us—and we just kind of try to understand

them better and—I don't know—look at them in a different way, too. After discussing it, you can see the opinions of other people and you know how they feel about it, too, and it helps me to

60 understand what the problem was—I mean, how to solve it.

ELINOR: I think we come here and sort of—more or less represent the problems of—and the feelings of a lot of people— unless some of the discussions we had aren't common to other people. But I think a lot of the problems we talked about are

65 more or less common to all high school kids and I think it helps the counselors and the people that are working with us to get an understanding of the kids, too.

FRAN: Kids have asked me, "What do you do in there?" "We discuss teen-age problems." "Like what, for instance?" "Like

70 how to get along with other people."

DOT: I think facing the reality of problems is important— solving them and getting along with other people, too.

COUNSELOR: What do you mean by facing the reality of problems?

75 DOT: Well, some people try to cover them up and—like it isn't there. I mean, they ask, "Do you have problems?" They sort of act like they don't have any problems. They make you look like a guinea pig.

BETTY: Everybody has problems.

80 DOT: Everybody has problems and I think it's just better to admit that you do because then you're on your way to solving them. You can't cover it up, otherwise you won't be able to get the solution to it.

CONNIE: Most kids have problems, but they probably don't

85 bring them out in the open or something.

DOT: Some kids have obvious problems. Like maybe one parent or no money. Things like that. They're real problems, but our problems are just as important to us as theirs.

CONNIE: Some kids don't think we could talk about things in

90 front of you.

BETTY: Some of the other girls thought it was a pretty good idea.

CONNIE:　I think it's got the boys interested.

DOT:　They don't want to admit that they do have problems.
95　They wouldn't want girls to know, but now that we've got an idea of what group counseling is, I don't think it would be so bad if they did it.

BETTY:　I've talked to some of the boys and they say, "Oh, that seems to be a good idea. I wish boys had a group for that."
100　The next day, they just sort of laugh at it. They can take it or leave it. I think they're afraid to admit that it sounds like a good idea.

(*Sounds of general agreement*)

COUNSELOR:　They blow hot and cold on it. Wasn't that the
105　way you felt before we started? What are your reactions now about going to counseling?

BETTY:　Well, nobody would have to tell me—I mean, to come talk to you. But some counselors seem not to be with it. Too old or something. I could never talk to them.

110　COUNSELOR:　I guess you're saying you don't think you could communicate with everyone.

BETTY:　I suppose that's what the kids think. I mean, we thought that about you once, too.

COUNSELOR:　You had reservations about me, too.

115　BETTY:　Yes. (*Sounds of general agreement*) But I was just watching some people and I could hear them talking and talking.

ELINOR:　Well, we get pretty deep and you feel like you couldn't really get that deep with just anyone.

BETTY:　Well, I have visions of someone sitting there telling me
120　I'm going through another stage and then I'd quit.

(*The girls agree that they would think twice about going to another counselor, but that they would think about it and would certainly go to someone who made a good impression on them. The counselor then asked them what skills a counselor
125　needs, what kind of counseling they want.*)

FRAN:　Understanding.

CONNIE:　Yeah. I was just going to say that, too.

ELINOR: Well, sometimes I've watched you and you just sort
of—when we get real wound up, you just sit back and listen.
130   I mean, I suppose there's things you felt like saying, but you
couldn't right at the time when we were talking because maybe
it would sort of shatter what we were trying to say. But you
still have to—you have to say something, but still you can't tell
us what to do because we've just resolved that we don't like
135   people always telling us how to do it. We have to sort of solve
it ourselves, but you have to help us—you have to know what
to say at the right time—that's what I'm trying to say.

FRAN: Well, lots of times, you try to go and talk to someone
and you go in there and you want to tell them something and—

140   BETTY: (*Interrupting*) We told them [*other individuals with
whom they had talked*] our problem and they said, "Well, what's
the problem now, girls? Can we get to that now?" And we'd
already told them and they didn't even know it.

CONNIE: They keep right on talking and don't let us say what
145   we want to say and they just try to tell you. They looked understanding about it, but they didn't know.

DOT: You have to stay cool and calm. You have to actually
know what's there.

BETTY: Well, I don't know, but I mean—like when I have a
150   problem or something. First, I beat around the bush for about
half an hour. You've got to be able to sort of understand what
the kid is trying to say. I mean, maybe they'll just mention it
once, but they're thinking about it so hard inside that you don't
know what you've said and what you're thinking so you just
155   sort—and you've got to be able to fit the pieces together.

DOT: I think you have to be like a detective guy. You have to
just sort of catch every little thing that they say and stuff because lots of times we don't know what we're talking about and
then again we do.

160   COUNSELOR: Then you want the counselor to be able to listen
and stay cool when everything is kind of all mixed up.

BETTY: And I don't want you to cry and it doesn't pay to get
all shook. I just have to get washed out inside me.

COUNSELOR: The counselor's got to be able to understand you,
165   is that it?

CONNIE: He shouldn't monopolize.

BETTY: He's got to sort of forget the good old days when he walked three miles to school, you know.

DOT: You have to sort of put yourself in our shoes. I mean
170   that's pretty hard to do—and I think you can overlook some stuff that goes on during the meetings.

COUNSELOR: Okay, shall we go on a bit? What do you think the group should be like?

DOT: I think you have to have some things in common.

175   (*Sounds of general agreement*)

CONNIE: Well, say like—most of us girls have dating problems and stuff and some other kids just think boys are really funny.

BETTY: I think, when you get to this age, it really makes a difference. I mean, the kids that have a boy friend and the kids
180   that laugh at boys and girls together.

ELINOR: And another thing that's helped is—well, I suppose if you're going to counseling, you're going for the purpose of talking. I mean, some kids are more reluctant to say things. I think it helps if your counselor knows the kids—like he has
185   to break them up into different groups—how willing they are to say things. I mean, you have to have a couple of leaders that are going to say stuff, but then you have to—the kids in the group have to all be willing to contribute or one person is going to get left out and you just don't know what they think about
190   the whole thing.

BETTY: Well, I think the kids in the group have to understand the other kids, too. Because it's sort of a two-way proposition because some kids like to—I mean, they'll just say anything that comes to their minds and other kids are more reluctant.

195   ELINOR: And the idea—if you have people who are going to talk, they sort of bring out the problems of the shyer people, too. I mean, they will mention the problem and then you can get the other kids started—so I mean—it's kind of hard to really say.

COUNSELOR: What's that about the shyer person?

200   ELINOR: If you have people that are going to state the problem, you can get the shyer person to come out and maybe he

can't state the problem the way he wants to, but you have to have people who are willing to say something to get other people involved in it. And you have to have differences, too, be-
205   cause—well, if you didn't—if we all agreed on the same thing, there wouldn't be much objective in it.

BETTY: Well, I don't know how to express it, but just how different is everybody? I mean what they're thinking and everybody is so much different, but we have things in common, too.

210   COUNSELOR: On the outside you might look alike, but inside you're still very much individuals.

BETTY: And I think that's one of the things we've all realized. Even though we do have common backgrounds and stuff, we each—we're individuals and we each have our own feelings. I
215   don't know, but I feel that everybody's been pretty nice to me in this group and have thought of me that way. And I try to think of everybody else that way, too—as an individual. I think I've gotten more critical of myself and less critical of other people.

220   DOT: Not to the point where you drag yourself down and you're in a hole that you can't get out of. I mean, you could do that, too. Maybe I've watched too much TV or something —you see those guys that are in a rut because they've got so much guilt and stuff like that. But it's helped us to realize our
225   own problems and that our ideas aren't always the right ideas and to help see others'.

CONNIE: You can't always think you're right. I mean, you realize that sometimes you probably aren't always right.

COUNSELOR: Are you saying that you're real critical of your
230   shortcomings or that you're just more aware that they exist?

DOT: I think that's a better way to say it really. You're more aware that it's there and you're trying to solve it. You aren't really criticizing it. You know it's there and you have to do something about it.

235   BETTY: The way I think—you know those fights that us girls used to have—they were caused because we didn't think about what we—we—

DOT: About other people.

FRAN: There's one thing I've been thinking about. We didn't
240   discuss as many things as I thought we would. We didn't get
on as many different subjects. I mean, it was mostly parents for
quite a while and then the same with what we believe is right
or wrong and then we were discussing boys and dating. But I
think the points that we did get were really good. They really
245   helped me.

BETTY: We didn't cover that long list we made at the first
meeting. Those were educational and everything.

COUNSELOR: Did you want to discuss those?

GROUP: No.

250   BETTY: Not as strong as what we did discuss. You could have
said, let's get down to school and grades and jobs and school,
school, school. But you didn't. I mean, we brought up our own
problems.

BIBLIOGRAPHICAL NOTE

The bibliographical note is designed to serve as a guide to the references we have found particularly useful and stimulating although we may not always agree with the point of view presented. The list can furnish the reader with some suggestions for his own investigations that hopefully will lead to other equally valuable materials.

Traditional separations among the behavioral sciences no longer hold true. One cannot neatly categorize books as anthropological, sociological, or psychological because all these sciences are utilizing the same or similar approaches and techniques in order better to understand man and his behavior. The materials themselves seem to fall more naturally into the groupings of general references, studies of special groups, approaches to motivation and personality, historical studies, and informal studies. Even these groupings are not mutually exclusive and have necessitated arbitrary judgments on our part. The sections, however, avoid the stereotyped separations among three sciences that can be viewed broadly as one.

GENERAL REFERENCES

The natural starting point in any of the separate fields is a general text of which many are available. The books we have included as general references are those that go somewhat beyond the ideological limits of the general text. For example, Raymond Firth's *Human Types* (a most misleading title) claims to be an introduction to social anthropology, but is far more meaningful to the person with some anthropological knowledge because it deals with broad issues in the field. Similarly, Dorothy Lee's

Freedom and Culture requires considerable background if the reader is to appreciate its original perceptions and thought-provoking qualities.

Barry, R. and Wolf, B. *An Epitaph for Vocational Guidance.* New York: Bureau of Publications, Teachers College, Columbia University, 1962.

Beck, C. *Philosophical Foundations of Guidance.*° Englewood Cliffs, N.J.: Prentice-Hall, 1963.

Becker, C. *The Heavenly City of the Eighteenth-Century Philosophers.*° New Haven: Yale University Press, 1932.

Bendix, R. and Lipset, S. (Eds.) *Class, Status, and Social Power.* Glencoe, Ill.: Free Press, 1953.

Benedict, R. *Patterns of Culture.*° Boston: Houghton Mifflin, 1934.

Berelson, B. (Ed.) *The Behavioral Sciences Today.*° New York: Harper, 1964.

Borow, H. (Ed.) *Man in a World at Work.* Boston: Houghton Mifflin, 1964.

Breckenridge, M. and Murphy, M. *Growth and Development of the Young Child.* Philadelphia: Saunders, 1963.

Brown, J. *The Social Psychology of Industry.*° Baltimore: Penguin, 1954.

Calverton, V. (Ed.) *The Making of Man.* New York: Modern Library, 1931.

Centers, R. *The Psychology of Social Classes.* Princeton: Princeton University Press, 1949.

Coon, C. *The Story of Man.* New York: Knopf, 1954.

Coon, C. and Hunt, E. (Eds.) *Anthropology A to Z.*° New York: Grosset and Dunlap, 1963.

Davis, A. *Social Class Influences upon Learning.* Cambridge, Mass.: Harvard University Press, 1948.

DeGrazia, S. *Of Time, Work and Leisure.* New York: Twentieth Century Fund, 1962.

Dunn, L. and Dobzhansky, T. *Heredity, Race and Society.*° New York: Mentor, 1952.

Eells, K., *et al. Intelligence and Cultural Differences.* Chicago: University of Chicago Press, 1951.

Eiseley, L. *The Firmament of Time.*° New York: Atheneum, 1960.

° An asterisk following the title of a book indicates its availability in paperback although we may not be citing or may not have used the paperback edition.

English, O. and Pearson, G. *Emotional Problems of Living.* New York: Norton, 1955.

Erikson, E. *Childhood and Society.*° New York: Norton, 1950.

Firth, R. *Human Types.*° New York: Mentor, 1958.

Fortune Magazine, Editors of. *The Exploding Metropolis.*° Garden City, N.Y.: Doubleday, 1958.

Fried, M. (Ed.) *Readings in Anthropology.*° New York: Crowell, 1959. 2 vols.

Galbraith, J. *The Affluent Society.* Boston: Houghton Mifflin, 1958.

Galdston, I. (Ed.) *Medicine and Anthropology.* New York: International Universities Press, 1959.

Getzels, J. and Jackson, P. *Creativity and Intelligence.* New York: Wiley, 1962.

Goodman, P. *Growing Up Absurd.*° New York: Random House, 1962.

Haimowitz, M. and N. *Human Development.*° New York: Crowell, 1960.

Hall, E. *The Silent Language.*° Greenwich, Conn.: Premier, 1961.

Havighurst, R. *Developmental Tasks and Education.*° New York: Longmans, Green, 1952.

Henry, Jules. *Culture Against Man.* New York: Random House, 1963.

Herskovits, M. *Economic Anthropology.* New York: Knopf, 1952.

Hilgard, E. *Theories of Learning.* New York: Appleton-Century-Crofts, 1948.

Homans, G. *The Human Group.* New York: Harcourt, Brace, 1950.

Jacob, P. *Changing Values in College.* New York: Harper, 1958.

Kahl, J. *The American Class Structure.* New York: Holt, Rinehart, and Winston, 1961.

Kardiner, A. *The Psychological Frontiers of Society.* New York: Columbia University Press, 1945.

Kimball, S. and McClellan, J. *Education and the New America.* New York: Random House, 1962.

Kluckhohn, C. *Mirror for Man.*° New York: Whittlesey House, 1949.

Kuhlen, R. and Thompson, G. (Eds.) *Psychological Studies of Human Development.*° New York: Appleton-Century-Crofts, 1963.

LaBarre, W. *The Human Animal.*° Chicago: University of Chicago Press, 1954.

LaPiere, R. *The Freudian Ethic.* New York: Duell, Sloan, Pearce, 1959.

Lee, D. *Freedom and Culture.*° Englewood Cliffs, N. J.: Prentice-Hall, 1959.

Lerner, M. *America as Civilization.*° New York: Simon and Schuster, 1958. 2 vols.

Levy, J. and Munroe, R. *The Happy Family.* New York: Knopf, 1938.

Linton, R. *The Tree of Culture.*° New York: Knopf, 1955.

Lloyd-Jones, E. and Westervelt, E. (Eds.) *Behavioral Science and Guidance.*° New York: Bureau of Publications, Teachers College, Columbia University, 1963.

Mayer, K. *Class and Society.*° New York: Random House, 1962.

Mead, M. *Male and Female.*° New York: Morrow, 1949.

Merton, R. *Social Theory and Social Structure.* Glencoe, Ill.: Free Press, 1957.

Merton, R., Broom, L., and Cottrell, L. (Eds.) *Sociology Today.* New York: Basic Books, 1959.

Merton, R. and Nisbet, R. *Contemporary Social Problems.* New York: Harcourt, Brace, 1961.

Miller, D. and Form, W. *Industrial Sociology.* New York: Harper, 1951.

Montagu, M. (Ed.) *Culture and the Evolution of Man.*° New York: Oxford Galaxy, 1962.

Mowrer, O. *The Crisis in Psychiatry and Religion.*° Princeton, N.J.: Van Nostrand, 1958.

National Society for the Study of Education. *Education for the Gifted.* 57th Yearbook, edited by N. Henry. Chicago: University of Chicago Press, 1958. Part 2.

————, *Child Psychology.* 62nd Yearbook, edited by H. Stevenson. Chicago: University of Chicago Press, 1963. Part 1.

Nosow, S. and Form, W. (Eds.) *Man, Work, and Society.* New York: Basic Books, 1962.

Pressey, S. and Kuhlen, R. *Psychological Development through the Life Span.* New York: Harper, 1957.

Riesman, D. *Individualism Reconsidered.*° Glencoe, Ill.: Free Press, 1954.

————. *The Lonely Crowd.*° New Haven: Yale University Press, 1950.

Rogoff, N. *Recent Trends in Occupational Mobility.* Glencoe, Ill.: Free Press, 1953.

Sanford, R. (Ed.) *The American College.* New York: Wiley, 1962.

Sapir, E. *Selected Writings of Edward Sapir in Language, Culture and Personality.* Berkeley: University of California Press, 1949.

Schneider, H. *The Puritan Mind.*° Ann Arbor: University of Michigan Press, 1958.

Sears, R., Maccoby, E., and Levin, H. *Patterns of Child Rearing.* Evanston, Ill.: Row, Peterson, 1957.

Shaffer, L. and Shoben, E. *The Psychology of Adjustment.* New York: Houghton Mifflin, 1956.

Shaw, F. and Ort, R. *Personal Adjustment in the American Culture*. New York: Harper, 1953.

Sherif, M. and Hovland, C. *Social Judgment*. New Haven: Yale University Press, 1961.

Smith, P. (Ed.) *Creativity*. New York: Hastings House, 1959.

Spindler, G. *Education and Culture.*° New York: Holt, Rinehart, and Winston, 1963.

Stone, L. and Church, J. *Childhood and Adolescence*. New York: Random House, 1957.

Sutherland, R., *et al.* (Eds.) *Personality Factors on the College Campus.*° Austin, Tex.: Hogg Foundation, 1962.

Taylor, C. and Barron, F. (Eds.) *Scientific Creativity*. New York: Wiley, 1963.

Thomson, R. *The Psychology of Thinking.*° Baltimore: Penguin, 1959.

Valentine, C. *The Normal Child and Some of His Abnormalities.*° Baltimore: Penguin, 1956.

Warner, W. *Social Class in America.*° New York: Harper, 1960.

———. *American Life.*° Chicago: University of Chicago Press, 1962.

Warner, W. and Abegglen, J. *Occupational Mobility in American Business, 1928–1952*. Minneapolis: University of Minnesota Press, 1955.

Whyte, W. (Ed.) *Industry and Society*. New York: McGraw-Hill, 1946.

———. *Men at Work*. Homewood, Ill.: Dorsey Press, 1961.

Wrenn, C. *The Counselor in a Changing World.*° Washington, D. C.: American Personnel and Guidance Association, 1962.

STUDIES OF SPECIAL GROUPS

The books included in this section offer the reader the opportunity to study the behavior of people in groups that may be similar or dissimilar to his own. These readings illuminate values, ways of thinking, and ways of doing and illustrate the meaning and importance of the social structure and mores to the individual. Wide reading of such studies as those listed can help any reader to recognize his own values and ways in contrast with those of others.

Barnett, H. *Being a Palauan.*° New York: Holt, Rinehart, and Winston, 1960.

Beattie, J. *Bunyoro.*° New York: Holt, Rinehart, and Winston, 1960.

Cash, W. *The Mind of the South.*° New York: Knopf, 1941.

Coleman, J. *The Adolescent Society.* Glencoe, Ill.: Free Press, 1961.

Conant, J. *Slums and Suburbs.*° New York: McGraw-Hill, 1961.

Davis, A. and Dollard, J. *Children of Bondage.*° New York: Harper, 1964.

de Huszar, G. (Ed.) *The Intellectuals.* Glencoe, Ill.: Free Press, 1960.

Dennis, W. *The Hopi Child.* New York: Appleton-Century-Crofts, 1940.

Dobriner, W. *Class in Suburbia.*° Englewood Cliffs, N.J.: Prentice-Hall, 1963.

Dollard, J. *Caste and Class in a Southern Town.*° New Haven: Yale University Press, 1937.

Drake, S. and Cayton, H. *Black Metropolis.*° New York: Harper, 1961. 2 vols.

DuBois, C. *The People of Alor.*° New York: Harper, 1961. 2 vols.

Eggan, F. (Ed.) *Social Anthropology of North American Tribes.* Chicago: University of Chicago Press, 1955.

Firth, R. *We, The Tikopia.*° Boston: Beacon Press, 1963.

Forde, C. *African Worlds.* London: Oxford University Press, 1954.

Fortune, R. *Sorcerers of Dobu.*° New York: Dutton, 1963.

Frazier, E. *Black Bourgeoisie.*° Glencoe, Ill.: Free Press, 1957.

————. *The Negro Family in the United States.* Chicago: University of Chicago Press, 1939.

Hart, C. and Pilling, A. *The Tiwi of North Australia.*° New York: Holt, Rinehart, and Winston, 1960.

Haveman, E. and West, P. *They Went to College.* New York: Harcourt, Brace, 1948.

Havighurst, R., *et al. Growing Up in River City.* New York: Wiley, 1962.

Havighurst, R. and Taba, H. *Adolescent Character and Personality.* New York: Wiley, 1949.

Heath, R. *The Reasonable Adventurer.*° Pittsburgh: University of Pittsburgh Press, 1964.

Herskovits, M. *The Human Factor in Changing Africa.* New York: Knopf, 1962.

Hoebel, E. *The Cheyennes.*° New York: Holt, Rinehart, and Winston, 1960.

Hollingshead, A. *Elmtown's Youth.*° New York: Wiley, 1949.

Hollingshead, A. and Redlich, F. *Social Class and Mental Illness.* New York: Wiley, 1958.

Hsu, F. *Americans and Chinese.* New York: Abelard-Schuman, 1953.

———. *Clan, Caste and Club.* Princeton, N.J.: Van Nostrand, 1963.

Jahn, J. *Muntu.** New York: Grove Press, 1961.

Jersild, A. *When Teachers Face Themselves.** New York: Bureau of Publications, Teachers College, Columbia University, 1955.

Kardiner, A. and Ovesey, L. *The Mark of Oppression.** Cleveland, Ohio: Meridian, 1961.

Kenyatta, J. *Facing Mount Kenya.** New York: Vintage, 1962.

Kluckhohn, C. and Leighton, D. *The Navaho.** Cambridge, Mass.: Harvard University Press, 1946.

Kravaceus, W. and Miller, W. *Delinquent Behavior.* Washington, D.C.: National Education Association, 1959.

Lewis, O. *Tepoztlan.* * New York: Holt, Rinehart, and Winston, 1960.

Lichter, S., *et al. The Drop-Outs.* Glencoe, Ill.: Free Press, 1962.

Lincoln, C. *The Black Muslims in America.** Boston: Beacon Press, 1963.

Lowie, R. *The Crow Indians.** New York: Farrar, Strauss, and Cudahy, 1935.

Lynd, R. and H. *Middletown.** New York: Harcourt, Brace, 1929.

———. *Middletown in Transition.* New York: Harcourt, Brace, 1937.

Malinowski, B. *Argonauts of the Western Pacific.** New York: Dutton, 1922.

———. *Magic, Science and Religion and Other Essays.** Glencoe, Ill.: Free Press, 1948.

———. *The Sexual Life of the Savages in Northwestern Melanesia.** New York: Liveright, 1929.

Mead, M. *Coming of Age in Samoa,** *Growing Up in New Guinea,** *Sex and Temperament in Three Primitive Societies** in *From the South Seas.* New York: Morrow, 1939. (Also available separately in Mentor Series.)

———. *New Lives for Old.** New York: Mentor, 1961.

Mead, M. and Wolfenstein, M. (Eds.) *Childhood in Contemporary Cultures.** Chicago: University of Chicago Press, 1955.

Mills, C. *White Collar.** New York: Oxford University Press, 1951.

Myrdal, G. *An American Dilemma.** New York: Harper, 1944.

Passow, A. (Ed.) *Education in Depressed Areas.** New York: Bureau of Publications, Teachers College, Columbia University, 1963.

Powdermaker, H. *Hollywood, the Dream Factory.** Boston: Universal Library, 1950.

Redfield, R. *A Village That Chose Progress.** Chicago: Phoenix, 1962.

Redfield, R. and Rojas, A. *Chan Kom.** Chicago: Phoenix, 1962.

Remmers, H. (Ed.) *Anti-Democratic Attitudes in American Schools.* Evanston, Ill.: Northwestern University Press, 1963.

Remmers, H. and Radler, D. *The American Teenager.** Indianapolis, Ind.: Bobbs-Merrill, 1957.

Reynolds, L. and Shister, J. *Job Horizons.* New York: Harper, 1949.

Seeley, J., Sim, R., and Loosley, E. *Crestwood Heights.** New York: Basic Books, 1956.

Thompson, L. and Joseph, A. *The Hopi Way.* Chicago: University of Chicago Press, 1945.

Torrance, E. *Guiding Creative Talent.* Englewood Cliffs, N.J.: Prentice-Hall, 1962.

Vidich, A. and Bensman, J. *Small Town in Mass Society.** Garden City, N.Y.: Anchor, 1960.

Warner, W., *et al. Democracy in Jonesville.** New York: Harper, 1949.

————. *Yankee City.** New Haven: Yale University Press, 1961.

Weyer, E. *Primitive Peoples Today.** Garden City, N.Y.: Dolphin Books, n.d.

Winstedt, R. *The Malays.* London: Routledge and Kegan Paul, 1958.

Whyte, W. *Street Corner Society.* Chicago: University of Chicago Press, 1955.

Zborowski, M. and Herzog, E. *Life Is With People.** New York: Schocken Books, 1962.

APPROACHES TO MOTIVATION AND PERSONALITY

As the heading indicates, the readings in this section are primarily concerned with motivation and personality development. Included in the list are several books that summarize theories. In general, these volumes are more useful to the reader who is acquainted with some of the original materials than they are to the beginner.

We are omitting the valuable and readily obtainable works of the early psychoanalytic theorists. We hope that most of our readers are already acquainted with these indispensable materials.

Adorno, T., *et al. The Authoritarian Personality.* New York: Harper, 1950.

Allport, G. *Becoming.** New Haven: Yale University Press, 1955.

————. *Pattern and Growth in Personality.* New York: Holt, Rinehart, and Winston, 1961.

Berelson, B. and Steiner, G. *Human Behavior.* New York: Harcourt, Brace, 1964.

Bindra, D. *Motivation.* New York: Ronald, 1959.

Birney, R. and Teevan, R. *Measuring Human Motivation.** Princeton, N.J.: Van Nostrand, Insight Books, 1962.

Blake, R. and Ramsey, G. (Eds.) *Perception.* New York: Ronald, 1951.

Brammer, L. and Shostrom, E. *Therapeutic Psychology.* Englewood Cliffs, N.J.: Prentice-Hall, 1960.

Cameron, N. *Personality Development and Psychopathology.* Boston: Houghton Mifflin, 1963.

Coleman, J. *Personality Dynamics and Effective Behavior.* Chicago: Scott, Foresman, 1960.

Dollard, J. and Miller, N. *Personality and Psychotherapy.* New York: McGraw-Hill, 1950.

Fromm, E. *Escape from Freedom.* New York: Farrar and Rinehart, 1941.

————. *The Forgotten Language.** New York: Rinehart, 1951.

————. *Man for Himself.* New York: Rinehart, 1947.

————. *The Sane Society.* New York: Rinehart, 1955.

Ginzberg, Eli, *et al. Occupational Choice.* New York: Columbia University Press, 1951.

Hall, C. and Lindzey, G. *Theories of Personality.* New York: Wiley, 1957.

Harper, R. *Psychoanalysis and Psychotherapy 36 Systems.** Englewood Cliffs, N.J.: Prentice-Hall, 1959.

Heidbreder, E. *Seven Psychologies.* New York: Appleton-Century, 1933.

Herzberg, F., Mausner, B., and Snyderman, B. *The Motivation to Work.* New York: Wiley, 1959.

Honigmann, J. *Culture and Personality.* New York: Harper, 1954.

Horney, K. *Our Inner Conflicts.* New York: Norton, 1945.

————. *Neuroses and Human Growth.* New York: Norton, 1950.

————. *The Neurotic Personality of Our Time.* New York: Norton, 1937.

Jourard, S. *The Transparent Self.* Princeton, N.J.: Van Nostrand, 1964.

Kagan, J. and Moss, H. *Birth to Maturity.* New York: Wiley, 1962.

Kaplan, B. (Ed.) *Studying Personality Cross-Culturally.* Evanston, Ill.: Row, Peterson, 1961.

Katz, M. *Decisions and Values.** New York: College Entrance Examination Board, 1963.

Kluckhohn, C. and Murray, H. (Eds.) *Personality in Nature, Society and Culture.* New York: Knopf, 1953.

Koch, S. (Ed.) *Formulations of the Person and the Social Context.* Vol. 3 of *Psychology.* New York: McGraw-Hill, 1959.

Kohler, W. *Gestalt Psychology.*° New York: Mentor, 1959.

Levy, D. *Maternal Overprotection.* New York: Columbia University Press, 1943.

Lewin, K. *A Dynamic Theory of Personality.*° New York: McGraw-Hill, 1935.

Lindzey, G. (Ed.) *Assessment of Human Motives.*° New York: Grove Press, 1960.

Linton, R. *The Cultural Background of Personality.*° New York: Appleton-Century-Crofts, 1945.

Lynd, H. *On Shame and the Search for Identity.*° New York: Harcourt, Brace, 1958.

McCary, J. (Ed.) *Psychology of Personality.*° New York: Grove Press, 1956.

McClelland, D. *Personality.* New York: Sloane, 1951.

———. (Ed.) *Studies in Motivation.* New York: Appleton-Century-Crofts, 1955.

McClelland, D., et al. *The Achievement Motive.* New York: Appleton-Century-Crofts, 1953.

Maslow, A. *Motivation and Personality.* New York: Harper, 1954.

———. *Toward a Psychology of Being.*° Princeton, N.J.: Van Nostrand, Insight Books, 1962.

———. (Ed.) *New Knowledge in Human Values.* New York: Harper, 1959.

May, R. *The Meaning of Anxiety.* New York: Ronald, 1950.

———. (Ed.) *Existential Psychology.*° New York: Random House, 1961.

May, R., et al. (Eds.) *Existence.* New York: Basic Books, 1958.

Menninger, K. *Love Against Hate.*° New York: Harcourt, Brace, 1942.

———. *Theory of Psychoanalytic Technique.*° New York: Science Editions, 1961.

Mowrer, O. *Learning Theory and Personality Dynamics.* New York: Ronald, 1950.

Mullahy, P. *Oedipus Myth and Complex.*° New York: Hermitage House, 1948.

———. (Ed.) *A Study of Interpersonal Relations.*° New York: Grove Press, 1949.

Munroe, R. *Schools of Psychoanalytic Thought.* New York: Dryden, 1955.

Murphy, G. *Human Potentialities*. New York: Basic Books, 1958.
——. *Personality*. New York: Harper, 1947.
Murray, H. *Explorations in Personality.*° New York: Oxford University Press, 1938.
Piaget, J. *The Construction of Reality in the Child*. New York: Basic Books, 1954.
——. *The Psychology of Intelligence.*° London: Routledge and Kegan Paul, 1951.
Roe, A. *The Psychology of Occupations*. New York: Wiley, 1956.
Roe, A. and Siegelman, M. *The Origin of Interests.*° Washington, D.C.: American Personnel and Guidance Association, 1964.
Rogers, C. *Client-Centered Therapy*. New York: Houghton Mifflin, 1951.
——. *Counseling and Psychotherapy*. New York: Houghton Mifflin, 1942.
——. *On Becoming a Person*. New York: Houghton Mifflin, 1961.
Rogers, C. and Dymond, R. (Eds.) *Psychotherapy and Personality Change*. Chicago: University of Chicago Press, 1954.
Schofield, W. *Psychotherapy.*° Englewood Cliffs, N.J.: Prentice-Hall, 1964.
Sherif, M. and Cantril, H. *The Psychology of Ego-Involvements*. New York: Wiley, 1947.
Snygg, D. and Combs, A. *Individual Behavior*. New York: Harper, 1949.
Staats, A. and C. *Complex Human Behavior*. New York: Holt, Rinehart, and Winston, 1963.
Stacey, C. and DeMartino, M. *Understanding Human Motivation*. Cleveland, Ohio: Howard Allen, 1958.
Sullivan, H. *Conceptions of Modern Psychiatry*. Washington, D. C.: William Alanson White Psychiatric Foundation, 1947.
——. *The Interpersonal Theory of Psychiatry*. New York: Norton, 1953.
Super, D. *The Psychology of Careers*. New York: Harper, 1957.
Super, D., et al. *Career Development.*° New York: College Entrance Examination Board, 1963.
Super, D., et al. *Vocational Development.*° New York: Bureau of Publications, Teachers College, Columbia University, 1957.
Szasz, T. *The Myth of Mental Illness*. New York: Hoeber-Harper, 1961.
Tiedeman, D. and O'Hara, R. *Career Development.*° New York: College Entrance Examination Board, 1963.
Whiting, J. and Child, I. *Child Training and Personality.*° New Haven: Yale University Press, 1953.

Whyte, W., *et al. Money and Motivation.* New York: Harper, 1955.
Young, P. *Motivation and Emotion.* New York: Wiley, 1961.

HISTORICAL STUDIES

There is no comprehensive history of the behavioral sciences. In fact, there is relatively little written that attempts to relate these various sciences to each other or even to study in depth the development of a single science in a sound historical manner. By and large, the reader wishing to see the relationships among these sciences must seek them out for himself. Many books contain short introductory historical chapters, but these vary greatly in quality. The books listed here also vary in quality and accuracy, but can serve as a starting point for those readers who agree with us that history provides insights and understandings not elsewhere obtainable.

Barnes, H. (Ed.) *Introduction to the History of Sociology.* Chicago: University of Chicago Press, 1948.

Boring, E. *A History of Experimental Psychology.* New York: Appleton-Century-Crofts, 1950.

Brinton, C. *A History of Western Morals.* New York: Harcourt, Brace, 1959.

Bromberg, W. *The Mind of Man.*° New York: Harper, 1959.

Burlingame, R. *The American Conscience.* New York: Knopf, 1957.

Hays, H. *From Ape to Angel.* New York: Knopf, 1958.

———. *In the Beginnings.* New York: Putnam's Sons, 1963.

Kardiner, A. and Preble, E. *They Studied Man.*° New York: Mentor, 1963.

Kroeber, A. and Kluckhohn, C. *Culture.*° New York: Vintage, 1963.

Linton, R. *The Tree of Culture.*° New York: Knopf, 1955.

Lowie, R. *History of Ethnological Theory.* New York: Holt, Rinehart, and Winston, 1937.

Murphy, G. *Historical Introduction to Modern Psychology.* New York: Harcourt, Brace, 1949.

Penniman, T. *A Hundred Years of Anthropology.* New York: Macmillan, 1952.

Thompson, C. *Psychoanalysis.*° New York: Hermitage House, 1950.

Walker, N. *A Short History of Psychotherapy in Theory and Practice.*° New York: Noonday, 1959.

Zilboorg, G. *A History of Medical Psychology*. New York: Norton, 1941.

INFORMAL STUDIES

The technical literature is not the only source of materials on motives, values, and realities. Novels, travel books, analyses of their own societies by foreign authors, and descriptions of life among people of different cultures provide interesting pictures of value conflicts and of varieties of ways of thinking and doing. The following list is a very limited sample of the informal studies we have found most intriguing.

Barzini, L. *The Italians*. New York: Atheneum, 1964.
Bjerre, J. *Kalahari*. New York: Hill and Wang, 1960.
Brongersma, L. and Venema, G. *To the Mountains of the Stars*. Garden City, N. Y.: Doubleday, 1963.
Dark, E. *The Timeless Land*. New York: Macmillan, 1941.
Durrell, G. *The Bafut Beagles.* New York: Ballantine, 1960.
Grimble, Sir A. *Return to the Islands.* New York: Morrow, 1957.
———. *We Chose the Islands*. New York: Morrow, 1952.
Knowles, J. *Double Vision*. New York: Macmillan, 1964.
Matthiessen, P. *Under the Mountain Wall*. New York: Viking, 1962.
Smith, B. *Portrait of India*. New York: Lippincott, 1962.
Thomas, E. *The Harmless People*. New York: Knopf, 1959.
van der Post, L. *The Heart of the Hunter*. New York: Morrow, 1961.
———. *The Lost World of the Kalahari.* New York: Morrow, 1958.

OTHER SOURCES

The many useful and stimulating articles appearing in the various professional journals defy listing here. For those, we refer the reader to the appropriate journals or to the indices germane to his field of interest.

Counseling and guidance-personnel materials, which often contain chapters on theory, will be included in the bibliographical note of our book, *Dynamic Developmental Counseling*.

INDEX